READER'S DIGEST
beginner's
GUIDE TO HOME
computing

READER'S DIGEST
beginner's
GUIDE TO HOME
computing

PUBLISHED BY THE READER'S DIGEST ASSOCIATION LIMITED
LONDON • NEW YORK • MONTREAL • SYDNEY • CAPE TOWN

A READER'S DIGEST BOOK

Published by The Reader's Digest Association Limited
11 Westferry Circus
Canary Wharf
London E14 4HE

Copyright © VNU Business Publications Ltd 1997, 1998

ISBN 0 276 42397 6

A CIP data record for this book is available from the British Library

This book was designed, edited and produced by Eaglemoss Publications Ltd
in association with VNU Business Publications Ltd,
based on the partwork *Easy PC*

Printed in Singapore

10 9 8 7 6 5 4 3

Contents

1 GETTING STARTED

Welcome!

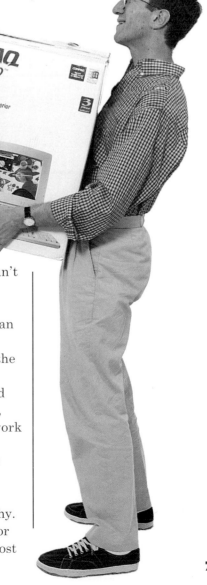

This is the essential guide to everything you need to know about computing for the home, the small office and, most important of all, the family. PCs are no longer a luxury. We all use them in one way or another – at work, in school or college and at home. Many have found their computers have become important for storing and using information, as well as for playing games. They have even opened up totally new ways of learning.

With a computer you can do some everyday things with more flair and ease. You can write letters, monitor your bank accounts and keep track of names and addresses. But, on top of that, there are a number of new things you can do with the more modern multimedia computers. These allow you to find information easily, show pictures and play sounds and movies.

Then there's the Internet, which allows you to search the world's computers for information on any topic you can think of, from aardvarks to zephyrs. You can also get in touch with other computer users worldwide and exchange information. And that's all for little more than the cost of a local phone call.

For many of us, computers still seem complicated and frightening. Yet anyone who has watched kids using computers will know that this can't really be true. Once you've broken through the barriers of jargon that surround using a computer, you'll find this box of electronics is no more difficult to work than a fax machine or a videocassette recorder. And it can do a whole lot more for you.

This beginner's book on home computing is here to guide you through the jargon. We'll explain in plain English what all the components do. We'll guide you towards the products you can buy. And we'll suggest useful and fun projects you can try out. Each section concentrates on specific topics, from using basic software to going on-line. This is a complete reference work for anyone new to the world of personal computers.

You'll soon find that a CD-ROM is no more a mystery than an audio CD player, and that details about computer memory are something you will understand and not have to think about. Computers are changing all the time, and here you'll find information on what is worth looking for and why. Whether you own a multimedia computer running Microsoft Windows 95 or 98 or an older PC running Windows 3.1, this book will help you get the most out of your PC. ●

Your PC

Green PCs

A PC has two main elements: the hardware and the software. The hardware consists of the parts of your PC that you can hold, touch and see. The computer itself, the monitor, the printer, the mouse, the modem, the add-on boards that plug into the PC, even the cables that connect it together, are all examples of hardware.

Computer manufacturers are aware that they have a responsibility to reduce their impact on the environment. The more responsible companies are ensuring that all packaging and plastics used are recyclable. They have removed CFCs from all stages of the manufacturing process. Look for a computer with a 'green motherboard', which has been manufactured with this in mind.

The concern continues with the operation of the computer. Green computers and monitors automatically switch off most of their systems when the PC is not being used, which saves considerably on the amount of energy used. Like TV screens, computer monitors produce tiny amounts of radiation. Before you start worrying, the levels are much lower than those you would normally be exposed to from going out in the sun. But to be on the safe side, low-radiation monitors have extra filtering built in especially to help protect people who sit in front of computer monitors all day, every day.

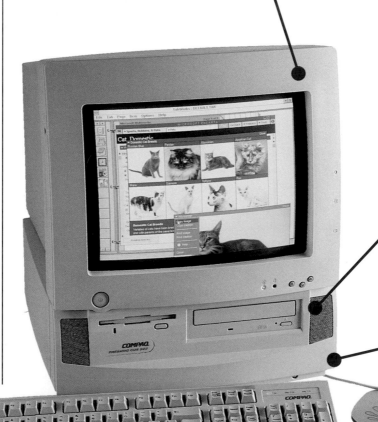

The *monitor* displays everything you are working on, usually in full colour. Portable computers use flat-screen LCD, or liquid crystal display, monitors that are not based on the same technology as TV-type monitors. They produce a less detailed image but weigh only a few pounds and use little electricity.

Your PC may have internal or external *speakers,* which you can use for stereo-quality sound when playing CDs and games.

The *system box* contains the computer's main electronics and additional parts, like the hard disk, memory and display cards.

The *keyboard* is used to enter text and numbers, control the software and move around the screen.

The *mouse* is used to control the software and move around the screen. You need a mouse pad or mat with an even but slightly rough surface to allow the mouse to move smoothly. This will also help it stay clean.

Why? a PC

Most people will buy a desktop PC, which is one that sits permanently on your desk, as opposed to a portable one that you carry around with you. In addition to the PC itself, you will probably buy extra pieces of hardware called peripherals, such as a printer or a modem.

The *printer* prints out your documents. There are black-and-white and colour printers, mains and portable printers, and low-cost good-quality and more expensive high-quality printers.

The computer may also have a *modem* that connects to your telephone line. This lets you join the worldwide community of computer users and receive and send faxes. (Modem not shown to scale.)

The computer we know as the PC is built around an original design created by IBM. Because IBM didn't mind if other people used its basic concepts, many other manufacturers started producing personal computers that copied the way the IBM PC functioned. As more of these copies of IBM PCs – called clones – came on the market, more software companies decided to start writing programs for them. In turn, that encouraged more manufacturers to make IBM PC-type computers.

The situation has snowballed to the point where the PC, PC components and software for the PC are now produced by hundreds of thousands of different organisations, making the PC the world's most successful type of computer. This is why we will be concentrating on PC products. Provided the computer is indeed a PC, whether it is made by Amstrad or Zenith, it will work in much the same way and it will run the same PC software.

Apple Macintosh

Apple started making its own type of personal computer at around the same time that the PC was born. Its system was incompatible with PC hardware and software. But Apple had a big advantage that made it successful. It was the first company to use pictures and windows – years before Microsoft Windows became popular. It also made plug-and-play machines. This meant people did not have to buy so many extra bits and pieces to do the things they wanted to do. For example, Apple machines already had a sound capability included, which made them easy and fun to use compared to the early PCs.

The Mac, as it is now affectionately called, became the preferred computer for people in the more creative fields, such as architects, musicians and designers, who needed a powerful and easy-to-use computer. The Mac is still the main alternative to the PC. There are not so many of them around because, unlike IBM, Apple has been reluctant to let anyone copy the design of its computers.

The rest

While many manufacturers followed the IBM PC design, others developed their own computer systems. These were incompatible with the PC, so hardware and software developed for one system won't work on the other. But, freed from IBM's way of doing things, these manufacturers could make home computers that were better in other respects. They may be much cheaper, better at playing games, or better at handling sound and pictures. Many of these computer systems are excellent but tend to be used mainly by people with an interest in a specific function.

Processors

The microprocessor, or processor – aka the CPU (central processing unit) – is the brain of the computer. It's the main chip on the motherboard and works almost like a supercalculator that does the calculations it is told to do by the computer programs.

To look at, the processor resembles an After Eight mint with small pins attached. You can identify a processor by the number on its top, which tells you how powerful it is.

One of the first PCs built used a processor designed by Intel. Intel gave it the reference number 8086. Since then, Intel has given each new generation of processors a new number: 80286, 80386 and 80486 – now shortened to 486. Intel has broken away from this tradition with its latest generation of processors, called Pentiums, although they are still referred to by some as the 586.

Processors are also measured by how fast they perform. This value is given in megahertz, abbreviated to MHz. The bigger the MHz number, the faster the processor.

Some software programs, like word processors, do not need much in the way of mathematical calculation power. Others, like spreadsheets or programs that display complex computer-created images, need lots of additional calculation power. Some 386 and 486 processors can have additional circuits, called coprocessors, to deal with these calculations. For a small cost, you can add a coprocessor to 386SX and 486SX computers to speed up their performance. All new 486 and Pentium computers have this coprocessor function already built into the main processor.

Inside your PC

Look inside any PC and you will see similar items of hardware. They all have motherboards, processors, disk drives, power supplies and memory chips. Many of these items are built to a fixed set of standards. This means that these parts are interchangeable and that computers can be fairly easily upgraded with additional items of hardware, which just plug into the main system.

It's worth getting to know your way around the insides of your PC. There may come a time when you want to add more memory or an expansion card for a special purpose, such as a fax/modem. But remember, never open your PC when it's connected to mains power.

Just as on other electronic items, on most PCs, the *LED* (light-emitting diode) lights show that the computer is on, and monitor the hard disk's activity.

The *on/off button* switches power to the computer and its power outlets.

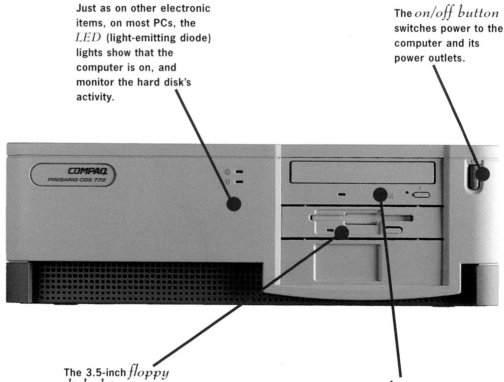

The 3.5-inch *floppy disk drive* lets you put software on your PC and store and exchange files. A floppy disk is a disk made of flexible plastic that stores computer data. It is housed in a rigid plastic case.

The *CD-ROM drive* has become an important part of the multimedia PC. Each CD-ROM disc can hold a vast amount of data, pictures, video and sound. But the standard CD-ROM discs are what is called 'read only'. You cannot store your own data on them, as you can with a floppy disk. In late 1997, DVD-ROM drives became available with some PCs. DVD, originally 'digital video disc', now stands for 'digital versatile disc'. DVD-ROM is a faster and more sophisticated multimedia tool than the CD-ROM.

Random access memory (RAM) chips are used by the computer for temporary storage of the program you are using and all the data you are working on. RAM is measured in megabytes (Mb).

Additional memory chips can be plugged into the *spare slots* to increase your PC's internal memory capacity.

The PC uses a small *battery* to supply power to several special memory chips when the computer is switched off. These chips store such information as the computer's setup details and the time and date.

The *motherboard* contains all the main electronics of your computer, including the main chip that does all the processing. The *BIOS chip* also lives on the motherboard. BIOS stands for 'basic input/output system' and is pronounced 'bye-oss'. This chip is responsible for making sure that all parts of the computer communicate with one another. It is permanently programmed with the instructions your computer needs to follow when it is switched on and loads the operating system from the disk. It also translates complex instructions from the CPU into information understood by devices like the keyboard.

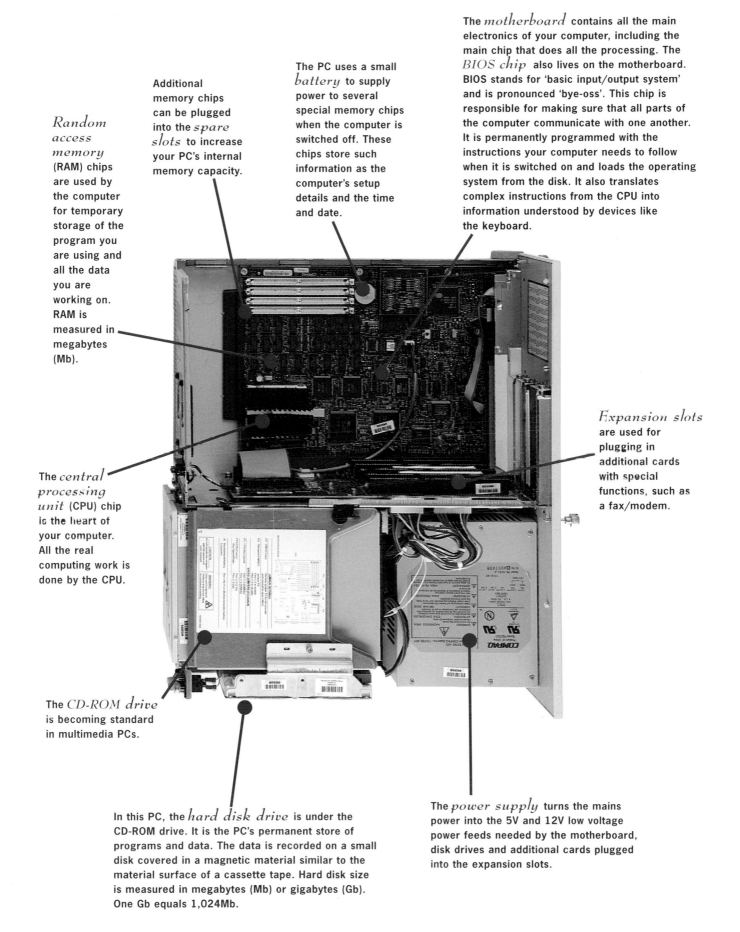

Expansion slots are used for plugging in additional cards with special functions, such as a fax/modem.

The *central processing unit* (CPU) chip is the heart of your computer. All the real computing work is done by the CPU.

The *CD-ROM drive* is becoming standard in multimedia PCs.

In this PC, the *hard disk drive* is under the CD-ROM drive. It is the PC's permanent store of programs and data. The data is recorded on a small disk covered in a magnetic material similar to the material surface of a cassette tape. Hard disk size is measured in megabytes (Mb) or gigabytes (Gb). One Gb equals 1,024Mb.

The *power supply* turns the mains power into the 5V and 12V low voltage power feeds needed by the motherboard, disk drives and additional cards plugged into the expansion slots.

Input

The computing process breaks down into three areas: input, processing and output. Inputting to the PC gets information into the system and gives you control over the instructions you send to the computer. Processing, which is carried out by the software and the computer processor, follows your instructions to do all the things you want to do with the information. Finally, output hands the results back to you.

It's just like a washing machine. You input water, dirty clothes and washing powder; the machine washes, or processes, the clothes by going through various wash, rinse and spin cycles; and the output is clean clothes.

There is a whole range of devices that will feed your computer information. The mouse and keyboard are the most obvious, but sound cards, modems, image scanners and digital cameras are all input devices that you may use. An input device can be anything that takes information from the outside world and turns it into data that the computer can understand. Every piece of information, whether it is being entered at that moment or has been taken from something prepared earlier and stored on disk, has first of all to go through an input device of some sort.

At a glance

- Keyboard
- Mouse
- Scanner
- Digital camera
- VR gloves and headsets
- TV/video card
- Modem

Keyboard and mouse

The input devices that everyone recognises are the keyboard and the mouse. The PC's keyboard is essential. It has a typewriter keyboard, a calculator number pad, a set of function keys that allow you to do specific tasks, and a set of direction keys with arrows for moving around the screen. The mouse is much better at the job of navigating around the screen and is good for software that calls for drawing and painting.

Sound

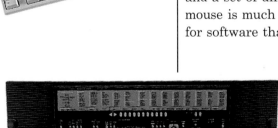

Sound cards turn sound into digital information a computer can handle. They take the sound from a CD, hi-fi or microphone and convert it into digital audio in the same way that sound is digitally recorded in a studio for a CD. The sound card can take in real sound and the special MIDI information used by music synthesisers and electronic keyboards. So a PC can be used as the heart of a home music studio. MIDI stands for 'musical instrument digital interface'. With the right sound card, you can plug a MIDI box into your computer. You can then plug the MIDI cables from your musical instruments into the box and have an orchestra on your hands!

Scanners

What sound cards do for sound, scanners do for pictures. The scanner uses sensors to pick up different colours and areas of light and dark on a printed picture or slide. This produces a digital version of the image, which is then passed to the PC. The scanner will scan the image into the PC in much the same way that a photocopier does. Then you will be able to see the image on the screen. You can also buy cheaper hand scanners, which you pass over the picture yourself.

Digital cameras

Digital cameras do away with the film you would normally use in a camera. They turn the image directly into a digital picture that your computer can use. You can take a picture with a digital camera, then connect it to your PC and download the image so you can see it on your computer screen.

Virtual reality

New input devices in the marketplace include various types of virtual-reality sensors, like gloves, headsets and body sensors. These pick up your body movements and send them directly to the PC. So, you can feel something in your hand that isn't physically there; the sensation is simulated by the computer.

TV and video

There are TV and video input cards that allow you to use your PC to watch, or even record, TV and videos on your computer.

Joysticks

As well as general input devices, like the keyboard and mouse, there are those designed for specific applications. There are joysticks and pilot controls for games and flight simulators, which are programs that imitate piloting an aeroplane.

Other computers

It's not only you who can communicate with your computer. Other computers can input information, too. In many offices, computers are connected electronically to form what's called a network. Once connected, you can take information from any of the other computers on the network and use it on your own PC.

The computers do not all have to be in the same building. By using a modem, which connects your computer to the telephone line, you can call a computer anywhere in the world and receive information from it in the form of messages and files. This is the whole basis of the Internet, which uses the national and international phone system to create a worldwide network of computers large and small. The Internet contains every type of information you could possibly want to access on your PC at home.

Output

At a glance

- **Monitor**
- **Inkjet/laser printer**
- **Sound card**
- **Headphones/speakers**

Being able to input information and process it would be a pointless exercise if you couldn't get it back out of your PC. As with input systems, there are some very common output devices. You obviously can't live without something as vital as a monitor, but when it comes to printers and sound cards, you may decide to buy these later. However, if you want to buy them from the start, you may find that you can get a good deal from the vendor.

Monitors

No PC can be without a monitor, or display. For PCs the display is a colour monitor, with more than a passing resemblance to a small colour TV. First, the computer sends the display information to the display card inside your PC. That turns it into a video signal that your monitor can display as a picture. Over the years, the quality of images produced by a PC has increased enormously. The first PCs could show only single-colour text, while today's display cards and monitors can produce more detail than a good TV and show over 16 million colours.

Portable computers have a flat-screen display that uses technology similar to that used in calculators. The difference is that these computer screens can show pictures and not just numbers. They are also available in colour.

Printers

The printer does the same job as the monitor, except the words and pictures are printed on paper rather than shown on a screen. The process is much the same. The computer sends the information to be printed to the printer card inside your PC. That turns it into an image of the page that your printer can reproduce on paper. There are two common types of printer for the home user: inkjet (some are called bubblejets) and laser. The best can produce copies of almost magazine quality – quietly, quickly and in full colour.

Inkjet printers work by spraying tiny dots of ink on to the paper. Inkjets are virtually silent in operation. They can print to a high quality, and some offer the option of printing in colour, which they do reasonably well. They are not that expensive and are the most popular type of printer for home computer users.

Laser printers work in much the same way as photocopiers. An image is beamed on to a metal drum using a small laser. Toner powder is transferred via the drum on to a sheet of

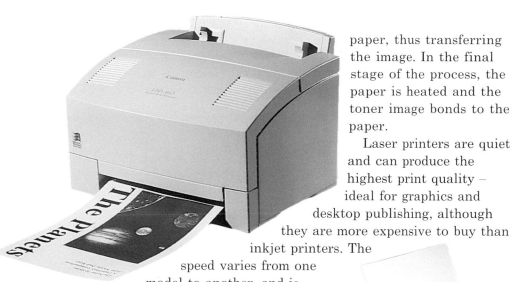

paper, thus transferring the image. In the final stage of the process, the paper is heated and the toner image bonds to the paper.

Laser printers are quiet and can produce the highest print quality – ideal for graphics and desktop publishing, although they are more expensive to buy than inkjet printers. The speed varies from one model to another, and is measured in pages per minute, abbreviated to ppm. The slowest is 4ppm, while anything above 8ppm is pretty fast. Colour laser printers are also available, but at an even higher price.

Sound cards

The sound card that records sound and music can also be used for play-back. When connected to a pair of speakers, your PC's stereo sound can be up to CD quality. PC sound is used for music and effects in games, as well as educational and reference software. It can also add small audio cues to everyday programs to tell you that the right or wrong keys have been pressed. There is a wide range of uses for sound on the PC, but one of the most common is simply to play audio CDs while you are working!

Headphones and speakers

There's no point in having a sound card if you can't hear what it is outputting. For that you need headphones or a set of speakers. You will probably have to buy these separately. You may find that you already have a set of headphones for a personal stereo system that will fit the audio output jack on the back of your PC. You can choose from all kinds of speakers, depending on the sound quality you want.

Processing

Processing is the job of the software and the computer's central processor. It takes the information you have entered and processes it the way you want. There is a huge range of software to handle different sorts of data in different ways, from word processing and painting to playing music on a synthesiser via your PC. The section on software on page 16 will give you a better idea of the range of software around. But, whatever the process, every software program produces a result that has to be sent to your PC's output so you can see or hear it.

Software

Software is the collective name for all types of computer programs. Software programs are simply a huge set of instructions that make your PC do something useful. They tell your PC what to do with the information you are feeding into it, what to show on screen and what to print.

Software is supplied on a set of floppy disks or CD-ROM discs, which you transfer to your PC's hard disk. When you buy a PC, the important software items, like Windows, should already be loaded on to the hard disk.

When you want to run a particular software program, such as a writing program or a word processor, you turn your PC on and choose the program you need. Programs are represented by a small picture, or icon, on the screen. The PC finds the program on the hard disk, loads it into the PC's memory bank and gets it ready for you to use.

In this book we concentrate on software that works with Microsoft Windows, which is the operating system used by most PCs today. Windows presents you with graphics, images, icons and lists of choices called menus, which make it easy to use. This type of software is called a graphical user interface or GUI (pronounced 'gooey'). When you look at the screen, 'what you see is what you get' when you start printing, so Windows is an example of what's become known as a WYSIWYG (pronounced 'wizzywig') program.

If you buy Windows-compatible programs, they will work with Windows. Once you have mastered the way Windows works, you can often work your way around any Windows-compatible program, no matter how new it is to you.

There is a software program for every conceivable job. Each main category of software will be covered in depth later in the book. Here we give you an introductory overview of the more important types of software.

Software for free!

Some companies sell their software by letting you try it first before you buy it. This is called shareware. Such programs are available at very low cost. They can be copied, shared and passed on to others. Some are full working programs, while others may be disabled so that you can, say, try out a word processor but it won't print out.

The shareware system is fair if everyone plays by the rules. You get a version of the program with most of the features it offers, and you can try it out on your PC for a while to see if you like it. If you do, you buy it by sending your credit card information to the software company. You then get back a full version of the program or a code number that you type in to authorise your shareware for further use.

Desktop publishing
If you want to produce a newsletter or a magazine, you will need a desktop publishing program – usually called DTP. These programs can handle graphics and fancy lettering.

Word processors
This is software for creating letters and documents. You can type in text and make it look the way you want it to on paper. Word processors often include a spell checker. If you are not sure of your spelling, the computer will check the spellings and give you the right ones.

Spreadsheets and accounting software
These are used mainly in business. They make manipulating rows of figures quick and simple. As well as doing calculations, they have excellent report-printing facilities that can extract essential information and present it neatly. There are also accounting programs to help you keep track of your personal finances.

Graphics

Graphics software offers almost limitless possibilities, from creating your own pictures to retouching photographs. Drawing and computer-aided drawing, or CAD, programs are ideal for creating highly accurate plans and drawings. CAD programs are usually very sophisticated. They often have the ability to draw in two or three dimensions and are generally used by architects and product designers.

Games

For some, games are the best excuse to buy a computer. Most titles that are available for games consoles also have PC versions, and there are many specially developed PC games with stunning visuals and sound.

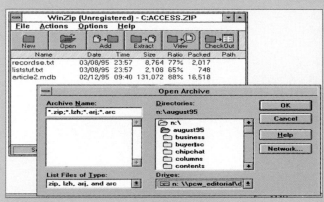

Utilities

Like most pieces of equipment, your computer needs to be maintained. Most of the maintenance work is done not with a screwdriver but with utility software. Utilities help check that everything is working well. They can organise your hard disk and clear out unwanted programs. They will back up files to floppy disks for safety and check for viruses.

Databases

These are filing-cabinet programs that enable you to store all kinds of lists and then instantly find the data you want. You can load as much information as you like and then ask the program to sort the entries.

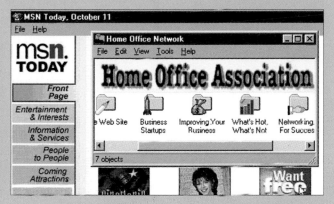

Communications

Increasingly, people want to use their computers to talk with others. There is a huge range of communications software to do this. This software can hunt out computers around the world on the Internet that contain information you might be interested in. You can also use the Internet to find out information on almost anything you can think of.

Edutainment

This software merges education with entertainment. It covers topics from architecture and animals to robots and reference works. Many programs mix text, graphics, sound, music, animation and movie clips, all in one program.

Will it work?

Some programs will run on very basic PCs. Others need lots of power and memory and several different extras, such as sound cards. Check out whether the software will work on your PC by looking on the panel at the back of the box. This tells you how powerful your computer must be and what facilities it needs to run the program. If the word *recommended* is used, beware! For example, it may say it requires 3Mb of RAM, but 10Mb is recommended. Usually this means you need 10Mb or the program won't perform up to expectations.

The program will take up at least 12Mb of *hard disk space*, so make certain you have plenty of spare room on your disk.

This program is on *CD-ROM*, so you need a CD-ROM drive to run it. All modern CD-ROM drives are at least double-speed.

To use Microsoft® 3D Movie Maker, you need:

- Multimedia PC with a 486SX/50MHz or higher processor
- Microsoft Windows® 95 operating system or Windows NT™ Workstation operating system version 3.51 or later; product does not run on Windows version 3.1 or earlier
- 8Mb of memory (RAM)
- 12Mb of available hard disk space
- Double-speed CD-ROM drive
- Super VGA monitor (256 colours) with local bus video
- Microsoft Mouse or compatible pointing device
- 16-bit sound card, and speakers or headphones
- Microphone required for recording

It needs a computer with a *486SX/50MHz processor* as a minimum. A faster processor will make the program run more smoothly.

When you buy a PC, it will normally be loaded with *Windows*. This duplicates the functions of the older MS-DOS operating system.

It needs at least 8Mb of *internal memory* to work.

Super VGA display means the monitor and the display card must be capable of showing at least *256 colours*. This is standard on all modern PCs.

If your *mouse* works with Windows, it will work with this program too.

This is a *multimedia program*, so you need a set of speakers or headphones to hear the sounds it contains, as well as a microphone if you want to make your own recordings.

This means you have to have a *16-bit sound card* for this program because it has speech, music and sound effects.

What to look for

When looking at ads for computers, remember to read the fine print. You will save yourself disappointment if you learn what to look out for before you place an order. Remember to check what is included in the price. If you are careful, you may get yourself a bargain.

The type of *processor* inside the PC. You'll need a Pentium 133MHz as a minimum. A faster processor would be better.

The amount of *memory* included. 16Mb is the minimum to look for; 24Mb or 32Mb will make things run more smoothly.

How big is the *hard disk*? The minimum should be 1.2Gb. Buy as big a hard disk as you can – you'll always find ways to fill it up.

The computer can be in a standard *desktop case*, which sits on your desk or a vertical tower.

The display card should be *SVGA*.

The *inputs* and *outputs* to connect the PC to the mouse, printer or other external devices.

The computer will come with a *mouse* and a *keyboard*.

The spare slots to plug in peripherals, such as *modems*. There are three types of slots: ISA, VESA(VLB) and PCI. Look for the VLB, PCI or a combination of VLB/PCI.

The electronics have been manufactured with minimum risk to the environment and have a *power-management* feature.

It's safest to buy by *credit card*, although many companies charge an extra 1 to 5 per cent for this. Check that the company will not debit your credit card until the item is sent.

Warranties vary greatly, so ask the salesperson to specify the terms of the warranty. The computer here is guaranteed for a year. On-site means the firm will repair it where you live, but check the response time.

Joe's BargainPCs

Check out our prices on PCs!

This month's best buy

~~£2,000~~

£1,200

- 133MHz Pentium processor
- 16Mb RAM
- 1.2Gb hard disk
- Desktop case
- 512Kb Accelerated Graphics Card
- 1 parallel and 2 serial Ports
- 102-key keyboard
- Mouse
- 3 VESA Local Bus slots
- Green motherboard

- 3.5in 1.44Mb Floppy Disk
- 17in 0.28 pitch Low-radiation SVGA Colour Monitor
- 16-bit SoundBlaster compatible sound card
- 24 Speed CD-ROM Drive

Includes free software!

Windows 98 loaded   MS Works

Plus 12-month on-site warranty

MasterCard or Visa accepted

Call our hotline now
0200 123456
Fax 0100 123456

JOE'S BARGAIN PCS
NORTH STREET
ANYTOWN AB1 2CD

NEXT-DAY DELIVERY

Make sure that the items advertised are *in stock*.

Make sure that the *price* advertised is what you will have to pay.

The *floppy drive* is used to load and store software.

This tells you how big the *monitor* is. 17 inch is normal for everyday use.

The *sound card* is also an option, but essential for multimedia and games. Highly recommended.

A *CD-ROM drive* is highly recommended.

Most computers come with *Windows* already up and running these days. Many dealers also add in other software, which is a cheap way of getting all the basic word-processing, a database and other software that you need. Check that the manuals are included.

You may be able to pick up the computer yourself and save on *delivery charges*.

Check when the computer can be *delivered* and whether this will cost extra.

What to buy

You should regard your computer as the machine you need to run your software. First decide on the sort of things you want to do with your home computer. You must decide what sort of software is going to be needed. Then you can choose a computer that is going to run that software properly.

The newest version of Windows is Windows 98. This is your starting point, as virtually everything you are going to do will run from within Windows. Windows 95 and 98 are easy-to-use software systems that control everything you do on your PC. But making it so easy to use means it eats up a lot of power and memory before you even start running application software, such as a word processor. If you don't have enough power or memory in your computer, then Windows and programs running under Windows may not work.

The most obvious way to tell if your computer is running slowly is whenever new images are shown on screen. You press a key and instead of an instant reaction, the computer busily whirs away for seconds – which seem like minutes – before anything new happens. When playing games, the animations and video footage may have slow or staggering action, and there may be breaks in the sound tracks as well.

To avoid this, you will need a computer that has at least a 120MHz Pentium processor and 16Mb of RAM. The more powerful the processor, the better the system will run, and the more likely it is to be able to handle the software that will come out in the future, which may require 166MHz/32Mb.

Most people are amazed that more RAM memory can make as big a performance difference as buying a faster processor. Many computers are

What size computer is for you?

Computers come in many shapes and sizes, and what you buy will depend on what you need it for as much as what you can afford.

Notebooks
These are portable computers light enough and small enough to fit into a briefcase. Many are as powerful as desktop computers and have a standard keyboard. They tend to be more expensive than their desktop computer equivalents.

Palmtops
Palmtop computers are more like electronic organisers. They are pocket-size and use a miniature keyboard. They are suitable for taking memos or for use as an address book rather than for heavy-duty computing work.

sold with 8Mb of RAM as standard because it is cheaper to do it that way. But this is simply not enough to run programs under Windows properly. You must go for at least 16Mb. If you can afford it, buy 24Mb or even 32Mb of RAM from the start. You can add extra memory by buying chips to insert into your PC.

The other main item to look out for is the size of the hard disk, which is where your computer will store all your programs. Since some collections of programs, or suites, can use up more than 100Mb of your hard disk, you will need a lot of hard disk space – at least 1.2Gb. If you have the option, it is worth spending a little extra to get a bigger hard disk from the outset. You'll soon find ways to fill it up.

All computers should come with a keyboard and mouse, a Super Video Graphics Array – abbreviated to SVGA – display card, and monitor. SVGA is the current standard for colour monitors and allows you to have a monitor with lots of colours at an affordable price.

After that, there is a range of optional extras that you may want. If you decide you want to have a multimedia computer, you will also need a CD-ROM drive, sound card and speakers. Chapter 13 will go into full details about what you need for multimedia. If you are interested in receiving faxes on your PC or using the Internet, you may want a modem that will connect your PC to the phone line.

It is also worth comparing the bundled software that different companies supply along with a computer. It's called bundled software because it comes with the computer, and it is often a very cheap way of buying hundreds or sometimes thousands of pounds worth of quality software.

Desktop

The most common form of PC is the desktop computer. This sits on your desk and has one box that contains the main electronics, along with a separate monitor, keyboard and mouse. The current trend is towards fixing the monitor to the system unit. Computer manufacturers are gradually packing more and more into one box. Over the next few years, people will increasingly buy their multimedia PC, TV, telephone, fax and modem as an all-in-one item.

Desktops are the best value for money because it is easier to upgrade them to take advantage of the technological advances expected in the future. They are also very versatile and can be used in the office as well as the home, for games as well as finance.

The good thing about choosing a desktop that is IBM-compatible is that they all adhere to the same standards. You can run a lot of software, and it is easy to buy extra RAM memory, expansion cards and peripherals, such as printers and CD-ROM drives.

Where to buy

Now that you have decided that your home will not be complete without a PC, where is the best place to buy one? There are several different types of computer suppliers. None of them has a monopoly on being the best or the worst, so look for the type of dealer that meets your needs.

COMPUTER DEALERS

Computer shops vary from small local dealers, which normally advertise in the local press, to the computer superstores that are springing up across the country. Smaller local shops will have a limited range of brands but can make up a system to match your needs exactly. They will test it all out and show you how it works. Although the price of the hardware is likely to be very attractive, they are less likely to be able to offer the bundled software packages that the bigger dealers can add in.

GOOD POINTS   **Local, will tailor a system to meet your needs exactly, good advice**

BAD POINTS   **Limited range of hardware, unlikely to be able to offer software bundles, can be variable in quality and reliability**

ADVICE ☺ ☺ ☺ ☺   PRICES ☺ ☺ ☺ ☺ ☺
RANGE ☺ ☺ ☺ ☺ ☺   FLEXIBILITY ☺ ☺ ☺ ☺ ☺
CONFIDENCE ☺ ☺ ☺ ☺ ☺

HIGH STREET STORES

The most convenient source of computers may be the computer department of a major high street electrical chain or one of the large department stores. You can see and use the computer, and you have the confidence that you are buying from a well-established retailer that is likely to be there next year should you have any problems. A high street store will sell you a complete package. But if you want a variation on the theme with a different printer, more memory or a larger hard disk, you may be out of luck. There may also be a larger number of credit deals available.

GOOD POINTS   **Local, supply ready-made systems, you've probably bought other electrical goods from them before**

BAD POINTS   **Little flexibility in altering parts of a system, knowledge not quite up to that of the specialist dealers**

ADVICE ☺ ☺ ☺ ☺   PRICES ☺ ☺ ☺ ☺ ☺
RANGE ☺ ☺ ☺ ☺ ☺   FLEXIBILITY ☺ ☺ ☺ ☺ ☺
CONFIDENCE ☺ ☺ ☺ ☺ ☺

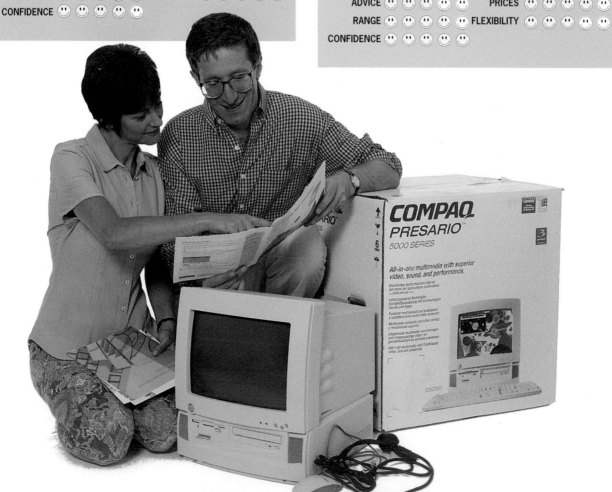

COMPUTER SUPERSTORES

The superstores are often located out of town, so you may have to travel. You are not going to get the same personal service as you will at your local shop, but they do offer a huge range of packages and systems.

GOOD POINTS	Supply ready-made systems and made-to-order systems, reasonable advice
BAD POINTS	You are lucky if they are local; like any superstore, professional but impersonal

ADVICE	☺ ☺ ☺ ☺ ☺
PRICES	☺ ☺ ☺ ☺ ☺
RANGE	☺ ☺ ☺ ☺ ☺
FLEXIBILITY	☺ ☺ ☺ ☺ ☺
CONFIDENCE	☺ ☺ ☺ ☺ ☺

SECONDHAND

Secondhand computers are cheap and normally reliable. But because they are generally a few years old, they are not likely to be powerful enough for today's needs, let alone for the future. At present, it is unlikely that the secondhand market will offer a really useful computer. You may save money in the short term, but don't think of it as a long-term investment. Plus, there won't be a warranty if something goes wrong, and you will have no redress, just as if you had bought a secondhand car. Take along a friend who can ask the right questions, and never buy one without seeing it working.

GOOD POINTS	Cheap, you can buy something with all the right parts so you don't have to buy extras yourself
BAD POINTS	No warranty, no backup, often no track record to rely on, and could be out-of-date

ADVICE	☺ ☺ ☺ ☺ ☺
PRICES	☺ ☺ ☺ ☺ ☺
RANGE	☺ ☺ ☺ ☺ ☺
FLEXIBILITY	☺ ☺ ☺ ☺ ☺
CONFIDENCE	☺ ☺ ☺ ☺ ☺

MAIL ORDER

It is difficult to flick through a computer magazine without finding hundreds of companies willing to sell you PCs, peripherals and software by mail. Many of these companies have been around for years and provide excellent service. They can match computers to your requirements and deliver them quickly. They also have flexible arrangements to make sure you stay happy if there is a problem. Choosing a mail-order supplier is no different from choosing a high street shop. Browse through the ads, and call the companies to ask them what they offer. Don't be afraid to ask for advice, and see who impresses you most. Always shop around.

GOOD POINTS	Specialist knowledge, can often make to your specification, lower prices
BAD POINTS	You need to know what you want, more difficult to return for repair, dealing with an unknown supplier you can't see face-to-face

ADVICE	☺ ☺ ☺ ☺ ☺
PRICES	☺ ☺ ☺ ☺ ☺
RANGE	☺ ☺ ☺ ☺ ☺
FLEXIBILITY	☺ ☺ ☺ ☺ ☺
CONFIDENCE	☺ ☺ ☺ ☺ ☺

Key

☺ ☺ ☺ ☺ ☺	Watch out!
☺ ☺ ☺ ☺ ☺	OK
☺ ☺ ☺ ☺ ☺	Good
☺ ☺ ☺ ☺ ☺	Very good
☺ ☺ ☺ ☺ ☺	Excellent

Stores

● Don't be afraid to ask questions and get a feel for the salespeople. Do they seem knowledgeable? Does the company give you confidence?

● State what you want the machine to do. Can they show you a PC running the software you will need?

● Where possible, pay by credit card, as this gives you extra protection.

Mail order

● Confirm the exact prices you are going to have to pay. You may find that once you've added delivery charges and VAT, the final price can be a shock.

● Check all the details by phone and find out how long delivery will take.

● Keep a copy of the order and any other correspondence. If you talk to anyone on the phone, keep a note of what was said and the person's name.

● Where possible, pay by credit card, as this gives you extra protection.

Shopping list

Make it easy to select the type of PC that will match your needs. Check the boxes for the facilities and functions you want, and fill in the shopping list with an idea of your requirements and the minimum and maximum specifications you think are realistic. You can then take it with you or copy it and use it when you talk to computer dealers. It will give them a clearer idea of what you want your PC for, and help them to advise you.

Steps to buying

1. Decide what you want your PC to be able to do, and make a shopping list of all the items this will require.
2. Choose a brand and a model.
3. Set a price. You may adjust this in light of your research. Initially, it will be what you can afford.
4. Choose where to buy, whether from a mail-order supplier or retail store.
5. Check prices by studying advertisements in newspapers and computer magazines, and adjust your budget if necessary.
6. Make your purchase.

Your easy checklist

Hardware

	MINIMUM	RECOMMENDED	HIGH-PERFORMANCE
PROCESSOR	☐ 133MHz Pentium	☐ 233MHz Pentium	☐ 300MHz Pentium
RAM	☐ 16Mb	☐ 32Mb	☐ 64Mb
HARD DISK	☐ 1.2Gb	☐ 2Gb	☐ 4Gb+
MONITOR	☐ 15in	☐ 17in	☐ 19/21in
GRAPHICS CARD	☐ 2Mb Video	☐ 4Mb Video	☐ 8Mb Video
PRINTER	☐ Black-and-white Inkjet	☐ Colour Inkjet	☐ Laser
SOUND CARD	☐ 16-bit	☐ 16-bit WaveTable	☐ 16-bit WaveTable
CD-ROM DRIVE	☐ 8-speed	☐ 12-speed	☐ 24-speed
FAX/MODEM	☐ 33.6K	☐ 56K	☐ 56K or ISDN
SCANNER	☐ Handheld colour	☐ Document colour	☐ Flatbed colour
WARRANTY PERIOD	☐ 6 months	☐ 12 months	☐ 3 years

Extras

GAMES JOYSTICK	☐ No	☐ Yes
SPEAKERS	☐ No	☐ Yes
COMPUTER ACCESSORIES	☐ Disks	☐ Disk boxes
	☐ Manuals	☐ Mouse mat
PRINTER ACCESSORIES	☐ Connecting cable	☐ Spare ink/toner

Software

INTEGRATED PACKAGE	☐ Yes	☐ No
WORD PROCESSING	☐ Yes	☐ No
DESKTOP PUBLISHING	☐ Yes	☐ No
GAMES	☐ Yes	☐ No
EDUTAINMENT	☐ Yes	☐ No
DRAWING & PAINTING	☐ Yes	☐ No
ACCOUNTING	☐ Yes	☐ No
SPREADSHEETS	☐ Yes	☐ No
DATABASES	☐ Yes	☐ No
COMMUNICATIONS	☐ Yes	☐ No

PRICE £ _____
DELIVERY £ _____
VAT £ _____
TOTAL £ _____

NAME OF SUPPLIER _____
TELEPHONE NO _____

2

UP AND RUNNING

Get Set!

In the first chapter, we took you through the basics of what a PC is and what it can do for you. In this chapter we explain how to get your computer up and running. We take you through the basics of unpacking your PC, connecting it and getting it working. We explain simply and clearly what all those plugs and cables do – and where they go. We also show you what you have to do to connect all the accessories, such as speakers and modems, and what the expansion slots inside your PC are for.

We will help you find your way around each of the important parts of your computer system, including the keyboard, the mouse, the monitor, the printer, the disks and the disk drives. You'll find out how they work and, more importantly, how you are going to get the most out of them. Plus, we give hints and tips on how to keep your computer in tip-top condition and how to look after the information you put on disk.

But it's not only your computer you have to take care of. Where you put your PC and how you operate it can affect your comfort. Placing the monitor at the correct height, getting the lighting right and making sure that you are sitting correctly all help to ensure that using your PC is a rewarding experience.

Finally, we cover what to do if setting up your PC doesn't go as smoothly as you had hoped. Our troubleshooting tips will give you a clearer picture of how to turn a collection of electronic components and packaged software into a working computer system. ●

Unpacking

Once you get your PC home, you have some work to do before you can start using it. This is a good time to learn a little about how your computer system goes together. If you have to move it or change anything later, you'll need some idea about what all the leads and cables do.

Usually there will be three boxes to unpack, unless you buy an all-in-one PC with the monitor attached. Generally, the box containing the computer is also likely to have the mouse, keyboard and cables packed with it. The monitor and the printer will come in separate boxes, which should also contain all the necessary cables, accessories and manuals. Clear enough space to work in and remove each unit from its packing, and make sure all the documents and accessories are kept with each unit.

At this point it is worth pausing to look through all the manuals. These will usually tell you where all the connectors are to be found and any additional advice on how to put your computer system together.

While you are setting up the system, it will be easier to place the PC with its back to you so that you can see where all the wires go.

If you have a standard desktop computer, the most common place to put the monitor is on top of it. This will save desk space and leave the monitor at about the right height. Tower PCs, on the other hand, are placed to one side of the monitor or under the desk. If you are right-handed, it is easier if the computer is to the right of the monitor. This is a more natural position to load disks into the PC and also means you don't have to trail the mouse cable across the back of the desk.

Wherever you are going to use your computer you will need adequate desk space and convenient mains sockets. You will need enough space for the computer, keyboard, mouse mat and any paperwork, and at least two mains power sockets. The computer and all the other peripherals, such as printers and monitors, use only moderate amounts of power, so you can use a multiway mains adapter on a single wall socket. However, it is better to use a power strip, which will fit under the desk and make it easier and safer to plug in additional items. If you are going to use a modem, you will also need a telephone socket nearby.

COMPAQ PRESARIO™ CDS 500 SERIES
MULTIMEDIA + MORE

Attractive, All-in-One design loaded with extraordinary multimedia features!

Des fonctions multimédia extraordinaires réunies en un produit complet et attrayant!

Attraktives, kompaktes Design mit einzigartigen Multimedia-Funktionen!

Design elegante e integrato con straordinarie caratteristiche multimediali!

¡Diseño atractivo y completo (todo en uno) cargado con funciones multimedia extraordinarias!

Aantrekkelijk, alles-in-één ontwerp vol bijzondere multimedia-mogelijkheden!

Attraktiv allt-i-ett-design full av extraordinära multimediafunktioner!

THREE-YEAR WARRANTY

& connecting

There should be two leads coming from the monitor. One is for the mains (1); the other feeds the monitor with data from the PC. Plug the power cable into the mains outlet on the PC and the D-shaped (5) cable into the monitor port at the back of the PC. Then connect the mouse (2 or 3) and keyboard (4) to the appropriate connections at the back of the PC. Connect the printer cable to the computer and the printer power lead directly to the mains. Finally, connect the computer's power cable to the mains socket.

Mouse and keyboard cables

The mouse will use either a small D-plug (2), so called because it looks like a letter D, or a round PS/2 connector (3). The PS/2 connector should go into the socket marked Mouse. The D-connector should be connected to the socket marked COM1 or SERIAL1. If COM1 is a large D-socket and your mouse has a small D-plug, you'll need an adapter.

Monitor cables

The monitor gets its power from the mains outlet at the back of your PC or from the wall outlet. A small D-plug with up to 15 pins (5) feeds it data from the PC. The socket your monitor's D-plug goes into should be marked either VGA, Monitor or Video.

Printer

The printer has to be connected to the mains socket. You should never try to connect more than one unit to the PC's power outlet. The printer lead has a large 15-pin D-plug (6) that goes in the socket marked LPT1 or Printer.

Ports

The PC needs to talk to the monitor, printer, mouse and keyboard. The outlets that do this are called ports. There are special ports for your monitor and for your keyboard. Your PC will have two serial ports, called COM1 and COM2, and a parallel port. COM1 is normally used to connect the mouse, and COM2 is a spare port for devices like modems. The single parallel port, LPT1, is normally used to connect the PC to your printer.

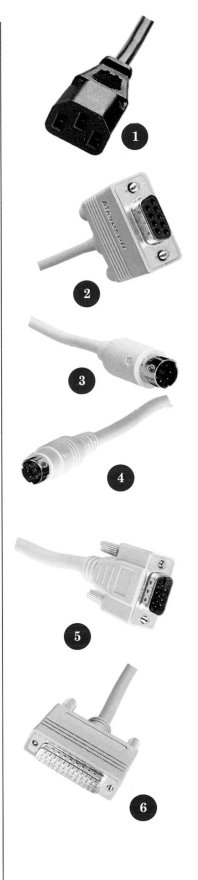

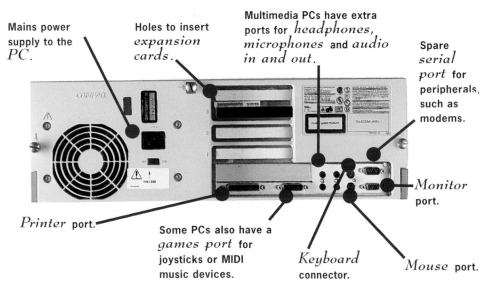

Mains power supply to the PC.

Holes to insert *expansion cards*.

Multimedia PCs have extra ports for *headphones, microphones* and *audio in and out*.

Spare *serial port* for peripherals, such as modems.

Monitor port.

Printer port.

Some PCs also have a *games port* for joysticks or MIDI music devices.

Keyboard connector.

Mouse port.

Keyboard

Every computer needs a keyboard to get information into it and to control the software. Some of the keys are there to enter text and numbers, and others are there to control what happens within the software or to move around the screen. Many keys can be used to do both, so the computer keyboard is a little more complicated than the one you find on a typewriter.

Keyboards can differ in layout, but they all have the same features. Most obvious are the main letters and numbers that are in the standard QWERTY layout (read the top five letters on the first row of letter keys) which has been used on keyboards since the invention of the typewriter. Numbers are laid out on the top line of the typewriter section and are repeated as a numeric pad on the right of the keyboard. The numeric pad is easier to use if you are entering a lot of numbers.

Across the top of the keyboard are the function keys, which software programs use as a quick way of accessing specific functions, such as printing a document or saving a file. The action each of these function keys performs varies from program to program, with the exception of the F1 key, which is nearly always used to summon the on-screen help feature. So if you get stuck in a program, you can usually just hit F1 for guidance.

Two-fingered exercise?

Most computer users manage to get by well with the trusty two-fingered typing technique. But if you are likely to be using the computer a lot, it is worth learning to type properly, as this speeds up everything you do and makes it that much easier to use. It also means that you are less likely to suffer from any health problems, as you will learn how to hold your hands correctly.

One option is to use a teach-yourself typewriting software package. These help you learn to type with all fingers and get more experience with the computer at the same time. They take you through different exercises and often let you know how you are doing by giving you speed tests. You can buy learn-to-type programs for kids, too. These are fun to use.

Clean up!

Keyboards will accumulate dust and a surprising amount of general debris over a period of time. To clean the keyboard, you should use a keyboard cleaning kit. This has a brush and a canister of compressed air to blow the dust out from underneath the keys. The key caps will also get grubby over a period of time. Use a barely damp cloth to clean them.

If your keyboard stops working or works erratically, clean it and check the connections. While it may be worth asking a computer engineer to look at it, you may find that it is cheaper simply to buy a new one.

Try not to spill drinks on your keyboard. If you do, switch off the computer as quickly as you can and then unplug the keyboard and shake any excess liquid out of it. Leave it somewhere warm (not hot!) to dry off.

The *Escape key* is the one key to help get you out of trouble. If you call up a function or menu box by mistake, pressing Esc should cancel it.

For upper case, or capital letters, you have to hold down the *Shift key* while you type. Pressing the *Caps Lock key* switches the whole typewriter keyboard over to capitals until you press it again to switch Caps Lock off.

The *Tab key* has the same function as the typewriter Tab key. It is also used to move across columns in tables and the cells – boxes where you enter in figures or words – in spreadsheets, as well as to move around some Windows menu boxes.

Twelve *function keys*, which the software uses to give you instant access to particular functions, such as printing and saving.

On many keyboards there are three *LED lights* to remind you whether the Num Lock, Caps Lock or Scroll Lock keys are currently depressed or not.

In most Windows programs, pressing the *F1 key* will call up the help information to guide you through the program.

The *Print Screen, Scroll Lock* and *Pause keys* are called the DOS keys because they are dedicated to functions in the DOS operating system. They are rarely needed when you are working in Windows.

Standard *typewriter keys* for letters, numbers and other characters.

Press *Backspace* and the cursor – the line or arrow on the screen that tells you where you are – will go back one space, deleting whatever letter is in the way. *Delete* moves the cursor forward one space, deleting whatever letter is in the way. If you switch *Insert* on when you type, you will then automatically type over any letters that are already on a line.

The *Cursor Control keys* let you move the cursor vertically and horizontally around the screen without using the mouse. You can jump up or down a page using *Page Up* and *Page Down* or to the beginning or the end of the line with *Home* and *End*.

The *Control* and *Alt keys* are used together with the typewriter and function keys to give you access to more of the software's functions. The commands in any Windows program menu bar can be selected by pressing Alt and its underlined letter.

The *Calculator* or *Number keys* are laid out calculator-style to form a numeric pad with divide (/), multiply (*), add (+) and subtract (-) keys. These are activated by pressing the *Num Lock key*. When Num Lock is off, these keys duplicate the functions of the Cursor Control keys.

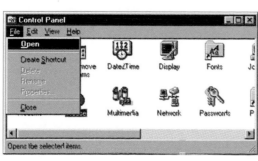

Mouse

The mouse is what makes moving through Windows so easy. You use your mouse to move around the screen and select Windows menus and commands. The mouse is always used in the same way, and you will find that the manuals that come with your software will tend to use the same words for the four basic mouse functions. *Point* is when you use the mouse to move the cursor over a particular item on the screen. *Click* is when you press the button once, either to fix the cursor at that position on the screen or to select a menu. *Double-click* is when you press the mouse button twice quickly to start a menu function or a program. *Drag* is when you hold the button down while moving the mouse.

Dangermouse

If you use a computer intensively, some muscles in the hand, wrist or arm can suffer strain from constantly repeating the mouse actions. Reduce the possibility of repetitive strain injury (RSI) by making certain you are using your mouse correctly and using keyboard shortcuts instead of the mouse when possible. Switching to a tracker ball can help. RSI usually hits those like designers and journalists, who use their computers intensively for long periods. Nevertheless, it is a good idea to be careful.

Mousehold

It is worth learning how to hold your mouse correctly. Hold it with your first and index fingers resting gently on the left and right buttons and your arm more or less horizontal. Make sure the mouse mat is close to your keyboard so you don't have to stretch your arm out too far to operate the mouse.

Now gently move the mouse around the mat. It is the action of the ball inside the mouse running against the mat that makes the cursor move. Lifting up the mouse and moving it, something common to those using a computer for the first time, will have no effect. It takes a little practice to master the point, click and drag techniques, but it will soon become automatic. When you feel expert at it, run Paintbrush in Windows, or any other drawing or painting program, and see how you can use the mouse to draw straight lines and circles freehand!

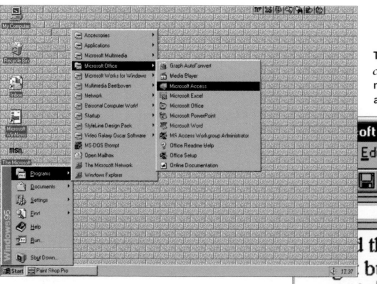

The mouse can be used both to *control* Windows functions and to move around the program's screen and *select* things.

Mousework

The mouse works by detecting the movements of the mouse ball. Two rollers, connected to sensors, press against the ball. One turns when you slide the mouse backwards and forwards, the other when the mouse goes from side to side. The information from the sensors is turned into electronic instructions for the movement of the on-screen cursor or arrow.

Mice of all kinds

The standard mouse uses a cable to connect it to the COM1 or PS/2 mouse port at the back of your PC. Some are designed to sit comfortably in your hand and others are designed just for fun. There are cordless mice that use an infrared beam instead of a cable. The alternative to a mouse is a tracker ball. It has the ball on the top rather than underneath, and you use your hand to roll the ball. Tracker balls take up less space and are often built into laptop PCs.

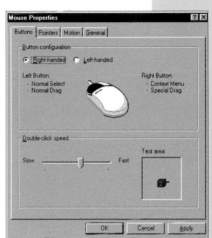

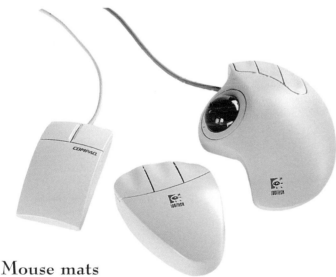

Mouse mats

Every mouse deserves a mat to play on. The mat has the right sort of surface, and provides just enough friction, to let the ball run without slipping or jumping. Mouse mats also permanently reserve a space on your desk on which to operate your mouse. They come in all shapes and sizes.

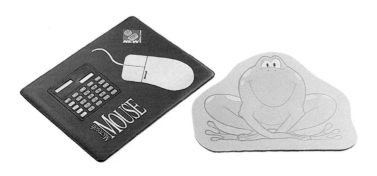

Adjusting your mouse

Some users like a mouse to respond very quickly to their movements and clicks. Others find that they like the action to be a bit slower so that they don't accidentally overshoot. By calling up the Mouse icon in the Windows Control Panel, Windows lets you choose the right tracking and double-click speed for you and even lets you swap the functions of left and right buttons if you are left-handed.

Ickey mouse?

The inside of the mouse can get dirty over a period of a few months. If the cursor loses its smooth action around the screen and jumps, then it is likely your mouse needs cleaning.

So, with the computer off, turn the mouse upside down. You will see a ring surrounding the mouse ball. The ring is released by either twisting or sliding it.

With the ring removed, take the ball out and then use adhesive tape to pick up any dust or lint on the surface of the ball. Wipe away dirt or lint inside the mouse socket. You can also blow gently to remove any dust. If anything is trapped inside the socket or on the rollers, use a cotton swab dipped in isopropryl alcohol to loosen it. Allow the surfaces to dry completely before cleaning. Replace the ball and secure the ring and you will have a smooth-running mouse again.

Monitor

A monitor is essentially a TV screen that takes its information from your computer and displays it for you in full colour. The instructions for what is to be shown on the monitor are created by the computer and the software and are then passed to the display card inside the PC. It is this card that turns that information into the red, blue and green signals that make up the screen images for the monitor to display.

The image you see is in fact made up from just three beams of electrons that fly across the screen, making groups of red, green and blue phosphor dots on the inside surface of the monitor's glass glow. Because the dots are grouped closely together, the eye does not see the individual dots, but a single spot, or pixel, of the colour that is made up from the three glowing dots. If all three guns are firing at full strength, the effect is of a single white pixel spot. If they are all firing at absolute minimum strength, you will see what looks like a black pixel spot on the screen. By changing the relative powers of each of the three beams, it is possible to create pixels in millions of different colours.

Controls

Your monitor has its own controls to adjust the look of the display on the screen. It is best to set up the monitor using a screen of black text on a white background. Turn the controls and you will feel a slight click at their centre point. Set all the controls to their centre point first and then make adjustments to suit your own needs.

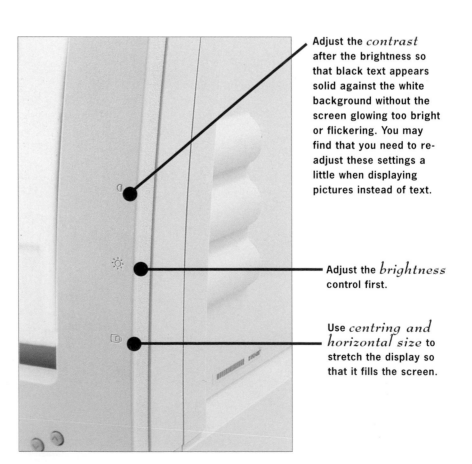

Adjust the *contrast* after the brightness so that black text appears solid against the white background without the screen glowing too bright or flickering. You may find that you need to re-adjust these settings a little when displaying pictures instead of text.

Adjust the *brightness* control first.

Use *centring and horizontal size* to stretch the display so that it fills the screen.

What's SVGA?

The standard display quality for Windows PCs now is Super Video Graphics Array (SVGA), which can produce a detailed image with photo-quality colour. To create a single SVGA image, the three beams are shot across the screen very quickly to create up to 600 lines of 800 pixels each. These images can be updated at over 70 times every second, so screen images can change instantly and the PC can display movement, animations, and video.

Your monitor and display card should be SVGA and so be able to display images 640 pixels wide by 480 pixels high (normally written as 640 x 480). You can choose to show anything from 256 to 16 million colours, which is the equivalent of photographic-quality colour.

Size and shape

For most home PC users, a 17-inch monitor will be just right. It is big enough to show all the detail needed for normal work and not too big to fit on the desk. Larger 20-inch monitors are used for professional desktop publishing and technical drawing, for which a large screen is essential.

Keep it clean

If your desktop monitor starts to get dusty or finger-marked, and does not have a mesh anti-glare coating, buy some screen wipes to clean the surface. If you can't find any, turn off the power to the system and the monitor. Then, with a soft cloth and window cleaner, clean the screen by squirting a little cleaner on to a damp cloth and applying it to the screen. Avoid using abrasives or solvents, as they will permanently damage the finish.

Portable computers use an entirely different display technology called *Liquid Crystal Display (LCD)* where small electrical currents make small squares in the screen go dark. Colour LCD screens are available, but they are not quite as clear and bright as a standard PC monitor.

Screen Savers

If an older PC is left on, but is not being used, the image can burn itself into the phosphor surface of the monitor, leaving a permanent shadow. To get around this, software developers came up with the idea of screen savers, which replace the display with a moving image after a few minutes. As soon as you press a key or touch the mouse, the screen saver disappears.

Screen savers have turned into an art form. Apart from being a fun way to personalise your PC, they can hide your on-screen information from prying eyes. You can set them so that you need to type in a password before the screen returns to normal. Windows comes with its own set of screen savers. You can buy additional screen savers, which display everything from the famous Flying Toasters to *Star Trek* images. Go to Display or Desktop in Windows and try out the screen saver options supplied with Windows.

Printer

There are three main types of printer: the dot-matrix, the inkjet and the laser. Although they print on to paper in different ways, they all use the same information from your PC and you normally use the same ports to hook them up. When you unpack your printer, make sure you read the instructions carefully before connecting it, since there may well be several parts, such as the paper feeder, that have to be fitted before it is ready for action.

When the printer is assembled, connect it to the PC's printer port, normally marked LPT1 or Printer, and then connect its mains lead directly to the mains socket on the wall, or power strip.

Windows uses software called Drivers to translate the image you see on your monitor screen into information your printer can understand. Before you start printing, you have to ensure that Windows has the right Driver installed for your printer. Selecting the Printer icon in the Control Panel will show you which Printer Drivers are installed and that the print information is being sent through the right port. The printer will then work with any Windows program you have now or will have in the future, without your having to do anything else.

Printer controls

While some printers are controlled entirely by on-screen software, most have some controls built into them with indicators to tell you more about the printer's current settings. The panel below is a typical example. Try out each of the controls so that you can see what they do. The power switch is usually found at the back of the printer. If you don't normally switch off at the wall socket when you finish working, you should switch off the printer using its own mains power button.

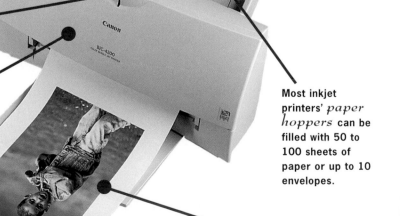

The paper tray is *adjustable* for different sizes of paper and envelopes.

Some printers have no *external controls* other than a power switch and are operated entirely through software on the PC.

The hinged *dust cover* protects the ink cartridge and minimises noise during printing.

Most inkjet printers' *paper hoppers* can be filled with 50 to 100 sheets of paper or up to 10 envelopes.

Printed documents emerge face up into the *output tray* to dry.

Printer drivers

When you send a job to a printer, the printer must have some way of knowing what you want it to put on the paper. It has to recognise italics, special fonts, bullets, pictures, graphs and all the other things that people want to print. To do this, it uses a piece of software called a printer driver. Each model of printer has its own driver, provided by the manufacturer. The driver contains all the information needed for the printer to interpret what you put into your documents so that the printed output looks exactly as you intended.

While each printer driver is particular to one printer, if you can't find exactly the right one, it is often worthwhile experimenting with the nearest you can get. A Hewlett-Packard LaserJet 4 driver will work almost perfectly with an HP LaserJet 4/M. But you cannot expect a Canon driver to work particularly well with a Fujitsu printer.

If nothing looks likely in the list of drivers, a lowest common denominator is often available. This will give a basic output. It is unlikely to do italics or bold and certainly won't handle graphics or fonts other than Courier. But at least you'll get text on to paper.

Easy**WINDOWS**

PORTS
Several of the sockets at the back of your computer are called ports. If you're lucky, these will be labelled on the back of your computer; if they aren't, you'll have to work it out (*see below*). You can plug your choice of peripherals into these ports.

SERIAL/PARALLEL
Your computer will have two types of ports for printers, called serial and parallel. Most computers sold now have two serial ports (known as COM1 and COM2) and one or two parallel ports (LPT1 and LPT2). Identification is usually simple, as serial ports are male (with pins) and parallel ports are usually female (with holes).

How to take control of your printer driver

STEP 1 Open the Control Panel, and look for the icon labelled Printers. You'll see from its arrow that it's a shortcut to somewhere else. In fact, if you used the Start, Settings route to the Control Panel, you might have noticed an entry in the Settings menu just below the one for Control Panel called Printers.

STEP 2 You can use either route to reach this window. Each installed printer driver has its own icon in the window, and what you see depends on which printers, if any, have been installed. There's also an Add Printer icon. Double-click on this ...

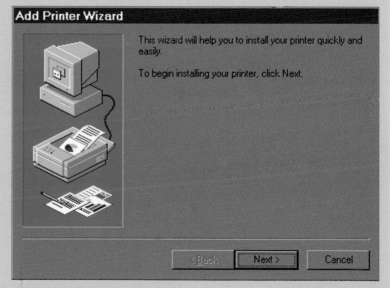

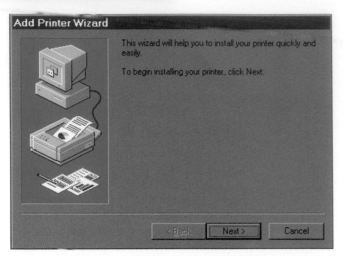

STEP 3 ... and you meet another helpful Wizard, the Add Printer Wizard. Click on the Next button to start the installation.

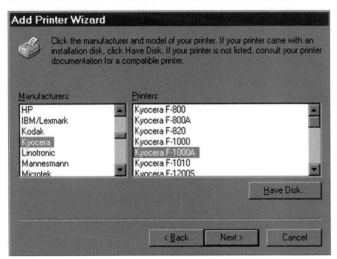

STEP 4 Here you're asked if your new printer is local or on a network. Choose local unless you are connected to a network, and click on Next. On the left a list of manufacturers appears; on the right, a list of models. Find the make of your printer and the list in the printers column will change to show all the drivers for that brand. Pretend you have a Kyocera. Your printer is an F-1000A, so double-click on that. If your printer came with its own driver, put the disk in the drive and click on Have Disk. Select the driver as before. If you can't find your printer, choose Generic and Generic/Text Only.

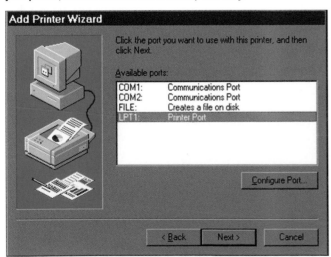

STEP 5 You are then asked about ports (see *Easy Windows*). The choice you are offered depends on your machine, but it's often between COM1, COM2, FILE, and LTP1. You can ignore the File option and the COM options, as most printers use parallel ports (see *Easy Windows*), so it's reasonable to choose the LPT1 option.

STEP 6 You're shown the make and model you've chosen and asked if you want this to be the default printer. Usually, you'll only have one printer, so it will have to be the default, so click this option and Next. Printing a test page is a good idea, so choose this, too. Finally, click on Finish. If the Wizard can't find the printer driver on your hard disk, it may ask you to insert the Windows CD-ROM.

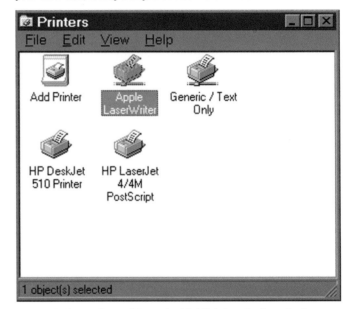

STEP 7 Delete printer drivers by highlighting the icon in the Printers section of the Control Panel and pressing Delete. Confirm the action and the driver will go away.

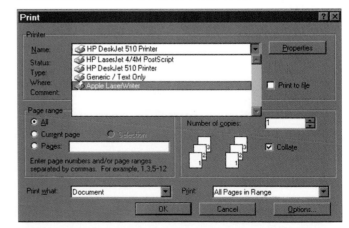

STEP 8 Following these steps, you can add any number of printers. If a friend comes over with a colour inkjet printer, you can have the driver installed and waiting. Unplug your usual printer and plug in the new one. The first time you want to print from, say, Word, click on File/Print to see this window. Where it says Printer Name, scroll down the menu, select the relevant driver, and print as usual. Don't just click on the Print icon, as this bypasses this Print window.

Peripherals

You may well have other peripherals to connect to your PC. While some devices, such as the modem, will use one of the PC's regular ports, others, such as scanners, sound systems and joysticks will use the sockets on the back of special cards that go into the expansion slots of your PC.

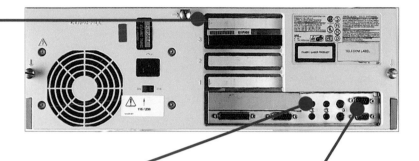

Bays for expansion cards for such devices as scanners and sound cards.

Ports for headphones, microphones and audio in and out.

Serial port for peripherals, such as fax/modems.

Sound

A sound card will have an output to feed a pair of speakers. These should be connected by inserting the 3.5mm stereo plug into the speaker or headphone socket of the sound card. Most sound cards have a D-connector, which is a games port. This is where you connect your games joystick if you have one. This port doubles as the MIDI connection for synthesisers and keyboards.

CD-ROM

The CD-ROM drive will be built into your PC and all the connections are done internally. If you want to listen to an ordinary audio CD, the CD-ROM drive also has a stereo jack socket at the front so you can plug in headphones, bypassing the rest of the computer's sound system.

Modem

The modem links your computer to the telephone line so you can send and receive files and messages from other computer users around the world using the Internet. Some modems are separate boxes (external modems) that connect to the COM2 port of your computer. These have to be connected to a telephone socket and also need a separate mains power supply. Internal modems are built on an expansion card that slots inside your PC. The only leads needed from these modems are to the phone socket.

Scanners

The other common peripheral is the scanner, used to scan pictures or text into the PC. These normally connect to their own cards in an expansion slot.

Memory

Your PC uses its own internal memory to store programs and files that you are currently working on. This storage area is called Random Access Memory (RAM) and is held on the memory chips inside your PC. Although the programs may still work if you do not have enough RAM, they will run more slowly. You will notice a big difference in the speed of your system if you increase the amount of RAM in your PC. Some computers come with only 8Mb of RAM, which is not enough to run Windows smoothly. You need at least 16Mb.

Store it as a file

All the information that your PC uses is stored on its internal hard disk, floppy disk or CD-ROM, in individual files. A computer file is just like a real file. You give it a name and file it away. When you want to get the file back, you just look for the file name on the disk and get your PC to open it up. By using My Computer as in Windows 95 (or File Manager as in Windows 3.1), you can see all the files on any of the disks in the PC, including the hard disk.

Floppy disks

The most common way to save files for transferring them to other PCs or just to keep for safety is the floppy disk. Floppy disks are cheap and reliable but have limited capacity – 720Kb for a standard disk or 1.44Mb for a high-density disk. While this isn't big enough for a large software program, the floppy disk is just the right size to hold quite a few of your documents or other files.

Hard disk drive

A hard disk drive has been fitted inside your PC. This is used as the PC's permanent store of programs and data. It is your PC's own library of programs and files. All of the programs that have already been loaded on to your PC are stored on the hard disk, so they are always available at the click of a mouse button. When you buy any new programs, the first thing you have to do is transfer it from the floppy disk or CD-ROM on to your hard disk.

Software programs are getting very big, so the hard disk needs to have a large storage capacity. If you have loaded Windows and several other programs, such as a word processor, a database, a spreadsheet and a drawing program, you will have already used up nearly 200–300Mb. You should be using at least a 1.2Gb hard disk to leave room for new files and programs.

Formatting

Formatting magnetically records empty tracks and indexes on to the surface of the disk. When it comes to recording and reading real data, this helps the disk drive know where on the disk particular bits of information have been stored.

Many floppy disks come pre-formatted. But if you need to format a floppy disk, put the blank disk into the drive and then use My Computer (or File Manager) in Windows to format it. You are always given a chance to cancel the formatting process if you have accidentally put in the wrong disk.

The hard disk will have already been formatted before you get your computer. Do not try to reformat your hard disk or you will erase every file and piece of information.

& storage

Bits and bytes

Computers store everything as streams of binary numbers. Binary numbers are simply a string of ones and zeros put together in groups to make up useful numbers. Our normal number system works in the same way, but whereas we work on the basis of multiples of tens, binary works on multiples of twos.

For example, the number 174 is made up of one set of 100, seven sets of 10 and four sets of 1:

100		10		1		
1		7		4		
100	+	70	+	4	=	**174**

The same number in binary is 10101110, made up of one set of 2, one set of 4, one set of 8, one set of 32 and one set of 128.

128	64	32	16	8	4	2	1
1	0	1	0	1	1	1	0

128+0 + 32+ 0 + 8 + 4 + 2 + 0 = **174**

Each of the ones and zeros are called bits and a group of 8 bits is called a byte.

1 or 0	=	**1 bit**
10101110	=	**1 byte**

CD-ROM drive

The CD-ROM is the latest way of distributing software. For most people the CD-ROM is a read-only system, which is what its name stands for: CD-Read-Only Memory. There are CD-ROM writers, but they cost more than a PC.

The big advantage of the CD-ROM is that it can hold up to 650Mb of data, which makes it ideal for distributing big software packages. (The new DVD-ROM holds several Gb of data.)

The software is installed on to the PC's hard disk from the CD-ROM in exactly the same way as it would be installed from a floppy disk, except that you don't have to keep changing disks. Once loaded, you can store the CD-ROM away, as it won't be needed again.

Zip drive

The Zip drive is an external drive that uses 100Mb Zip disks from Iomega Corporation. These are becoming an increasingly popular medium for storing larger files such as those produced by sound, video or multimedia software programs. Zip drives are supplied with software called DiskFit Direct which is designed to make it simpler to back up your files.

You can speed up your PC by adding extra *RAM chips*.

Kilobytes, megabytes and gigabytes

RAM is always measured by the number of bits it can store. For Windows work you need at least 16 megabytes of RAM. Because a byte is such a small unit of storage, hard disks and floppy disks are measured in terms of thousands of bytes (kilobyte or Kb) or millions of bytes (megabyte or Mb), and the largest hard drives can hold more than a billion bytes (gigabyte or Gb).

What does this mean in real terms? A word processor file of 1,000 words will take up around 15Kb, and a half-screen, full-colour picture will be about 150Kb. So the average floppy disk will hold around 100 short letters or 10 images. The hard disk needs to be much bigger because it permanently stores all the programs you are going to use.

	Storage space	Number of bytes	Number of megabytes
Double-density floppy disk	720Kb	737,280	0.72
High-density floppy disk	1.44Mb	1,440,000	1.44
Average hard disk	2Gb	2,000,000,000	2,000
CD-ROM	650Mb	650,000,000	650
Large hard disk	4Gb	4,000,000,000	4,000

Drives

T he magnetic surface of a floppy disk is safely tucked away in its plastic outer shell. When you put the disk in the drive, the motor locks on to the metal hub of the disk and starts it spinning. The metal shutter is pulled aside, exposing the disk's surface, and a recording head – a bit like those used on a cassette deck – records (writes) or reads data.

Metal *shutter* springs closed to cover the write window so the disk's recording surface cannot be touched.

Plastic *outer shell* protects the magnetic disk inside.

The *write-protect tab*. With the tab up and the hole exposed, the disk drive will simply refuse to write on to it. This protects you from accidentally overwriting important files.

Adhesive *label* to identify what's on the disk. Use different-colour labels for different types of files.

The *HD tab* tells the drive whether the disk is a double-density or high-density disk.

Looking after your floppy disks and drive

You need to treat your floppy disks with care. You should always take them out of the drive when you have finished with them. Buy a disk box to keep them in. The disks can be affected by stray magnetism, so avoid putting them on top of your PC or near any speakers. Use the write-protect tab to make it impossible to accidentally write over important files. The heads on the floppy disk drive may get dirty. Clean them with a floppy disk cleaning kit.

Hard disk

The data is recorded on a small disk covered in a magnetic material similar to the material on the surface of a cassette tape. The write/read head floats just above the surface of the spinning magnetic disk to read or write data on to it. The drives are very intricate devices, which is why they can store so much data on a very small magnetic disk, typically only 3.5in wide.

CD-ROM drive

The data is stored on the CD as small pits backed by a reflective aluminium surface. A small laser is focused on the CD and light reflected off the pits is registered on a light sensor and then translated back into data.

Maintaining your CD-ROM discs and drive

CDs are not indestructible. Scratches and dirt will stop them from working. So handle the disks by their edges and put them away after use. Empty CD cases are available at music stores and are a worthwhile investment. The lens on the CD-ROM drive's laser can get dirty. Use a CD-ROM cleaning kit.

Expansion

Computer makers know that each person will want to use their PC for different things and will need different peripherals. Some of the PC's basic facilities, such as the display card and the electronics that control the hard disk and floppy disk, can also differ depending on how you want your PC to work. All home PCs need a display card that can instantly deliver Windows screens. Others will also want to play video and animations smoothly. So instead of building these functions into the main PC board, manufacturers give you expansion slots. This also means you can upgrade cards easily. Expansion slots work a bit like ports, except they link straight into the computer's electronics so that the expansion card can communicate directly with the computer's internal processor and memory systems.

These expansion slots can also be used for peripherals that need to be closely linked into the computer's electronics. Typical peripherals that come as plug-in expansion cards are sound cards, display/video cards, fax/modems, scanner interface cards and network cards.

Fitting an expansion card

You need just a screwdriver to fit a PC card. With the power disconnected, remove the lid of the computer, find a spare slot of the right type, slide the card in and lock it in place with the securing screw. Be careful to hold the card by its edges only. And touch a piece of earthed metal first so that you don't pass static on to the card. Then replace the lid, switch on the computer and run the software that comes with the card. This tells the computer how to communicate with its new electronics.

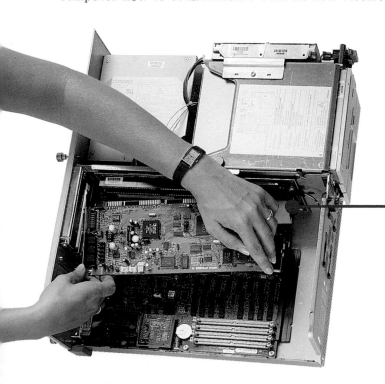

Easy to fit, the *expansion card* simply slides into the slot.

8-, 16- & 32-bit

PCs handle data as binary numbers (bits). The early PCs moved around numbers that were made up of eight bits (like 10101011), which cover a range from 0 to 255. Modern computers move around 16-bit (1101010001001010) or 32-bit (11010100010010101011010100 01001010) numbers. The bigger the number the computer can handle at any one time, the faster it can operate. The channel that the computer uses to move data around is called a bus and plug-in expansion cards link directly into these buses.

Waiting for the bus

The ISA (Industry Standard Architecture) expansion slots were first used on the early PCs with their 8-bit buses and ISA has remained the basic standard for expansion slots ever since. When computers improved, the ISA connectors were extended to handle 16-bit data buses, and now every computer has at least two or three ISA slots that can take 8-bit bus or 16-bit bus ISA expansion cards.

ISA can't handle all the demands of the latest generation of add-on cards, and there are new types of internal slots that are better. The most common is the PCI (peripheral component interconnect). PCs come with a combination of the ISA and PCI slots, so you can use both old and new expansion cards.

Any new PC card must match the type of expansion slot you have left free inside your PC.

Your PC at

Where you put your computer depends on the PC and the people who use it. It is important that there is space between the back of the PC and the wall, to maintain a good air flow. Your monitor also generates heat, so don't cover it up. You should have plenty of mains sockets so each unit can have a plug. Make sure your desk is sturdy enough. Be careful with cups, so that you don't spill anything on the keyboard. Ideally, you should have a drawer to store floppy disks and accessories, and a shelf for manuals.

You need the screen at the right height. A natural position is with the centre of the screen level with your chin and with the monitor angled back a little. If putting the monitor on top of the PC makes it too high, move the computer to one side and put the monitor on the desk. You may need an additional monitor stand, or even a pile of telephone directories, to raise it.

Try to hold your forearms horizontal and not to flex your wrists up or down while typing. Ensure that the *height* of the desk is such that your arms and wrists are comfortable.

If you suffer from *glare* or *reflection* on your screen, take a look at the lighting. You may need to buy blinds for a nearby window. By moving your PC to a different part of the room, you may avoid the glare of overhead lighting. You might even consider buying an uplighter so there is no overhead glare. Always make sure that the screen image is stable and flicker-free and that you can read anything on screen easily.

Allow enough space in front of the *keyboard* to support your hands and wrists during pauses in typing. You can buy separate hand and wrist supports to attach to the work surface if necessary.

Make sure that you can adjust the height and the tilt of the *chair* that you will use to provide good lumbar support.

Make sure there is *adequate space* under the desk for thighs, knees, lower legs and feet and that there is plenty of room to allow for changes in posture while using a computer. Prolonged sitting in one position can be harmful.

If your feet do not rest flat on the floor, you can either buy a *footrest* or use an old box to rest your feet on comfortably. Do not use a footrest when it is not necessary, as this can result in poor posture.

home

Like all TV screens, computer monitors produce ionising and non-ionising radiation. The amounts are minuscule, but you should sit so that your face is at least a couple of feet from the front of the screen.

The room should have good lighting. Try to avoid putting the monitor in a position where it is facing bright lights or a window. These will be reflected in the screen, making it difficult to see.

The right seating position is with elbows level with the keyboard so your arms are horizontal when you type. Use an adjustable chair, such as a typist's chair so that you can customise your seating position.

If your children are going to use the computer, make certain that the chair and monitor heights are suitable for them as well as you. If necessary, buy them a desk and chair. Show them how to switch the system on and off and which way the floppy disks have to be inserted.

Add a bit of greenery

Plants help the general working atmosphere, but do not place any plant directly above the computer hardware, as you might risk spilling water into the electronics.

Extras shopping list

Once you have your PC system, here are a few things you may need to complete your PC 'office'.

- Furniture: desk, adjustable chair, such as a typist's chair, desk lamp.
- Storage: floppy disk boxes, CD rack, spare CD cases.
- Consumables: paper, blank floppy disks, spare printer ribbon, or ink cartridge.
- Cleaning: keyboard cleaning kit, floppy-disk cleaner, monitor wipes.
- Others: mouse mat, wrist support, document holder, security tags.

Security

Along with VCRs and TVs, computers are a high-tech item loved by housebreakers. You should mark every item with your postcode using a permanent marker or an invisible ultraviolet marker. This will at least help you identify the units as yours. There are computer security systems that attach the computer to the desk with a strong metal cable, which makes it difficult to remove the computer quickly.

You should include your PC in your household contents insurance policy. If you have a laptop, check that your insurance covers it when it is out of the home.

Finally, remember the value of copying important documents on to floppy disks. For many people, losing vital information stored on the hard disk is a much more serious problem than losing the computer itself.

Switching on & off

When you switch on your PC, the monitor screen will be black with a few simple lines of text. The PC searches its hardware, checking that everything is working. Both the hard disk and the floppy disk will then whir into action. When it is happy that everything is OK, your PC will beep and look through the hard disk for two files: AUTOEXEC.BAT and CONFIG.SYS. These used to give it setup information but in Windows 95 they are there only to provide compatibility with older software. Then your PC will launch Windows.

In the meantime, your printer is going through a similar routine. When your PC is ready, the monitor will display the Windows Desktop and play the startup sound clip (provided that you have a sound card).

Operator error

The majority of problems people experience with their PCs are not flaws at all. They are what are called operator errors. Typical examples of operator error are not switching on the monitor or printer, finding that it is not plugged into the mains or is disconnected at the computer end, or finding that the monitor brightness has been turned all the way down.

The message 'non-system disk' is more likely to mean you have left a floppy disk in the drive, and 'keyboard error' may be caused by books resting on the keys. If you have a problem, first make a note of any information the PC is giving you and write down the symptoms.

Then switch off the PC and check absolutely everything. Only when you have done this and the problem still persists is it time to contact your dealer, manufacturer or PC service centre. ●

Use the mains switch

There is no reason why you shouldn't use the mains switch instead of the computer's Power button as your main on/off button, especially if you have all the computer peripherals connected using a mains adapter. Then, by clicking just one switch, you will send power to all the parts of your computer system. ●

Switching off

It is not a good idea to switch your PC off without closing down your programs first, as you could lose a file you have been working on. If you have finished working, remove any floppy disks or CD-ROMs and put them away.

Now you are ready to shut down Windows by clicking on Shut Down or Exit Windows.

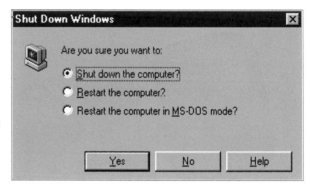

After a few seconds you will get a message saying it is safe to switch off your PC, or you will return to the black DOS screen, with its C:> prompt. Either way, you can now safely switch off your computer.

Computer crashes

The one time you may have to switch off your computer without going through this routine is when the software crashes. A crash is when something happens in the software that confuses your PC. The program stops working, the screen freezes, and pressing the keys or moving the mouse has no effect.

The first thing to do is press the Ctrl, Alt and Delete keys simultaneously. This might let you close down the current program but keep Windows working.

If pressing Ctrl-Alt-Delete does nothing, you have to press the Reset button on your PC. This will put the PC back into its switch-on sequence and should clear any problem. You will lose work that hasn't been saved.

Crashes are, unfortunately, quite common, so try to save your work regularly. Many programs include an auto-save feature that will save your work to the hard disk every few minutes. The saving is done behind the scenes, as a background operation, so it doesn't stop you from working.

Problems switching on

If there is trouble during powering up, you will normally hear two bleeps and a message will appear on the screen that indicates that your PC has detected a problem with some of the hardware. The computer will then display its own diagnostic screens, which may give you some idea what is wrong. Make a note of all the information on the screen and contact your supplier or the manufacturer, who will be able to tell you what to do.

3

WINDOWS

View-finder

Windows is a replacement for a system called DOS, which was the only way of operating PCs when they first came out. DOS was controlled via the keyboard and involved learning complicated commands to type in. Windows is a graphical user interface (known as a GUI, pronounced 'gooey') that allows you to operate the PC with a mouse on your desk and images on the screen.

But what does Windows do? It has been described as an 'enabler', an ugly word, but descriptive. Windows, in isolation, doesn't do very much. On its own it doesn't let you write letters, keep track of accounts, or catalogue your record collection. But it does enable you to run the programs – or, as they are sometimes called, applications – that allow you to do these things. So, if you want to write a letter, you use a word processor from within Windows. If you want to keep your business accounts on the PC, you can use an accounting program under Windows.

Think of your computer as a car. The engine (program) does the work, but you drive the car with the steering wheel and pedals (Windows) rather than directly with the engine. We'll be looking at how you can control Windows itself and set it up to suit your way of using your PC. It is worth learning to do that because Windows provides the interface for all the programs that you run (see *Easy Windows* box). Once you understand the Windows interface, you have the basic knowledge needed to run all Windows programs.

Suppose that you are using a word processor to write a letter to the bank manager, asking for a loan. In another program you have all the figures that justify your request to the bank for the money. Windows enables you to pick up the relevant numbers from the second program and drop them into the letter. Even if some of your data is in graphical form (say, a graph of your earnings and expenditures), you can still move it into the letter.

Windows has been regularly updated to make it more powerful and easier to use. We'll be concentrating on Windows 95, but Windows 98 is the newest.

STEP 1 A typical opening screen in Windows.

Let's assume that you have just bought a PC with Windows. Having had the fun of unpacking the computer and plugging it in, you turn it on. After hearing some clicking and whirring, you should see a screen that looks like Step 1 (page 45). Your screen may differ from this, but don't worry. Windows is meant to be configurable – that means it can be changed to suit the PC you have. The supplier of your PC may have configured it for you already. For example, the supplier may have put a picture on the background or there may be extra icons (see *Easy Windows* box on page 45).

Step 2 shows all the different things that can appear, but the ones you can probably see on your screen are the desktop (which is essentially the Menu bar and the background area on the screen), some icons and the task bar.

The best way to learn what these do, and how to use Windows itself, is by doing practical things. Microsoft, the company that makes Windows, supplies several free programs with it, including a word processor and several games. We'll start by opening up the word processor, as an example of a program, and closing it down again.

You'll find the task bar at the bottom of the screen. On the left of the task bar is a button labelled 'Start'. Remember that you have real buttons on your mouse and buttons which are part of the interface on the screen. To avoid confusion when referring to these, the usual convention is to say 'Click the Start button.' So click the Start button.

A menu – that's a list of choices – will appear. This menu stays in place, even if you remove your finger from the button. As you move the mouse cursor over the menu, different options are highlighted. If you click on one, or allow the mouse cursor to linger, a sub-menu will appear for all options with a small arrow on the right. The first four options on the menu shown in Step 3 have an arrow, so they have a sub-menu. This is

STEP 2 All of the common items that you are likely to encounter when you use Windows.

A *shortcut* is a way of navigating rapidly around Windows.

A *window* is a rectangular working area on the screen, normally containing one application and one document.

An *icon* is a small picture that represents something.

A *folder* is a container for icons and documents.

A *document* is an icon that represents your data, which could be a picture or a sound clip. Double-clicking on this will take you to it.

The *task bar* typically appears at the bottom of the screen. But you can move it by clicking on it, holding down the mouse button, and moving it to any of the other three edges of the screen.

the first of many conventions to remember.

Work your way down the menu system so that you have selected Programs and Accessories, as in Step 3. One of the Accessories is a program called WordPad, so click that option. After a brief pause, the program will appear in a window, ready for you to use it. Another Accessory, NotePad, is a less versatile version so choose WordPad.

To close the word processor, find the small button in the top-right corner labelled with an X and click on it. To close Windows entirely, click the Start button again and select Shut Down. A new window will appear, and you can click on the Yes button in that window.

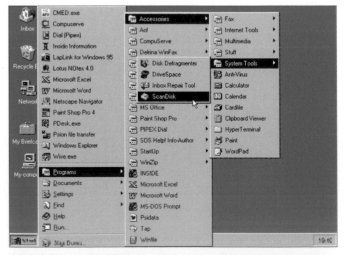

STEP 3 This is the Windows menu system that you are likely to see from the Start button, giving you a list of choices.

Playing with words

Now you know the very basics of Windows. You'll notice from the pictures of our PC screen on the next page that we've already begun the task of changing, or configuring, Windows to our liking by moving the Menu bar from its default position at the bottom of the screen to the top (see *Easy Windows* box on page 45). Windows normally reads from the top down rather than from the bottom up, so having menus at the top seems the better option.

First steps

The best way of learning Windows is to use one of the applications, and the easiest one to use is the word processor. So, let's write a thank-you letter to an aunt in New Zealand.

With Windows running, open up WordPad. In Step 1 (page 48) you can see the three levels of menu and submenus that appear when you click on the Start button. In the first main menu, Programs was chosen. Accessories was picked in the first sub-menu and WordPad in the second sub-menu.

After a pause, the duration of which will depend on the speed of your PC, WordPad will appear in a window (see Step 2). The header bar says Document – WordPad, and below it is a grey bar with six menus from which you can choose. The bulk of the window is filled with plain white space where you'll compose your letter.

You simply need to type something to fill up the space, as in Step 3. This is the start of the thank-you letter, with the salutation and some of the body text typed in. As you fill a whole line, you'll see that the next line automatically wraps around without your having to press the Enter key.

If WordPad has opened in a small window, you may find you cannot see a whole line of text at once. As with most things in Windows, you can change the small window to one that occupies a full screen (see Step 4). WordPad is now said to be running in full-screen mode.

We haven't made much progress with our thank-you letter. But we'll save it anyway, accepting the default options for the saving process. Call your document something memorable like Thanks. Now close WordPad.

Easy WINDOWS

CONFIGURING WINDOWS

If you decide that you'd prefer the Menu bar to appear across the top of your screen rather than across the bottom, moving it is easy. Put the mouse cursor on the Menu bar somewhere where there is no button, and press and hold down the left mouse button. Drag the cursor up to the top of the screen and you'll see a grey outline indicating the space the Menu bar will take up in its new position. Releasing the mouse button effects the move, and the Menu bar will now stay at the top of the screen. You can also experiment with the Menu bar on the left or right edges of your screen. You're free to choose whichever you prefer and to change it whenever you wish.

ENTER

The Enter key can also be called the Return key, and you'll often find instructions like 'Press Enter' or 'Hit Return'. The naming of this key comes from the days of manual typewriters, which had a lever for returning the carriage to the left-hand side of a document and moving down to the next line. Modern keyboards often have a symbol of an arrow with a tail sticking upwards and a head pointing to the left.

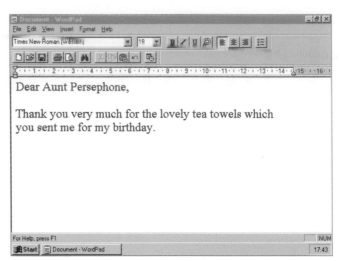

STEP 1 To open up WordPad, click on the Start button. In the menu that appears, move the mouse cursor to highlight the Programs item, then highlight the Accessories item in the next list. Finally, move the cursor right down to the last item on the third list, to highlight WordPad.

STEP 4 To give yourself a better view, click on the centre button of the three at the top-right corner of the WordPad window. It shows a rectangle with a thick line at the top, symbolising a window with a title bar across its top. WordPad now fills all of the available screen.

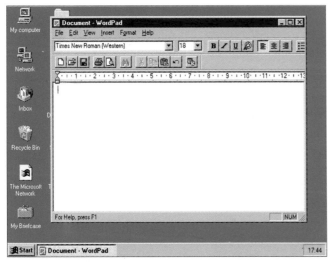

STEP 2 This is what you'll see on opening the WordPad word-processing application. The white space is like a blank page in a writing pad. There's a thin line blinking in the top-left corner called a cursor that tells you where the computer's attention is focused; this is where your text will appear.

STEP 5 Click on File in the Menu bar at the top of the screen, and then click on Save. The Save As window will appear. Type 'Thanks' into the highlighted File Name box. The rest of the settings can be accepted just as they are for now. To save the letter, click on the Save button on the bottom right.

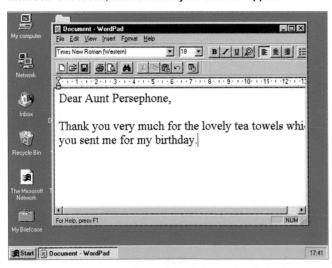

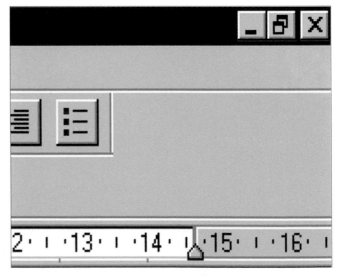

STEP 3 Type 'Dear Aunt Persephone,'. Press the Enter key twice (see *Easy Windows* page 47). This will give you a line space underneath the salutation and take you to a new line, where you'll begin the letter itself. Write 'Thank you very much for the lovely tea towels' and so on.

STEP 6 Now you can close down WordPad. There are three buttons to the right of the menu bar. The one farthest to the right has an X on it. This button appears on many menus and means close the current application. Click on it now.

Windows wonderland

By the end of the last pages, we had an unfinished letter that was saved somewhat hurriedly. This time we'll start WordPad and retrieve that letter. So launch WordPad (see *Easy Windows* box) the way you did last time. Pull down the File Menu to Open. Click the 'Thanks' file.

Now you should have your letter in front of you. Its appearance can be improved by adding your aunt's address and today's date, which can be done from the menu (see Steps 3 and 4, page 50).

Changing windows

You have the ability to move windows around and resize them. Last time, we changed the WordPad window to a full-screen window by clicking on the middle of the three buttons at the top right of the menu bar. There are other options that give even more control over a window's size.

Return to the smaller window by clicking on the same button. It should now be showing two overlapping window symbols. To move the whole window, put the mouse cursor in the header bar at the top of the window, click on the left mouse button and keep your finger pressed down while you move the mouse around on the mat. You'll see a grey rectangular outline that moves as you move the mouse. This represents the window, and when that rectangle reaches the place on the screen where you want the window to be, release the mouse button. You can move almost all windows in this manner – it's known as dragging – and you can move them as many times as you like.

It's also possible to change the size of the window by stretching out its borders. To make a window wider, place the cursor over the right-hand border of the window. You can tell the cursor is in the correct position for a stretching operation when the cursor changes to a double-headed arrow. Click on the mouse button, keep your finger down and move the cursor till the line that represents the edge of the box is where you want it, and release the button.

You can make windows larger or smaller and can take hold of any of their four sides to do so. To make a window wider and taller in one operation, put the mouse cursor on the bottom-left corner. You can tell you're in the right place when the double-headed arrow appears. This time it will not appear vertically or horizontally (as it does with the sides and the top/bottom) but at an angle. Drag with the mouse and release when the window is the size you want. With your window re-sized, finish your letter. Windows will even show you on screen what it will look like when it's printed (see Step 6, page 50).

WINDOWS

LAUNCHING APPLICATIONS

Launch is a term you'll see sometimes in reference to computer manuals and magazines, and it simply means to start a program or application running.

MOVING UP AND DOWN

To move to the top of a document, you can use the up arrow key on the keyboard, or you can press the Ctrl and Home keys at the same time. This is typical of Windows. It often gives you two or three different ways of doing the same thing. Did we say three? OK, you can also use the mouse and the scroll bar to move around the document. More on scroll bars on page 65.

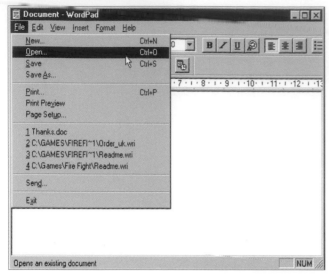

STEP 1 Click on File and then Open because you want to open an existing document. A window called Open appears (see below). The main part shows a list that includes a picture of a notebook. Next to this is the name you gave your letter.

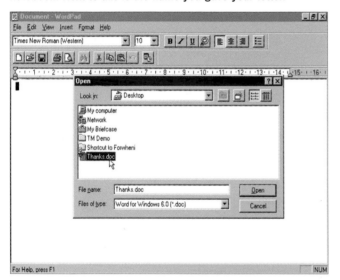

STEP 2 To retrieve this document into WordPad, click either on the icon or on the name. The icon will change colour, and the name will acquire a darker background. Then click on the Open button at the bottom of the window. You could also double-click on the document icon or its name.

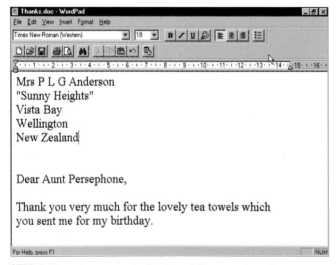

STEP 3 Move the cursor to the top of the page (see *Easy Windows* on page 49). Type in the address. Notice that this time you have to press Enter at the end of each line. This is because each line of an address is very short and the word-wrap feature only works on lines that stretch across the width of the page.

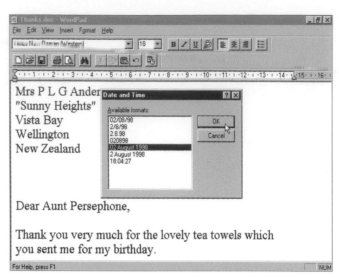

STEP 4 Click on Insert in the menu. Choose Date and Time. A window will show you the ways in which the date and time can be introduced automatically into your document. When you click on one you like – the last one is probably best for a friendly letter – the date instantly appears.

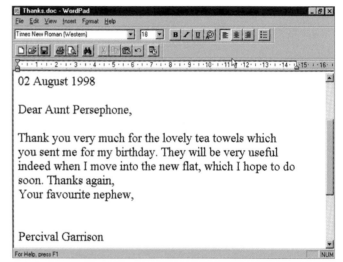

STEP 5 Move to the end of your letter, add a line space and type the closing phrase 'See you soon' or 'Your favourite niece/nephew'. Then leave a few lines of free space, into which you will insert your signature when the letter is printed, before typing your name.

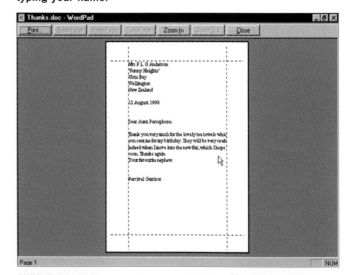

STEP 6 To see how your letter will look when printed, click on Print Preview in the File menu. Here is a preview of the finished letter. It looks OK, but it could be improved by adding a few line spaces at the top of the page. Add those and it's just about perfect.

Save and prosper

You've already used the word-processor application that comes with Windows to create a document and write a simple letter. The task of saving the letter for future reference was accomplished with little explanation. Now is a good time to look at saving files in more detail.

Windows is described as 'document-centric'. This simply means that, unlike older computer systems, Windows allows you to think mainly about documents, such as your letters, reports, newsletters etc., and not about the software that was used to create the documents.

Imagine that you have created a report using a word processor for text, a spreadsheet for pie charts, and a drawing package for clip art and logo. If you choose to open this report, Windows will automatically open all the applications used in its creation. All three would be ready and waiting for use with the open report.

So it's perfectly legitimate to click on the icon that represents your thank-you letter. Then WordPad will open and you'll have the text in front of you. It is equally effective to open WordPad and retrieve the document as you did last time. It's another example of the flexibility of Windows, and in time you'll work out your own favourite methods.

Saving a WordPad file

In the screen views on the next page, we return to the process of saving a WordPad file and look at the choices you can make. These cover where you save the file, either on a floppy disk or on the computer's hard disk. WordPad gives you the option of saving your file in several formats so that you can edit it with different word processors. Not all word processors save documents in the same format, so this is particularly useful if you need to pass a copy of your document on a floppy disk or via e-mail on to a friend who uses a different word processor. Also, if you are passing files from a PC to a Macintosh computer, or moving files from one kind of application, such as a word processor, to another, such as a desktop-publishing program, you want to make sure they are in a format that can be read. Rich Text Format is supported by most modern word processors, and Text Only provides a lowest common denominator format that can be read by any word processor.

Easy WINDOWS

TEXT BOXES AND DROP-DOWN LISTS

On many occasions as you work with Windows you'll see text boxes. They are places where you can make a choice if you wish to. Usually, a text box has a title, describing its role in life, and a sculpted oblong area where you enter your choice. If you look at the Save As window in Step 2 on page 52, you'll see one near the bottom of the screen that is labelled File Name, and the text box itself is where you'd type the name by which your file is to be saved.

Some text boxes have on their right edge a button that shows a downward-pointing arrow. A text box with one of these is called a drop-down-list box. It does exactly the same job, but it's more helpful. If you click on the button, a list pops down, giving all the options available. You simply choose the one you want by clicking on it, rather than racking your brains for something to type in that might fit the bill.

HIGHLIGHTING

To highlight a word, position the pointer to one side of the word. Click the left mouse button and hold it down, and move the mouse to highlight the whole word. Release the button.

If you're highlighting an existing entry in a text box, it is often easier to start from the right edge of the word and move the mouse to the left. There is often free space to the right of an entry, and you can place your pointer anywhere within it to begin. You need to place the pointer more accurately when starting from the left.

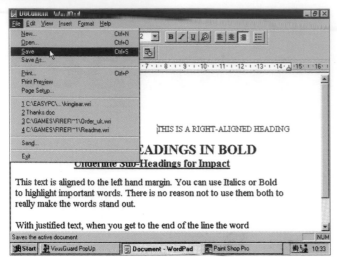

STEP 1 Open WordPad and type a few words into a new document – for example, 'testing, testing'. Click on the File menu and on Save. A Save As window opens in which you enter details of a file to be saved for the first time. Alongside the words Save In near the top of the window is an oblong area that says Desktop, with an appropriate icon. Your Desktop is what you see when you start Windows.

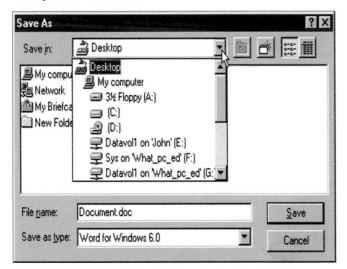

STEP 2 You will notice a button on the right-hand side of the word Desktop. It has a downward-pointing arrow on it (see *Easy Windows* on page 51). Click on it and it will list all the places where you can save your file.

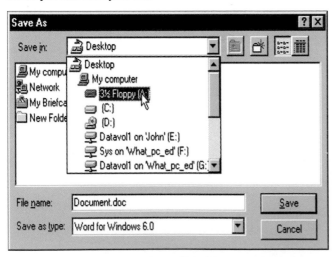

STEP 3 My Computer has a floppy-disk drive and a hard-disk drive C:. To save your file to a floppy, insert a disk into the drive. Highlight the floppy-drive option by moving the pointer to it, then click.

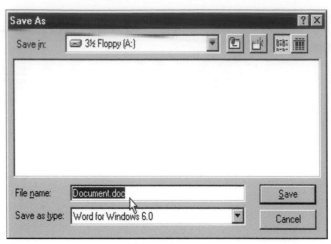

STEP 4 The destination is entered in the box. The next thing is to give your file a name. When the Save As window first opened, the default name Document was highlighted. If you'd wanted to accept the default location for your file, you could have just typed a file name and it would replace the default. Changing a file's destination or making other choices means the default file name will no longer be highlighted. Highlight the word and type in a name (see *Easy Windows* on page 51).

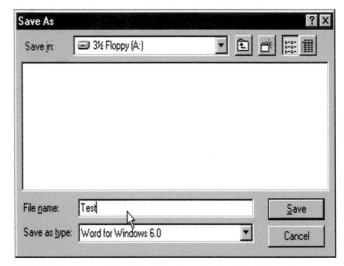

STEP 5 You can delete the default entry first, but there's no need to. Simply start typing. There are a few constraints on naming files in Windows, so just call it Test for now.

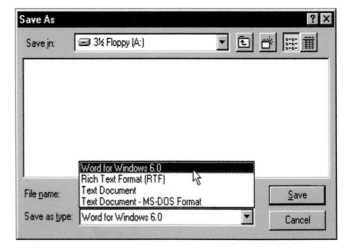

STEP 6 At the bottom of the screen is a box labelled Save As Type, and Word for Windows 6 is the default. Clicking on the button will show you the other available formats: Rich Text Format (sometimes shortened to RTF) and Text Only. Change the format only if you know your document will be needed by someone without WordPad or Microsoft Word 6.

Filing made simple

The word *folder* appears in Windows time and time again. The use of folders is one of the main ways in which Windows 95 and 98 differ from the previous versions of Windows and DOS; and, to the users of those two systems, these folders may at first seem strange. If you have ever used an Apple Macintosh, however, you'll feel quite at home because Macs have been using folders for many years.

If you're used to Windows or DOS, you'll probably already know all about directories, sub-directories and files. These tie in nicely with the idea of paperwork stored in a filing cabinet. Think of your hard disk, drive C:, as a filing cabinet. This equates to a directory. It's also called the root directory because it is the lowest level in describing the contents of a disk. The filing cabinet has three drawers, labelled Correspondence, Reports and Personal, which equate to sub-directories. In each drawer live many manila folders which represent the files.

So where do folders come in, then? In essence, all that has happened is that the terminology has changed. A folder is a directory, nothing more complicated than that. On screen a folder is represented by an icon that depicts a typical thin, card-board folder.

If you haven't used an earlier version of Windows before, life is actually easier. You don't need to know how directories work with folders, you can just think of folders as places for grouping documents together.

Remember the thank-you letter that you wrote using the WordPad word processor? Suppose that you have decided that it would be a good idea to keep all such personal correspondence together, and that you would like to create a new folder for it. You can do this when you save a document, and you can also move documents that already exist into a folder. We will take you through the procedure on the next page.

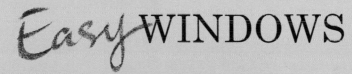

Easy WINDOWS

BUTTON LABELS

Icons on buttons are helpful as long as you can interpret the tiny graphics correctly. Who wouldn't guess, for instance, that the folder is the icon for creating a new empty folder? But they are not always immediately obvious. Windows 95 will help you to identify the buttons that you do not understand. All you have to do is put your mouse pointer on the obscure button and wait for a second. A little label pops out with a brief explanation of that button's role.

FILES

A file is the means of storing all information for use on a computer, and there are many different types of files. In Windows 95 each type of file is represented by a different icon.

Files are divided broadly into two categories: the files that you or other people have created using such applications as word processors, spreadsheets, graphics packages and the like (these are known as documents) and the files created by programmers, which are for use by the computer itself.

As you have already seen, files created by WordPad have icons that look like sheets of paper from a notepad with blue lines and a red A on them. Files such as these can be opened up and the contents can be inspected and edited. Files for the computer's internal consumption are not really meant to be read by people, and mostly their file names are not listed when you're within an application, such as a word processor. If you want to see them, you can – and marvel at all the completely indecipherable icons used to represent the different types of computer file.

In WordPad, for instance, you can see them by setting the All Files option in the Files of Type: text box. Then take a look at the root directory of drive C: or a directory called DOS. A multitude of files with strange icons appears. When you have finished looking at them, simply change the option back to Word files.

If you make a mistake and try to load one of these files into WordPad, nothing worse than an error message transpires, saying that it cannot load a file of that type. Just click on the OK button to continue as if nothing had happened.

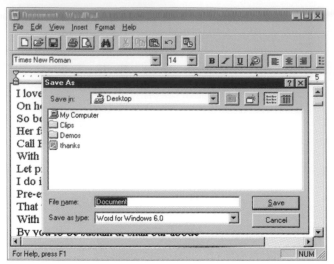

STEP 1 Open WordPad and start a document of a personal nature – a list or whatever. Click on File and on Save, as you did last time.

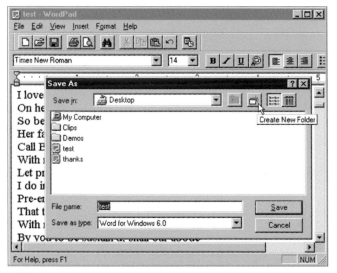

STEP 2 Your old friend the Save As window opens. Look at the collection of buttons to the right of the Save In: text box. The second one from the left shows a folder with whiskers growing from its top-right-hand corner. Rest your mouse on it for a second and a help label appears, saying, "Create new folder" (see *Easy Windows* on page 53).

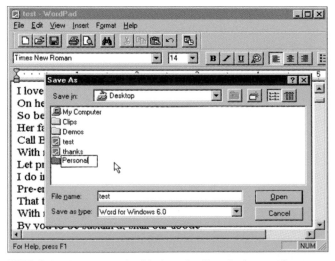

STEP 3 Click on it, and added to the list of places where you can already store files is a folder icon labelled New Folder. The folder icon and the name are both highlighted, and now is your chance to change the name to something more relevant to you. Type Personal (or whatever) and press Enter.

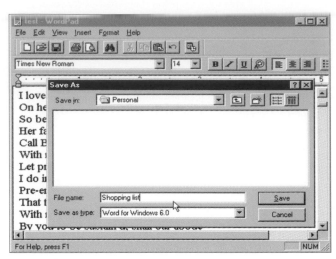

STEP 4 Choose your new folder as the destination for your list. Click on the button on the Save In: drop-down-list box. Select the new folder, then fill in a name for your new file, just as you did last time. Clicking on the Save button completes the operation.

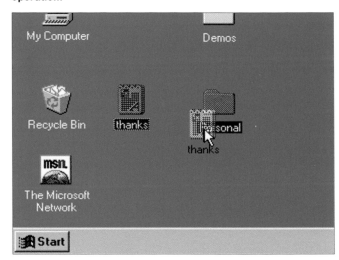

STEP 5 Return to the Desktop by clicking on the Minimize button in WordPad, which is on the top right – the one showing a bar in a box. You'll see the icon for your new folder floating there, as well as the icon for your WordPad document called Thanks. To move the Thanks file into the Personal folder, click on the file icon and, keeping the button down, slide the icon over and place it on top of the folder icon.

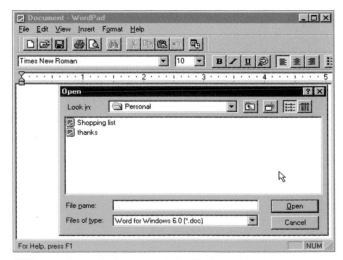

STEP 6 Release the button and the file is magically transferred. Return to WordPad and click on File, Open. Select your Personal folder to look in (using the same technique as telling Windows where to save your files) and your list and your thank-you letter are both filed neatly in the Personal folder.

On the hunt

O ne of the most inevitable things when you are using a PC is that at some stage you'll lose a file or a folder. You know it exists, you're almost sure you remember what it was called, but now that you want to retrieve it, it's not where you thought it was.

Windows 95 has a special tool for searching for these errant files and it is both flexible and easy to use. You can search for a name or part of a name. You can search for files created on the date you created or last used the missing file, or for the file type. And you can search through a specific part of your hard disk or all of it, and on a CD-ROM drive and floppy drive as well.

This wonderfully useful tool is called, simply, Find. You can get hold of it in two different ways: either from the Start menu, where it appears as the fourth item from the top of the menu, or from Explorer, where Find appears as an option under Tools.

How to find a missing file or folder

STEP 1 Using the Start Menu method, click on Start, Find and Files or Folders. A window called Find: All Files appears. This is where you define the parameters of your search. There are three options available, and the default is Name and Location. If you think that the missing file was called Aardvark but you can never remember how to spell it, you can search for the part of the word that you're sure about. Where it says Named, type in rdv. You don't have to bother with wild cards yet (see *Easy Windows* on page 56).

Choosing My Computer searches every available drive, although, of course, if there is no disk in the floppy drive and no CD in the CD-ROM drive, these won't be searched. The most common place to lose files is on the hard disk, so click on the C: drive option. Searching the whole hard disk is amazingly rapid considering the amount of data on the average hard disk.

Make sure the Include Subfolders box is checked, otherwise Find will ignore any nested folders and your search will not be complete. If you want to specify the folder in which the search should start (if you think the file should be in the Personal folder, for instance), click on the Browse button and select that folder, moving through the storage structure just as you would if using Explorer. Click on the Find Now button. The magnifying glass will move around aimlessly while a file list is constructed in an extension to the window that appears. ●

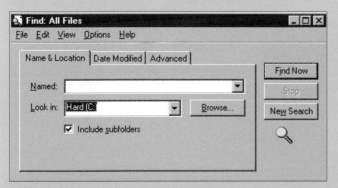

STEP 2 The only thing you have to tell Windows is where you want the search to be carried out. You must tell Find where to search, although you don't have to search by file name. Instead, you can use the Date Modified and Advanced options to search using other parameters. Clicking on the arrow to the right of the Look In box pops down a list of the available drives.

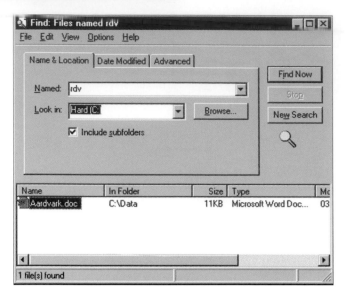

STEP 3 This view shows the result of the search. In fact, only one file has been located, and it looks like the long-lost Aardvark is no longer missing. If you want to start a new search, click the New Search button.

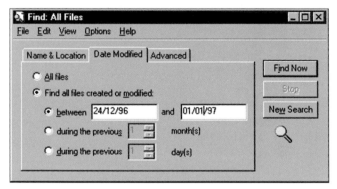

STEP 4 The other search options are Date Modified and Advanced, and they both refine the search defined in the Name & Location option. Click the Date Modified tab. Here the default selection is All Files, so to use the features offered, click to select Find All Files Created or Modified and fill in the criteria. You can specify the dates between which the file was created. You can also search for files created or modified in the last month or few months, or in the last day or so.

Here we are searching for thank-you letters that were written some time between Christmas and New Year.

If you're using the creation or modification dates to locate files, beware of your computer's clock. It stamps the current time and date on to any new file or updates that information on an existing file if it is edited and saved. If your computer's clock is not set correctly, it will stamp the wrong time and date on all your files, thus making it impossible to search for them with the handy tool provided by Find.

*Easy*WINDOWS

WILD CARDS

These are symbols that are used to represent 'anything' when you're working with file names. An asterisk represents any number of characters, while a question mark represents a single unknown character. Typing A*.* will find any file beginning with A, from a Word file called Alice.doc to a program file called Alligator.exe. Typing Aardvark.* will find the document file called Aardvark.doc, the picture file Aardvark.pcx, and any other type of file called Aardvark. Typing Aardvar?.doc will find any document called Aardvara.doc to Aardvarz.doc or other variations on the aardvark theme.

STEP 5 To check the date and time, click on Start, Settings and Control Panel. Look for the icon Date/Time, showing a clock face in front of a calendar. Double-click on this icon.

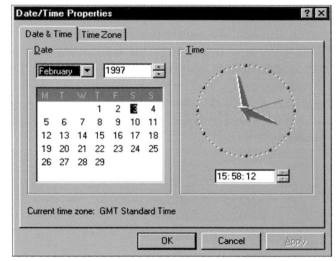

STEP 6 A window called Date/Time Properties opens and shows you a calendar and a clock face. Check that the year and month shown above the calendar are correct and that today's date is highlighted. If any of the settings is wrong, correct it. Then check the time shown on the clock. To change the hour, click on the hour in the box, then use the arrow buttons. Change the minutes and seconds in the same way. When everything is correct, click on Apply and on OK to finish.

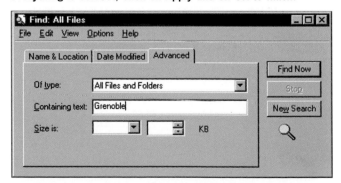

STEP 7 Returning to Find, in Advanced options you can choose to search for types of file, any text you know it contains, or a specific file size. The text search is most useful, especially if you can remember an unusual word used in the lost file. Searching for files containing 'the' will call up a multitude of candidates, but searching for 'Grenoble' will result in a much smaller list.

A helping hand

What should I do if I get confused about what to do? How can I easily remember the steps needed to do a certain job? Help is at hand. The Help system can also enable you to learn more about your computer. For example, you can use Help to teach you about wallpaper, a set of patterns that you can access in the Windows system, that enables you to enhance the appearance of your screen (see Steps 1–6, page 58).

With fanfare, the Windows Help system takes the stage. This is an on-line, context-sensitive help system (see *Easy Windows* box) that is always available to you on your PC, whatever you happen to be doing.

The computerised help system contains all the information you need to answer your questions about Windows. Instead of printing millions of copies of a paperback of monstrous proportions, and destroying thousands of trees, the text is all contained in documents held in your computer.

This way help is always at your fingertips. No longer will you reach for the manual, only to discover someone has borrowed it – and without asking first. Help systems usually have an index, so you can look things up, just as you would in the index of a book. They also usually have a way of showing you the various topics that are covered, just like the table of contents in the front of a book. There is often a way of printing out sections of the help system, so you can print out the information on adjusting the rate at which your cursor blinks and study it while relaxing in the bath.

To look for assistance in the Help system, click on Start and then on Help. A window opens up with a list of the contents, and there are tabs near the top of the window for moving to other help areas. The first area is Contents, where you start by default, and also Index and Find. Starting Help in this manner will always get you to the Contents screen. This time we'll concentrate on the help available here.

Another way of accessing Help is simply to press the F1 button (see *Easy Windows* box). If you are already using an application such as WordPad, pressing F1 will take you to the Index section and show you a list of all the help topics appertaining to WordPad. If you just want the Contents list, press F1 with the cursor anywhere outside the current active application window.

Easy WINDOWS

ON-LINE HELP

This means that help is always there waiting for your call. You don't have to do anything except tell it you need it by pressing **F1** or selecting Help from the menu.

CONTEXT-SENSITIVE HELP

This means that Windows is aware of what you're doing at the time you call for help. If you're in the Paint application, it will offer you Paint-oriented help.

THE F1 KEY

At the top of your keyboard is a row of keys marked **F1** to **F12**. The F stands for function, and these keys are known as function keys. Programs running under DOS in the days before Windows made great use of function keys as a means of operating the software without the use of a mouse. In Windows 95 they are used as part of shortcut keystrokes. For instance, pressing **Alt-F4** will close an application. Function keys are occasionally used alone, as with the **F1** key for calling up help. It has become a convention that F1 calls up help, and one to which most manufacturers adhere.

HYPERTEXT HELP

This term is used for help that comes to you in layers. In the initial chunk of information, certain words or phrases are highlighted in some way to make them stand out from the rest of the text. Clicking on these words pulls out another layer of explanation of the word in question. That explanation can also contain highlighted words from which you can see further information. This could go on indefinitely, but as it's easy to become confused after more than a couple of layers, most help systems stop at one or two.

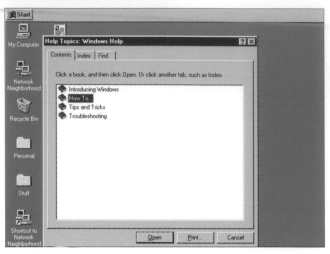

STEP 1 Click on Start and Help, and this is the window you'll see. There is a list of four items: Introducing Windows, How To, Tips and Tricks, and Troubleshooting. Your goal is to learn more about your computer, so try How To. Click on it and on the Open button, or double-click on How To.

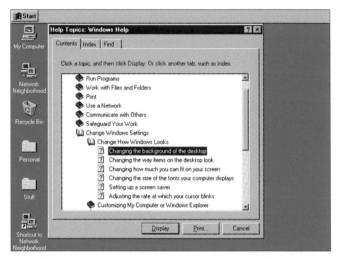

STEP 2 Another list appears. Change Windows Settings sounds promising, so double-click here and, in the subsequent list, the one labelled Change How Windows Looks is ideal. Double-click here, too, and you arrive at a list. At last some information is available, shown by the question mark. The book icons mean there are further choices to make, but the question marks indicate a piece of real information.

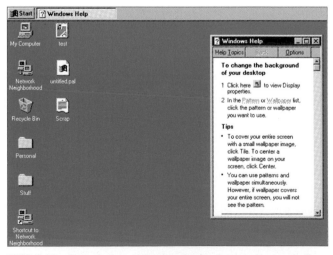

STEP 3 The first choice, changing the background, sounds fine. Double-click on it and a Windows Help window opens. At the top are three buttons: the one labelled Help Topics will take you back to the menu where you made the last choice. The Back button, now greyed out, will let you return to pages that you've already looked at. We'll look at the Options button later.

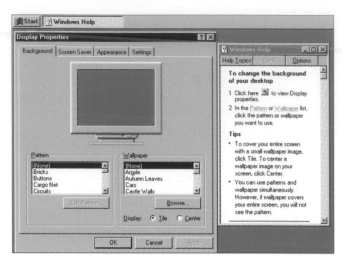

STEP 4 The window contains instructions on how to change the background of your desktop in a numbered list. Point 1 has a tiny button with an arrow pointing left. This is a good sign: it shows Windows knows what you need and that it entails running another application. Clicking on that button will automatically run that program so it is available for you to use. Click on it and a window entitled Display Properties opens.

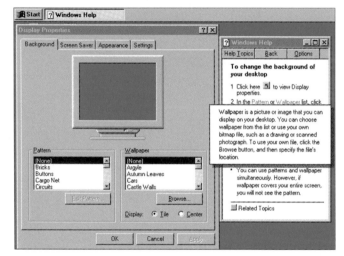

STEP 5 This is part of a program called the Control Panel. In the Help window, you'll see that there are two words written in green. When your mouse cursor points at one of these words, the cursor will change into a pointing hand. If you click on one of the words, an explanation of the word pops up in a little box. When you're new to Windows and its terminology, this help, often referred to as hypertext help (see *Easy Windows* on page 57), is invaluable.

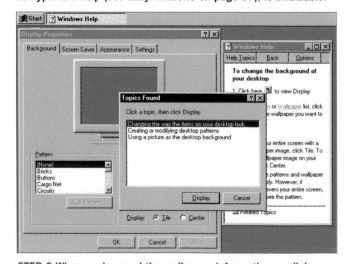

STEP 6 When you've read the wallpaper information, a click anywhere in the Help window puts it away. You're also given a couple of tips and another button at the bottom of the window for investigating related topics. Click on it to see what's available.

Playing it safe

Backup is a computer term that makes some individuals feel smug while the rest of us suffer feelings of unease, guilt and anxiety.

A backup is a copy of the files on your PC, made for the day that your hard disk fails or your computer decides it's had enough and won't boot. There are several different kinds of backup. You can keep a copy of the entire contents of your hard disk, or just some important files. Backups are usually of data files only. You should have the original disks or CD-ROMs for the applications you use in a safe place anyway. You can back up only the file or files from a single project if it is especially important.

The most common backup medium for home computers is the floppy disk. Floppy disks are cheap, easy to use and readily available. Their disadvantage is that they make the backup process time-consuming because you must stay around to change disks. A more convenient method is to use a Zip drive which uses the 100Mb Zip disks developed by Iomega Corporation. This comes with backup software called DiskFit Direct which speeds up the chore by cleverly backing up only the files you changed since the last backup.

In either case, if the worst happens and you have to replace your hard disk, you can copy the files back on to the new hard disk and everything from the last backup you made will be transferred.

If your data is really important – the complete files of your small business, for example – your backups should be stored off-site, in a fire-proof safe. Even a dry place in a garage would be better than on the desk alongside your PC.

It is up to you to decide how often to back up. Hard disks have become more reliable in recent years, and the temptation to trust them is strong. You have to weigh the hassle of backing up against the potential misery and despair if the worst should happen.

If you decide that backing up will help you sleep better, develop a routine, using three sets of floppies. If you are using 100Mb Zip disks, you can easily back up individual files, whole folders or even the entire contents of your hard disk. These disks are particularly useful if you start to work with the larger files produced by sound, video or multimedia software programs.

Easy WINDOWS

BACKUP
A backup is a copy of a file or files from your hard disk.

BOOT
A term meaning to turn on the computer and have it reach a stage where it's ready and able to do your bidding.

How to back up word-processor documents

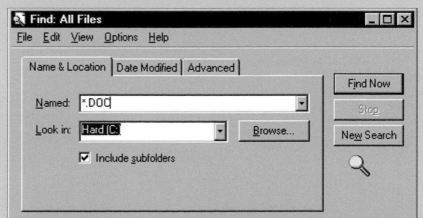

STEP 1 The easiest way to back up files is to use Find and Copy. If you decide you'd like a backup because you've worked on a lot of word-processor documents, first locate the files in question. Launch Explorer via Start, Find, and Files or Folders. The dialogue box opens at its Name and Location section. You can use wild cards to pick out all the word-processor files. If you're using Word, the default file extension is .DOC, so type in *.DOC. Next, enter the location, though the default of C:\ will usually be correct, and check that the Include Sub-Directories box is ticked.

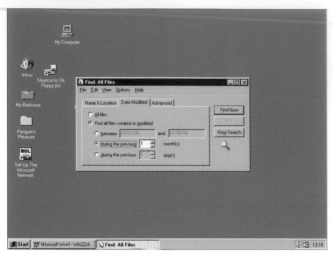

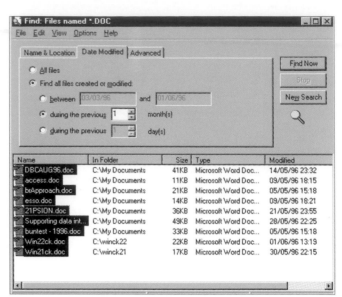

STEP 2 Click on the Date Modified tab, and then on the option labelled 'Find all files created or modified in the previous x month(s)'. The default is one month, which is fine. As you'll see from the dialogue box, the other options are to specify a number of days or to type in the dates between which you want to find all created or modified files. With the time span set to one month, click on the Find Now button.

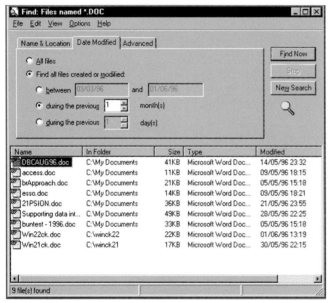

STEP 3 Your hard disk will whir for a while during the search. Then, in an area below that in which you specified your search, a file list will be built. Drag the bottom edge of the window to increase its size so you can see all of the list. If the list is very long, you'll have to resort to the scroll bars to move through it. Just as you requested, all the word-processor files that were created or modified within the past month are shown, regardless of their location on the hard disk. Displayed along with those locations are the file size and type and the date of the last modification.

STEP 4 Manoeuvre the screen into a position where you can see the list of files created by Find and a shortcut to drive A:\. Put a clean, empty floppy in the drive. Highlight the complete list of files by clicking on the first one, then click on the last one while holding down the Shift key. All the files in between will also become highlighted. Click somewhere in the highlighted block and drag it across to the shortcut. You'll see a skeletal outline of the highlights travelling under the mouse cursor, and a small plus sign will appear as you near the shortcut icon. Once the icon becomes highlighted, release the mouse button...

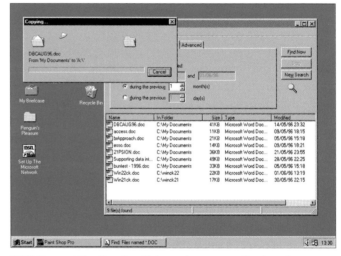

STEP 5 ...and the Copying dialogue box opens. Copies of your documents drift across the screen from one folder to the other. When this is finished, copies of all the document files will have been placed safely on the floppy disk. Store it in a safe place.

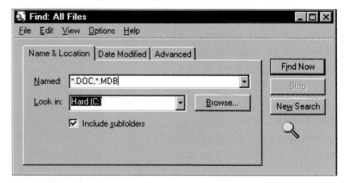

STEP 6 If you've been working on database files in MS Access as well, you can search for both types of files at once. In the Name and Location section of Find where you asked for all *.DOC files, you simply add a comma and type in *.MDB (the Access file extension). Both types of files will now appear.

The great explorers

Once you've built up a number of applications, folders and files that you use regularly, you will probably feel the need for some method of navigating around them all. You will need an easy way of finding, copying, moving and generally keeping house. Windows provides you with two ways of doing just this.

Tools that perform the tasks described above are called file managers because that's exactly what they let you do: manage your files. The file managers for Windows are My Computer and Explorer. My Computer is easier, slightly friendlier and more graphic, while Explorer is more serious about its role. They both offer very much the same type of features.

Let's start with My Computer. It can always be found on the desktop, and you're stuck with it, because it's one of the few things you can't delete. But you can change its name to Fred or something else. Click the right-hand button of the mouse on the icon, click on Rename and type in your preferred name.

*Easy*WINDOWS

ROOT
This is the name given to the first level of storage possible on a disk. The path for any file held in the root of drive C: will be C:\Filename. There is no folder containing the file; it's just sitting there on drive C:. The same is true of floppy disks (except that the drive letter will be A: or B:) and with these it's common not to use folders at all but to put everything into the root.

FILE MANAGERS

Explorer
With Explorer you can also view folders on other PCs in a network. To start Explorer, click on the Start button, then choose Programs/Explorer.

My Computer
My Computer is a more graphic file manager (*see opposite*). If your PC has two floppy-disk drives, another icon will appear labelled [B:]. Double-clicking on the control panel icon gives access to the tools, and double-clicking on the printer icon gives access to information about the printer or printers.

How to find your way around using My Computer

STEP 1 Double-click on the icon and a window appears called My Computer. In the window are several icons. Some represent drives and some, Windows tools. There are three types of drive icons, one for 3.5in floppy disks (A:), one for the hard drive (C:) and one for the CD-ROM drive (D:). Older computers have a fourth icon (B:) for 5.25in floppies. If your PC has a 3.5in floppy drive (which is common these days), a hard disk and a CD-ROM drive, your view of My Computer will be much the same as the one in this picture.

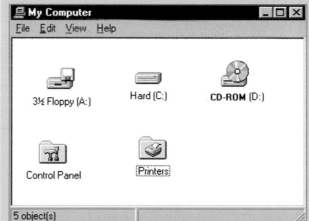

STEP 2 Slip a floppy disk into your disk drive and double-click on the appropriate icon. A window will open showing a collection of icons with file names written underneath. These are representations of the files and folders on the disk. If Windows can tell which application was used to create the file, it will display the corresponding icon. If it's not sure, it will use the all-purpose Windows flag icon. Close this view by clicking on the Close button (top right) or via the menu with File Close.

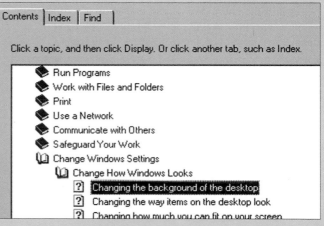

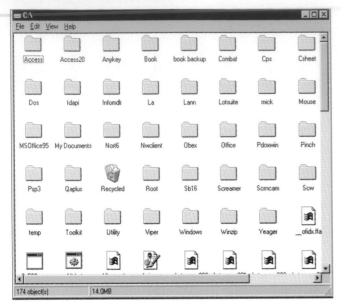

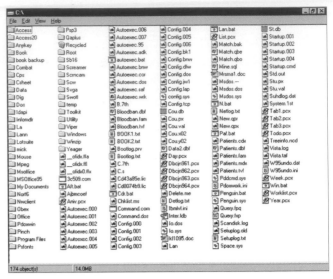

STEP 3 Now search the contents of your hard disk: double-click on its icon and you'll see its icons and file names. Use the slider bars to get a feel for how many there are. If there are lots, this is not a good method of searching for them – you'd be sliding around forever in your search for a particular file.

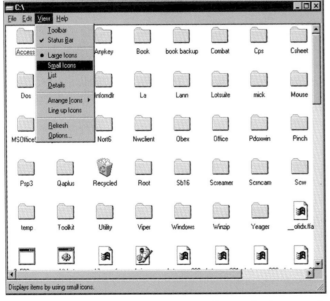

STEP 4 Click on View in the menu across the top. In the second section of the menu that pops out, you'll see that there is a bullet against the entry Large Icons, indicating that this is the view you're currently seeing. Below this are three other options: Small Icons, List and Details. Try Small Icons ...

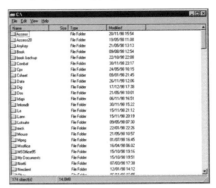

STEP 5 ...That's better. You still get the icons to help identify the types of file, but you can see more of them. Using the horizontal slider bar reveals quite a few more files than will fit on the screen, even if you click on the Maximise button to view the window at its full screen size. Let's try the other options.

STEP 6 List doesn't look much different from Small Icons, but the full depth of the screen is used, thus showing more files. With the window maximised, you're likely to be able to see everything. Finally, try the Details view.

STEP 7 This gives a long list of files, showing their names, size, type and the date and time they were last modified. Unless you need this information, List looks like the most helpful and most compact view. Looking at the contents of drive C: with the List view, you're looking at everything stored directly in the root of drive C: (see *Easy Windows*, page 61). The first files to be listed are folders. They show the folder icon to the left of their name, and they're listed alphabetically. To see the contents of a folder, double-click on it; another window of icons will open. If there are folders in this window, you can double-click on the icon to see what's in them. In this way, you can move through your folders until you find what you want. If you get confused, check the name of the folder you're inspecting. It's shown at the top of the window, although if you've moved through several layers of folders, the name may be truncated. Maximise the window to read it all. You can also stop the whole process by clicking the Close button, then start again.

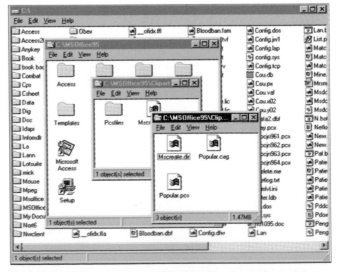

STEP 8 Here we're looking at the contents of a folder inside a folder inside a folder inside a folder. You can see all the steps taken to reach it in the windows behind the current one.

4

WORD PROCESSING

Take note!

Yo've seen how your PC goes together and how it works. Now it's time to look at the most important software package of them all: the word processor. A word processor is the one piece of software that has universal appeal. Not everyone needs a database or a spreadsheet. Not everyone wants to play games on their PC. But it is almost impossible to use a PC without typing a letter or a note.

When word processors first appeared it was easy to see what they could be used for, and people soon realised the advantages they had over a typewriter. This made word processing the driving force behind the PC's popularity in offices around the world. And, with Windows, word processors now show you on screen exactly what you are going to get on the page. This makes it simple for even the most inexperienced user to create good-looking documents.

In this chapter, we'll take you through word-processing techniques. We'll cover the basics of how to enter text and edit it. And we'll show you how to create all sorts of documents, from letters and envelopes to newsletters.

If you are planning to buy a PC, this will give you some idea of what you can do with a word processor. It will help you decide what sort of word-processing software is right for you. Is it worth spending money on one of the larger packages? Or should you stick with the simple WordPad and NotePad word processors that comes with Windows 95, or the Write word processor bundled with Windows 3.1?

If you already have a PC, you will know how to use a word processor for entering and editing text. We will guide you through the other functions your software offers. You will discover how to use your word processor to set up document styles that keep your work looking good, and how it can check your spelling and grammar.

In dealing with businesses, correctly spelled and well-presented letters are always a help. But using a word processor doesn't always have to be serious. There's a lot of fun to be had making your own newsletters, badges, bookmarks, labels, stickers, cards and invitations. The list is practically endless. If it can be printed, you can do it yourself with your PC and a word processor. ●

What is a word processor?

Word-processor software turns your PC into a computerised typewriter. But when you use a typewriter you put your words straight on to paper. If you make a mistake or want to change things, you have to start again. The most important difference with a word processor is that you see everything on screen first, so you can make all the changes you like. Only when you are happy with the result do you go ahead and print it.

And whereas a typewriter can only deal with letters and numbers, a word processor can do a great deal more. You can use any type of lettering style. You can make the letters bigger or smaller. And you can add pictures and lay the pages out any way you like. You are not restricted to producing pages of print, either. You can create images that are used for slides, for overhead projection, or just to be viewed on a computer screen.

Which word processor?

Word processors come in all shapes and sizes, from the modest WordPad that comes free with Windows, to more sophisticated processors like Microsoft Word, WordPerfect and Lotus Ami Pro.

You can buy your word processor on its own or as part of an integrated suite. Suites put together a bundle of commonly used software like a word processor, a spreadsheet and a database. Microsoft Works and Microsoft Office, Claris Works, Lotus SmartSuite and Corel PerfectOffice are good examples of integrated suites. A good time to buy your word processor is when you buy your PC because many companies offer special deals.

What do I need?

Sophisticated word processors give you more in the way of layout features, so you can do more interesting things with your text. They also have extras like spelling and grammar checkers, the ability to speed up functions using macros, better help facilities, and even simple drawing tools.

If you are only going to write a few letters, you need go no further than the WordPad or NotePad word processors that come with Windows 95, or the Write word processor that comes with Windows 3.1. But as soon as you think you want to do more, consider buying a more powerful word processor.

Specialised word processors

If you are working in a specialist area, you may need a specialised word processor. For example, not every word processor can show formulas, so, if you are working in science or mathematics, you will need to look for a word processor that includes an equation editor. Translators may also find a specialised word processor useful. A word processor designed for international languages will automatically reset the keyboard settings so that the keys equate to the right letters and symbols for each language.

Easy Word Processing Examples

The basic editing functions in this chapter will be found on all word processors. Some of the things that you can do with the more powerful ones are also included.

You will see that any reference to a word-processor function has a capital letter. So you know it is something to look for on the Tool bar or in one of the Menus. To guide you through a Menu list, you might see something like 'Format, Columns'. This is a quick way of saying look for the Columns functions in the Format menu.

Although we are using Microsoft's Word for the illustrations, you will find your word processor uses much the same layout and techniques. Your word processor may be using a different word to describe a set of functions or listing them in a slightly different way, so if you cannot find a function mentioned, check with the on-screen help or your manual to find it.

The *Menu bar* which covers every feature.

The *Toolbar* with buttons for instant access to key functions.

Information boxes tell you about type and document styles. You can change the size and style of a font here using the arrow buttons.

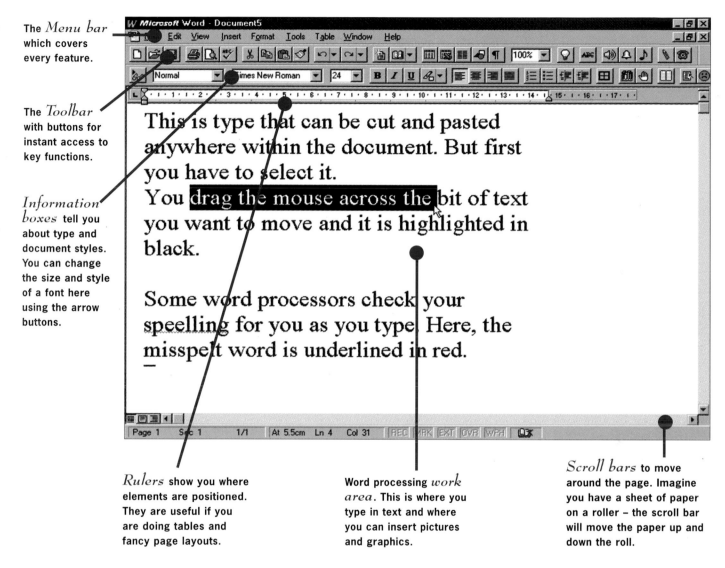

W Microsoft Word - Document5

Edit View Insert Format Tools Table Window Help

Normal   Times New Roman   24   **B** *I* U

This is type that can be cut and pasted anywhere within the document. But first you have to select it.
You drag the mouse across the bit of text you want to move and it is highlighted in black.

Some word processors check your speelling for you as you type. Here, the misspelt word is underlined in red.

Page 1   Sec 1   1/1   At 5.5cm   Ln 4   Col 31   REC MRK EXT OVR WPH

Rulers show you where elements are positioned. They are useful if you are doing tables and fancy page layouts.

Word processing *work area*. This is where you type in text and where you can insert pictures and graphics.

Scroll bars to move around the page. Imagine you have a sheet of paper on a roller – the scroll bar will move the paper up and down the roll.

Know your way around

Whichever word processor you use, you will find the layout of the screen much the same. As with all Windows programs, you have a Menu bar at the top of the screen where you can access every function the software offers. Down the side and across the bottom of the screen you have the scroll bars that let you move around all the pages of the document.

Below the Menu bar will be at least one, and probably two, Toolbars. These contain all the important functions that you will use for saving, printing, editing and formatting text. They are all shown as buttons you click on with the mouse. Get acquainted with the meaning of each button. It is not always obvious. If you are doing some complicated layout work, you can also get your PC to display on-screen rulers across the top and down the side so that you can position text and pictures accurately.

Somewhere on the screen, either in one of the Toolbars or in the bottom bar, will be a display that tells you the type and size of the font – that's the lettering – being used. It will show the line number, column, section and page that you are working on. And it will display the name of the format that you have applied to the document or the paragraph.

What sort of PC?

Word processors use little computer power. They will be happy running on a 486-based PC with Windows and equipped with 8Mb of RAM.

The biggest programs take up around 50Mb of hard disk space, although many will fit happily in under 20Mb. You will need more space to store your own documents. What you create on your word processor could be anything from an envelope to a newsletter, so we use *document* to mean any type of file that you are working on. Word-processor files are generally quite small unless you include a lot of pictures.

Getting started

Y ou can start your word processor by clicking on its icon – the small picture like one of these 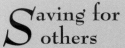 that represents it on the screen (see page 46). You will then be faced with the word-processor window, with a blank space to type into. If you want to continue doing work on an existing document, you can go to the File menu and choose the Open command. Alternatively, you can use Windows to find the document you want to work on. When you double-click on it, Windows will automatically start your word processor and load the document. You don't have to finish with one document before starting another. Word processors can have several files open at once, and you can switch between them and transfer information from one document to another.

Typing

What you see in the work area is often not the whole document. You use the scroll bars to move that window around the pages. Typing text is simple. Just key in the words and they appear on the screen. You do not have to tell the word processor that you have come to the end of a line. It will automatically start a new line when you have run out of space. Pressing the Return key will start a new line, but what really is happening is that the word processor perceives this as starting a new paragraph.

Moving around

The cursor that tells you where your typing is going to appear on the screen – what's called the Insert Point – is a flashing vertical line. When it is in the typing area, your mouse pointer appears as a vertical 'I' and reverts to being the normal mouse arrow when it is in the Toolbars.

If you want to insert an extra word in a sentence, you can use the mouse to go to the spot and a single click will put the cursor where you have placed your mouse's 'I' pointer. Alternatively, you can use the keyboard arrow keys to move around the screen to get the cursor in the right position.

Selecting text

Before you can change anything on screen, you've got to tell your word processor what it is you want to change by selecting, or highlighting, it.

Say you want to get rid of a sentence. You select it by using the mouse to put the cursor by the first letter of the sentence. Then you drag the mouse across the whole sentence. You do this by holding the left mouse button down while you move the mouse to the right. Anything you select is highlighted on screen and turned into white text on a black background.

Now just go to Cut in the Edit menu and the sentence disappears. At this point you realise you liked the sentence after all. Don't worry. Your word processor keeps track of what you have been doing and can go back at least one step to Undo your last command or action. To restore your sentence, go to Undo in the Edit menu and your sentence reappears on screen. Selecting and Undoing applies to virtually every editing and formatting – that is changing the way the text looks – function your word processor offers.

S aving for others

When you save a document, everything it contains (text, pictures and formatting) is stored together in a format that is particular to your word-processing package. If you are using only one word processor, this is no problem. But you may want to send your document on disk to someone else, or you may want to use your text in another type of software system, such as a desktop publishing (DTP) package. Then you have to file your text in a format that the other software package can understand.

Some word processor and DTP packages can translate files created by other packages. But if you want to be sure, save your words as a text file. Doing so saves each letter and symbol as an internationally agreed code number called ASCII (pronounced 'askey'), which every word processor can read. You can be sure all the letters and numbers are handled properly, but ASCII text files cannot contain any formatting information. Also watch out for some symbols, such as the £ sign, which may not be correctly translated and could appear as a ú in someone else's package.

Copy, paste and cut

Once you have selected a piece of text, use Copy to put a copy of it into your PC's Clipboard, which is your PC's temporary storage area. This text can then be pasted somewhere else in your document by moving the cursor to where you want the text to go and pressing Paste. A copy of the text you have selected remains in the Clipboard until you use the Copy function again to put something else in the Clipboard instead. So, if you have something you want to repeat many times, just keep pasting copies of it into your document.

Cut simply lifts the selected text so you can put it somewhere else and rearrange what you have written. Remember, if you have several documents open at once, you can Copy, Cut and Paste text between documents as well as within a single document.

Easy searching

Your word processor can search out words in your text for you, using the Find command. This is handy if you spelt someone's name wrongly, like McTavish rather than Mactavish, and it appears several times in your text. As an extra bonus, you can use the Find and Replace to do all that work for you. You tell your word processor which word is wrong and what to replace it with, and it will hunt through the entire written file and delete the wrong word and insert the right one.

Saving

Saving word-processing files is the same as saving any other Windows file. You call up Save in the File Menu.

Over a period of a few months you can easily create hundreds of word-processor files, so it is a good idea to create lots of separate folders or directories and sub-directories (using My Computer or File Manager) so that you can easily find your work again. Some people find it easier to file work by month, so you would have folders for January, February and so on. Others like to file by the type of documents they are: Letters, Faxes, Notes and so on. So before you start, think of a folder structure that will suit the way you work best.

FonTs

All Windows word processors are WYSIWYG (pronounced 'wizzywig'), which stands for 'What You See Is What You Get'. In other words, what appears on screen is what your printed page is going to look like. Make your text bigger and bolder, and it will appear bigger and bolder on screen, just as it will when you print it out. This may seem obvious, but all the early word processors could only show you typewriter-like text on screen, which gave you no idea of exactly how it would look when you printed it out.

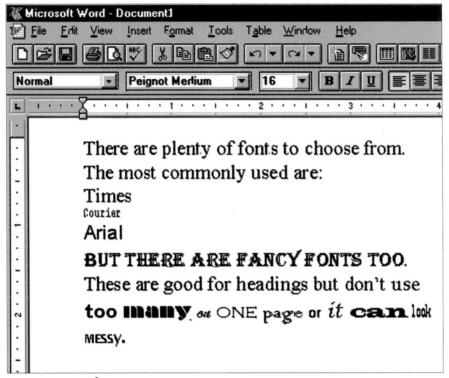

Lots of different *fonts* – also known as typefaces – are available.

Typefaces

The shape of the letters you see on screen is determined by the typeface, or font, that you choose. Windows stores these as font files on your PC's hard disk. Your word processor will come with a set of fonts, which will include Times, Courier and Helvetica. These are already available for Windows. For letters and documents, it is usual to use a single font, but you can liven up the presentation by using others.

Sizes

The size of your text is always measured in points (pt). This is a typesetting term, and one point is equal to 0.35mm ($^1/_{72}$in). As a guide, the text used for the words you are reading now on this page is in 10pt. The heading at the top of this page is 80pt. Remember that your text has to be big enough to be readable. If it is likely to be used by someone with less than perfect eyesight, why not use a bigger type, so that it is easier to read?

Making it stand out

When you want to highlight a particular word or sentence, you can do it by using *italic* or **bold** text or <u>underlining certain words</u>. Select which you want before starting typing by clicking on the relevant button or choice in the Toolbar (the **B**, *I*, <u>U</u> buttons) or Menu under Format. Now when you type, everything will come out as **bold**, *italic* or <u>underlined</u>. The alternative is to type everything normally, Select the text you want changed and apply the Italic, Bold or Underline formatting.

Keep it simple

You can use as many type styles as you want, but remember not to fall into the trap of using too many in one document. For good results, keep the general text the same all the way through and use the fancy typefaces for headings, where they will have the most effect.

Buying more fonts

There are many collections of shareware and freeware typefaces that you can buy very cheaply on floppy disk or CD-ROM. These disks usually come with software to view and load your choices on to your hard disk. Fonts take up a significant amount of disk space and memory, so only load the ones that you are going to be using.

99% Wysiwyg

Windows Wysiwyg is not quite 100% perfect. The problem is that your PC has to use special display font files to display your text on the monitor and separate printer font files to send the text to the printer. While font developers do their best to make sure the screen and printer versions of the font match perfectly, sometimes there are tiny differences. This normally won't be noticed, but occasionally the printed text may take a little more or less room on the page than you expected. This can change the layout a little. Always check any complex layout by printing it. Getting it perfect on paper may mean having to alter the layout so it doesn't look right on screen.

Other languages

Most fonts include all the letters of the English language. They also have the numbers and symbols you find on the keyboard, and most, if not all, of the special letters used in other European languages. Fonts are available for most of the non-European languages, although you would need a matching keyboard to make these useful for regular work.

Not every font is pure lettering. Look in your file of fonts using the Character and Format menus and look at the font called Wingdings. This is a font file with no letters or numbers but a lot of neat symbols that you can always find a use for.

Page layout

Your word processor can show you your work in several ways. You enter text in Normal View, which gives you some idea of the layout. But when you want to start putting in pictures and multiple columns, you also need to use the Page Layout view, which shows an image of the page as it will be printed. For a quick check before printing, you may also want a Print Preview. This puts pages on screen in the layout that will appear on the page.

Margins

First go to Page Setup under File and choose how far in from the sides and the top and bottom edges of the page you want your text. Try setting the margins at 17.8mm (0.75in) all the way round and then at 38mm (1.5in) to see the difference. Once you have set the margins, your word processor will keep that space clear on every page.

Aligning the text

Most letters have the paragraphs aligned to the left, so the first letter of each line starts on the edge of the margin. With Left Align you get a ragged look at the right of the paragraph, which is good for letter writing because it makes what you have written look a little more personal.

Now look at a newspaper. In each column, both the left and right of the text are straight. This is called justification. When you justify a paragraph, the word processor works out how many words it can fit on the line and then stretches the spaces between the letters and words so that they fit.

You can also Right Align the text. This puts it on the right of the page, ending at the right margin. This is good for headings. A more useful effect is to Centre your text. The word processor places the text so that it is centred on the page. This is excellent for headings and titles.

Macros

Advanced word processors have their own programming language that can automate some of your word-processing work. These programs are called macros, and a typical example is using a macro to get your word processor to automatically print an envelope using the address information from the letter you have just typed. The word processor comes with some macros, but you have to do some fairly serious studying of your manual to master the art of writing your own.

Tabs and indents

Use tabs to indent the start of the line. When you press Tab, the cursor jumps to the first Tab position on the line, marked on the on-screen ruler. You can clear the default settings and put in your own.

Indent each paragraph you type by pressing the Tab key; or use the Paragraph Formatting menu to pre-set the indent of the first line of each paragraph. Tabs are useful for putting your text into columns. Set Tabs to 50.8mm (2in), 101.6mm (4in) and 152.4mm (6in) and type in a list of names, job titles and telephone numbers, pressing Tab after each. You will end up with a nicely aligned set of columns.

Give yourself space

If the page is cramped, your word processor can allow more space between the lines or words. In Paragraph Formatting, for example, you can set Spacing Between lines at 1.5 lines and the Spacing After each paragraph at 2.5 lines. Type a couple

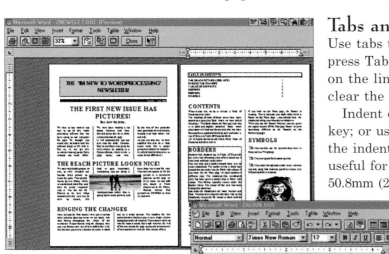

See your page as it will be printed using the *Page Layout view* (above).

Different *paragraph alignments* suit different sections (right).

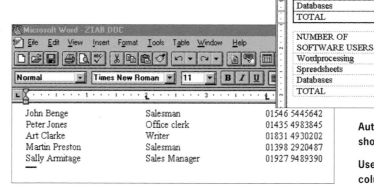

of short paragraphs and you'll see how they have opened up. Now Select a couple of lines and use the Character Formatting menu to increase the spacing between letters. Each line will expand across the page.

Automatically create *tables* to show data (above).

Use *tabs* to produce neat columns (left).

How many columns?

Letters are usually typed in one column with the text going right across the page. But newsletters and magazines always run text into several columns. You can do the same with little effort. When you choose multiple columns, the word processor takes over all the work of laying out your text.

If you select a two-column layout, the word processor will fill the left column first. When that is full, it starts putting your text into the right column. When that is finished, the word processor goes to the next page and starts filling up the columns on that. Remember, you will only see the full effect of your multiple-column layout when you go to Page Layout view.

Make a break

When a page is full, your word processor moves on to the next. Sometimes you might want to choose where to start the next page – maybe at the end of a paragraph. You can do this by inserting a Page Break (in the Insert menu), which tells the word processor to move on to the next page.

Fields

You will often find it useful to put in standard text, such as the date or the page number, on your page. Your word processor puts these into the page as Fields, which it will automatically update. A Date Field in a letter will always insert the current date, for example. Try using Insert, Date and note how the date is always correct when you open the document.

Tables

Most word processors include a Tables function, which you can use to make tables of any size you like. Each box in a Table is called a cell, and if there is a Table function then there is usually a calculator function, too, so the word processor can do all the adding up of lines and columns. Tables can be boxed in with grid lines or left open.

Headers and footers

These are special areas that fit at the top or the bottom of the page that can be used to repeat the document, section or chapter title on every page and include the page number (using the Page Number Field). You can put the same information in the Footer instead, if you prefer it at the bottom of the page.

Store your Style sheets

Every element of your paragraph — the type of foNt used, the font size, whether it is *italics* or **bold**, the tabs and the s p a c i n g – can all be grouped as a Style.

If you work on the same type of document regularly, you will want to get the same look each time. You can store this information and instantly apply it to the text in a new document.

To do this, select Format Style, click on New and give the style a name, such as 'My Style'. Then choose your text style from the options under Format. A preview of your text appears in the preview window. When you are satisfied, click Apply to add the style to the style sheet. Click Add to template to use the new style for other documents, too. When you start a new document, just call up the template. By applying 'My Style' to your text, it will automatically follow the style you have created.

You can even create a style for each heading and paragraph and store it separately, giving each one a different name. By applying your heading style to your heading text, it is automatically turned into the big bold heading centred on the page. Type in the introduction and apply the Intro Style and your indented italics section is instantly there.

Letters & envelopes

Here is a letter and envelope layout that uses a lot of the word-processing tools you have read about so far. The letter uses an A4 page, and your word processor will have several standard envelope-sized pages as options in the Page Setup menu. This envelope makes clever use of the Margins and Paragraph Indents, which is possible to do with many, although not all, word-processing packages.

The envelope's left margin is set to 89mm (3.5in) so that when you put the address in, it is placed where it should be, half-way across the envelope. But to get the message to appear near the left edge of the envelope, we have given it an indent of –76.2mm (–3in), so it moves to the left of the margin by that amount. It is now positioned 12.7mm (0.5in) from the edge of the envelope.

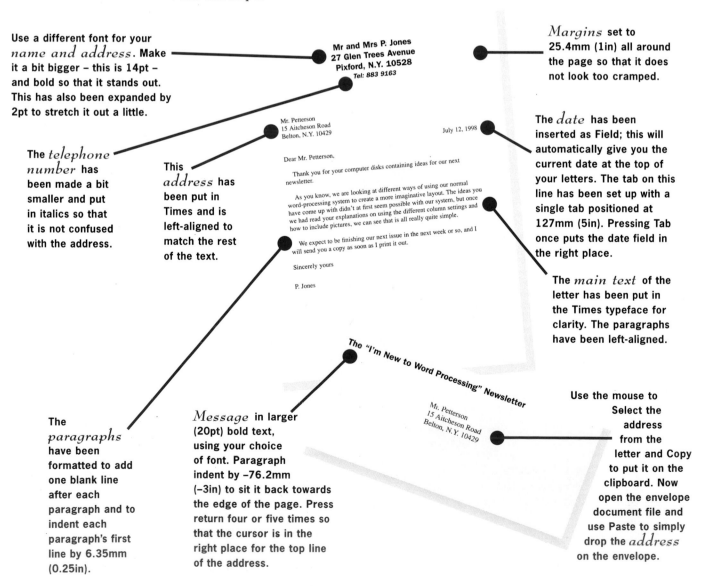

Use a different font for your *name and address*. Make it a bit bigger – this is 14pt – and bold so that it stands out. This has also been expanded by 2pt to stretch it out a little.

The *telephone number* has been made a bit smaller and put in italics so that it is not confused with the address.

This *address* has been put in Times and is left-aligned to match the rest of the text.

The *paragraphs* have been formatted to add one blank line after each paragraph and to indent each paragraph's first line by 6.35mm (0.25in).

Message in larger (20pt) bold text, using your choice of font. Paragraph indent by –76.2mm (–3in) to sit it back towards the edge of the page. Press return four or five times so that the cursor is in the right place for the top line of the address.

Margins set to 25.4mm (1in) all around the page so that it does not look too cramped.

The *date* has been inserted as Field; this will automatically give you the current date at the top of your letters. The tab on this line has been set up with a single tab positioned at 127mm (5in). Pressing Tab once puts the date field in the right place.

The *main text* of the letter has been put in the Times typeface for clarity. The paragraphs have been left-aligned.

Use the mouse to Select the address from the letter and Copy to put it on the clipboard. Now open the envelope document file and use Paste to simply drop the *address* on the envelope.

Mr and Mrs P. Jones
27 Glen Trees Avenue
Pixford, N.Y. 10528
Tel: 883 9163

Mr. Petterson
15 Aitcheson Road
Belton, N.Y. 10429

July 12, 1998

Dear Mr. Petterson,

Thank you for your computer disks containing ideas for our next newsletter.

As you know, we are looking at different ways of using our normal word-processing system to create a more imaginative layout. The ideas you have come up with didn't at first seem possible with our system, but once we had read your explanations on using the different column settings and how to include pictures, we can see that is all really quite simple.

We expect to be finishing our next issue in the next week or so, and I will send you a copy as soon as I print it out.

Sincerely yours

P. Jones

The "I'm New to Word Processing" Newsletter

Mr. Petterson
15 Aitcheson Road
Belton, N.Y. 10429

Fancy features

ll the best word processors build in a whole host of additional features that take you way beyond simply typing in and laying out a document. Many are there to make life easier for you and to guarantee that your documents are presented at their best.

How's your spelling?

Whether you trip up on really unusual words or just tend to put your *e* before your *i* when it's not after *c*, your word processor can come to the rescue. Once you've finished your work, press the Spelling button and your word processor will go through your text. It will compare every word you have written against a large dictionary with hundreds of thousands of words. This dictionary is stored on your hard disk as part of the word-processor software. If it finds a word you have typed that doesn't match anything it has to offer, it will highlight it and offer some alternatives. Because the misspelling is nearly always a matter of only a letter or two, nine times out of ten it has a pretty good guess at which word you really wanted. More sophisticated spelling checkers monitor your typing. If you regularly make the same mistake, they will automatically replace the wrong spellings as you go along.

Ain't no good at grammar?

One of the more helpful features of a good word processor is its grammar checker. This works just like the spelling checker, but instead of looking for words that are misspelled, it looks for sentences that break the rules. You may think your English is quite good until the grammar check goes to work on your split infinitives, misplaced modifiers and vague quantifiers.

The grammar checker will not only show you where you have gone wrong but also give you explanations and suggestions on how to make corrections and improvements. As a final help, you can ask the word processor to give you a readability report on your efforts. This will tell you the average length of each sentence and how easy it is to read.

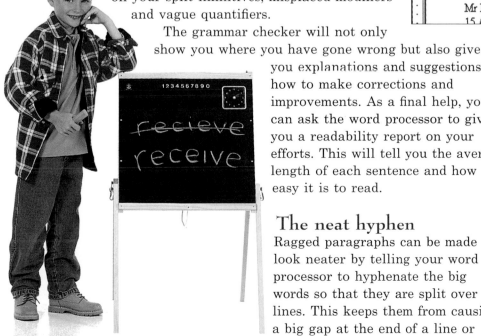

The neat hyphen

Ragged paragraphs can be made to look neater by telling your word processor to hyphenate the big words so that they are split over two lines. This keeps them from causing a big gap at the end of a line or making justified text too spread out.

Stuck for a word?

Then call up your word processor's Thesaurus. This lists all the alternatives you could use for a given word and also the word's antonyms (words with the opposite meaning). If you choose one of the alternatives offered, you don't even have to type it, as your word processor will instantly insert it in place of your original word.

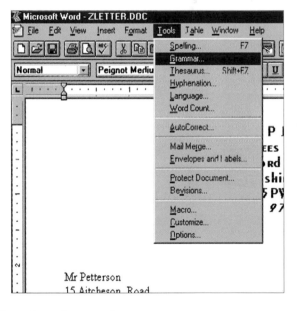

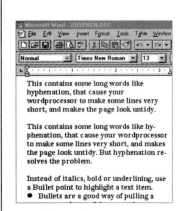

Hyphenation **helps to neaten your pages.**

Desktop Publishing

Here we have put together a newsletter using most of the word processor's important functions. The general explanation of what has been done is in the Newsletter itself. We have also given the formatting details of each element, which may give you some tips for your own work. Come back to these when you have tried out some of the ideas yourself.

Newsletter title or *masthead* using large (30pt) font in black. The paragraph is Centre-Aligned and set for one Column. The background is dark blue (called cyan by printers).

THE 'I'M NEW TO WORD PROCESSING' NEWSLETTER

Issue 5   June 1998

Issue number and date as small text (10pt) in white. Paragraph is Right-Aligned with a Border Filled in Black.

THE FIRST NEW ISSUE HAS PICTURES!
See how it's done.

Main headline. Same size as Masthead, but now normal black text.

We have at last worked out how to use all this word-processing software that has been sitting on our computer for ages. We thought you could only do letters and the ordinary things in life with it. But no, we can get this newsletter looking pretty fancy without too much effort. We have

been reading a lot about columns and have decided to run this bit in three columns across the page.

It will automatically put our text into the three columns. But we can force it to go to the next column by putting in a Column Break, which is like a page break, just here.

So the rest of this particular item goes on to the end column, making it all look nice and neat.

As you can also see, we have justified this text so it looks much more like a real printed newsletter or magazine. It is these touches that seem to make all the difference!

Heading 24pt Bold. Paragraph is Left-Aligned and set for one Column. This information is saved as a Style called 'Heading 1.'

THE BEACH PICTURE LOOKS NICE!

We said we would add a picture or two, so we've included our vacation beach picture to make the point. This picture has to go in a Frame, which is inserted and sized first and then the picture imported into it. You can set the Frames so the text wraps around it like this. As can be

seen by anyone, this look is quite impressive, considering you are using a word processor

rather than going down to the printers, and having them lay it out for you. You have the option to fix the picture in a permanent position on the page or let it move as you add text above it. These choices are in the Frame, Format Menus. Buy pictures on CD-ROM or scan in your own.

Main text in 12pt. Paragraphs Justified (saved as Normal Style) and put in three Columns with a Line Between Columns (normally in the Column Menus). Column Breaks (look for the Break Menu) force the text into three short Columns. The picture is Inserted into the frame. The frame is readjusted to crop and size the picture.

VARY THE FORMAT

Now just because the first stories were put in across three columns does not mean we are stuck with that format throughout the whole newsletter. Although it must be said that it is easier to stick with one format throughout.

But if your want to vary the design, then you can format each set of text differently. For example, this

has been put in two columns to make it stand out as a single section. The headline for this particular item has been put in as a single column paragraph and Left-Aligned. This means it takes up just the room it needs but it still reserves the rest of the line across the page so that the second column of text starts level with the first column of text.

Next headline was formatted by applying the 'Headline 1' Style.

Text same as before, but now in two Columns. Select all the text of this item and use Column Format, Two Columns, applied to the selected text.

Title in medium-size (14pt) Bold, Paragraph Left-Aligned, set for single Column and with black Border line.

Table of contents entered as a Table of Contents Field. The Field includes all paragraphs that have the 'Heading 1' Style with the page number they appear on.

CONTENTS

What is also nice to do is include a Table of Contents or an Index.

The headings of each of these items have been stored as a particular Style, which we have called Heading 1. This Style details the font type and that it is bold and slightly stretched. Some word processors will look out for any text that has been formatted in a particular Heading style and make a list of them in a Table of Contents Field.

All we had to do was to use Insert, Field, Table of Contents, and there it all is.

Title 24pt Bold, Paragraph Left-Aligned, set for single Column.

This section has been given a simple *Border line.*

BORDERS

Borders with shadows are a nice way of making a line of text stand out a little more and look a little neater.

You can also put a border around some text to make it stand out. The border is like a black box around the text, and it can be filled with colour if you want. On the front page we used borders in different ways. The Masthead (the newsletter's title) has been given a border that is filled with colour. This facility normally comes under the Border Menu. The colour of the text has been changed to stand out.

Just under the Masthead is the Issue Number and Date. This has been created in the same way as the Masthead, except the fill colour is black and the text colour is white.

The rest of the *main text* is set in two Columns.

FOOTERS

At the bottom of this page is a footer that the word processor has put in for us automatically.

We have told it what to write and to put a Page Number Field after the words "Page Number". Each following page will have the same text but the page number will change.

"I'm New to Word Processing" Newsletter

This *Footer text* will appear at the bottom of every page.

If you look on the front page, the Footer is missing. This is because you don't really need a footer on the front page — you already have the Masthead telling you what the newsletter is.

When you use the Footer function, you are given the option to turn off the first-page footer or print something different in the Footers on the following pages.

SYMBOLS

You can also use the symbols that come in such fonts as Wingdings.

They are good for illustrating a list.

They make things look a little more interesting and, using Insert, only take a second or so to include. Colouring them is a bonus.

Caption: Clip art is cheap and simple to add

The next pages should follow this basic look as we have now set the page style up. It is a straightforward exercise to fill the page style with text and drop pictures in where you need to.

Clip art imported from a CD-ROM clip art disc.

A Frame with small (10pt) Bold text put just below the picture's Frame.

Page Number 2

These *symbols* have been Inserted from the Wingdings font in Dark Red.

This is a *Page Number Field* for automatic page numbering by your word processor.

HAMILTON HURRICANE
School Play Special
20p

SCHOOL PLAY TRIUMPH!

MOVE TO WEST END OFFERED

This year's school play was rated the best theatrical event of the season by several of the country's leading theatre critics. The juvenile lead Michael Ashfoot, was hailed as the new Macaulie McCalkin. It is rumoured that Hollywood director George Spiegleberg has rushed talent scouts over from the U.S. to sign him up for the next Indiana Smith movie.

The play, performed to packed out audiences of parents, brothers and sisters brought encores and a 15 minute standing ovation for the performers.

FLOYD WEBBER VENTURE LIKELY

The incidental music written for the performance has attracted the attention of Julian Floyd Webber who wants to expand it into a full-length performance piece to premier at next year's Promenade Concerts. 'The finest music I have heard in ages,' he was quoted as saying.

CAROUSEL FOR NEXT YEAR?

Plans for next year's performance are believed to be centring on Carousel, with a complete Merry Go Round as the centrepiece of the stage.

A horse has been seen in the woodworking department being used as a model for the carvings.

Already the staff are looking for likely candidates for key roles in the performance.

Promising young talent (years 5, 6 and 7) should apply to the English Department before the end of term.

ALSO IN THIS ISSUE

Sports Day -Olympic hopefuls
Year 7 -Sweep the Blooker prizes

● You can make *newsletters* look less formal and more fun.

Printing

The last part of the word-processing job is to print out your document. The quality of your work will depend ultimately on the quality of your printer. If you use a dot-matrix printer, the results will be satisfactory. An inkjet will improve matters and give you the option of working in colour if you have a colour inkjet. The best quality is delivered by a laser printer, although you are restricted to black-and-white unless you have very deep pockets.

Colour

Colour can make a big impact on your work. Colour inkjet printers are only a little more expensive than ones that can only handle black and white. With a colour inkjet printer, colour photographs are printed acceptably but by no means to magazine printing standards. It is worth using colour where it will look best, in small blocks and to highlight text. If you are undecided about whether to buy a colour printer, it is probably worth taking the plunge and doing it. You will find you will like to add a small splash of colour to your printing every now and then.

Paper makes a difference

Quality is also affected by the paper you use. If you are doing a special project and want it to look its best, you should buy paper designed for your particular printer. There are special papers for inkjet and laser printers. These give you sharper images. There is a growing range of fancy papers – some with elegant borders, some that look like blank certificates and awards. You can use these to do all sorts of fun projects.

Stick it

Use a blank sheet of self-adhesive labels to create anything from a mailing label to a home-made jam sticker. If you think you are going to make a lot of labels, you can buy special label-making word-processing software that makes the job easier. Always treat sheets of labels with care. If there are any labels lifting off the page, they may get stuck in the printer and be very difficult to remove. If in doubt, use a fresh page of labels.

Fax it

Another use for your word processor is to create and send faxes using a PC fax/modem. The document is created in the usual way, but instead of printing it, you use the Send facility to fax it to someone. The fax system creates an image of your page, so what comes out of the fax is exactly what you would have seen from your own printer (see pages 119-26).

Project it

You can use your word processor to create slides. Simply send them on a floppy disk to a bureau that will use a special camera system to turn them into full-colour 35mm slides. You do need to check that the bureau can handle your particular word processor's file standard, as it is still uncommon to do this from a word processor rather than a slide-making presentation program.

5
DATABASES

Facts & files

After the word processor, databases are probably the next most important type of software you can run on your computer. But databases have got a terrible reputation for being complex things that are of use only to big businesses that need to keep track of hundreds of customers and thousands of sales. In fact, a database is nothing more than a collection of information on a particular topic.

Databases are nothing new. Look around and you'll find you've already got databases all over the house – the telephone directory, the train timetable, your address book, even your TV listings, are all databases.

The databases on your PC are no different. They, too, are just a collection of facts and information, but in a great big table of data. The big difference lies in what your PC can do with the information once it has all been loaded. For example, finding a particular name in a telephone directory is fairly simple. Your PC can do it quicker, but it's nothing you couldn't handle without your computer. Now think about trying to list all the people called Jones who live in London and Chicago. That's going to take some time by hand, and you might miss a few, too. But for your PC's database system, this is no more difficult than looking for one name – and it won't miss any. Once it has created the list of the Joneses, the system can then print out those details in a list or, if desired, print out individual envelopes for a mailing.

So the database system lets you do a lot of different things with the sort of data that you use every day. In this chapter, we will be creating a database of your friends and relatives. Then we'll show you how to sort the information, find entries and create useful lists, and automatically print out letters to them.

The methods you use to create and use a home database are exactly the same as those companies use for the databases that are essential to running their business. You may find that a database on your home PC will be just as useful. ●

What is a

Look in the databases around your home, such as your address book or the TV listings. Each contains lists of information on a particular subject: your friends' names and addresses, the TV programs' titles along with the times and days scheduled. These basic categories are laid out in the same format for every entry.

A PC database is exactly the same – a long list, or table, of information about anything from a company's stock and the prices of products to a list of the videos, tapes and CDs that you have at home. The important part of the database software is not so much the list of data itself but the way your PC can search through it to pull out hidden information. Although we call such systems databases, it is more descriptive to call them by their full name, which is database management systems (DBMS), since their advantage is in the way that they let your PC mix and match huge lists of information.

Types of databases

A database is built up of several parts. You may have a separate table of data that relates to a particular topic. So you may want to store the addresses and phone numbers of all your family and friends in one database, while another database may be for your video collection. And the kids might want their own database, cataloguing all their books and computer games.

The collection of data on one overall topic can also be arranged as a catalogue of several separate database tables. For example, a business might have separate database tables of its stock, the products' prices and its customers' details. All the sales and invoices may be entered into a separate database. Put together, this catalogue of databases can track every part of the company's activities.

Lists that talk to each other

There are two types of databases: flat-file and relational. With a flat-file database you put the details, such as names and addresses, into a single database. You can then search and sort through this list (find 'Bloggs, Joe' or 'anyone who lives in London'), but you can't get flat-file databases to merge with other databases to get complex details from your information.

Relational databases are more flexible. Instead of putting all the information in one file, you create separate database files that contain related information. You could create a list of friends in one file and a separate list of the ones to whom you are sending Christmas cards. The two files have a relationship – something in common – which is the names of your friends. The relational database management system can use the files together. When Christmas comes, it will use the Christmas-card list as a set of instructions to pull out all the relevant names and addresses from the other database and print out address labels for all the Christmas cards.

A *database catalogue* is a drawer full of related information. Each file (or table) contains sets of individual entries. Open the drawer and you can find any single entry or start comparing entries in one file with those in another file.

database?

No limits and no hunting

Traditional pen-and-paper databases, such as address books, have a limited amount of space to write things in, so you tend to include only the more important names and addresses. A database on your PC can be huge, and most give you the ability to put in thousands of entries per database.

Since the database can sort through even big lists in a fraction of a second, you can put even the rarely used entries into your database. Unless you know *a lot* of people, it won't make it any slower to find the important entries, and you'll always know that the name is in there.

Specialised databases

Using general database software, you can create an infinite range of databases to handle even the most unusual lists. But there are a number of common projects that lots of people could use a database for. Cataloguing any form of collection or building up a family tree are pure database functions, and you will find there are ready-made software packages that are fine-tuned for these jobs. Simple database software is deep within these programs, and they save you the effort of having to organise it yourself. Alternatively, your database may have formats, or templates, for some of these jobs, ready for you to use.

You can use a database to *catalogue* all kinds of collections and keep lists of everyday items.

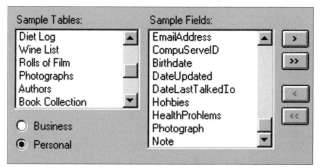

What you need

Databases are not very demanding on your computer, and any PC that can handle Windows will be able to handle a database management system. But if you are going to be working with large databases, especially if they include pictures, you'll need plenty of hard disk space. A fast processor and lots of RAM will help speed up the sorting and finding processes.

Which database?

While you can buy a database on its own, they tend to be costly. Most people will find they already have a database system, along with a word processor and a spreadsheet, in a combined suite of programs already installed on their PC. So if you have yet to buy your PC, look for one that is loaded with a software suite that includes a database.

Hidden databases

Word processors and spreadsheets both have simple database facilities. The mail merge function, where you have a list of names and addresses that can be added to individualise a letter, is a basic form of database, as are software address books or the phone and fax directories supplied with modems. If you have Windows 3.1 you'll also have Cardfile, which is a flat-file database at its most simple, and is ideal for lists of people and their phone numbers.

Creating a

Before you can start entering your data in a database, you have to create a form or table to load it into. Each line is called a record and contains all the information about an entry. Each little bit of information, whether it's a first name, a birth date or a product number, is given a little box of its own called a field. Once organised like this, it is easy for your database program to start making lists and sorting and finding all sorts of information for you.

Before you begin, you must write down what details you want to put into your database. For a database of friends, you will want first and last name, two to three lines for the road and town details, a field for the county and a field for the postcode. Then there are the other details, such as phone number (make that two if your friends have mobile phones as well), and you may want to put in birthday and anniversary dates, too.

All your information is contained in a single *table*.

Each column contains the same category of information with the *field* name at the top.

Christian Name	Surname	Address - line 1	Address - line 2	Town	C	Postcode
Peter	Jermin	Flat 5a	14 Kamhala Road	Battersea	LONDON	SW11 5QT
Tim	Forest	107 Guardhouse Me	South Johnston	Luton	BEDS	LF4 9KF
Katy	Brown	23 Westridge Ave	Bosbam Grange	Bosham	SUSSEX	CD19 5HF
Chris	Domin	22 Iotteridge Brl		East Wycombe	BUCKS	HP36 9XX
Martin	Andrews	15 Belvere Road	Eastcote	Worthing	W Sussex	BN23 2BX
Lin	Herhert	12 Hill Ave	The Broadway	Rickmansworth	Rerks	SL2 5DX
Mike	Jones	29 Deansbrook Ave	Baldon	Marlborougb	Wilts	SN18 2ZZ
Alison	Crompton	56 Oak Hill Park	Burgess Hill	Ahbots Langley	Herts	ZA18 8TQ
Hamish	Moore	14 McLean Drive	West St	Strensall	Suffolk	NR98 8WW
Sal	Nabe	15 Estella Drive		Northdene	Bucks	HP83 6TY
Janet	Whitehead	65 Tudor Hill	Heanton	Watford	Herts	WD42 ZFZ
Rohin	Rousell	1018 Prelmade Ave	Alhany	California	USA	CA R3997
Hannah	Lovell	14 Kenilman Road		Pagham	W Susses	PO85 9WQ
Rachel	Gispy	The Quarry	Dammead	Inverleithen	Peebleshire	SCO 9TR
Mike	Galitz	92 Chruch Road		Stanmore	Middx	MD36 8WQ
Sian	Cousins	50 Narcote Road	Dawley	Telforrl	Shropshire	FT31 8PY
Ray	Coombs	16 Beechtree Ave.		Wendover	Bucks	HP83 (0P
Heather	Kelling	50 Parish Piece	Heanton	Barnstable	Staffs	ST96 9RF
Jane	Coombs	16 Beechtree Ave		Wendover	Bucks	HP83 (0P
Hayley	Coombs	16 Beechtree Ave		Wendover	Bucks	HP83 (0P
Lauren	Coombs	16 Beechtree Ave		Wendover	Bucks	HP83 (0P

Record: 1 of 21

Each line contains a complete record, or *entry*.

No place like home

Let's look at creating a database of your friends and relatives by making a new file called Home. You've already decided on the names of the fields you are going to need, so you can open up the database's table and start entering the field names. These should make clear what information should be entered into the field.

Along with the field's name, your database will also want to know a little more about the sort of information or data that is going to be entered. The first-name fields are going to contain text rather than numbers or a date. You also need to tell the system how much space it should reserve for the field's information. Here it is set to 12 letters. You can make the field longer, but the database file will always reserve this amount of space for the entry, whether it is used or not. So if you make each field unnecessarily long, then the database file itself will needlessly get very large.

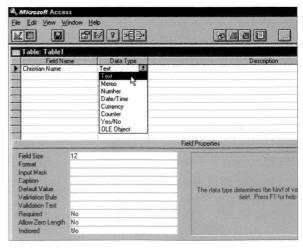

database

Your PC can do the home/work

If you want to add a few business contacts to your list, you can add a field to distinguish between home and work entries. If most are going to be home entries, instead of typing in 'home' every time you add a friend to the list, you can set up your field to use 'home' as the default, which means the database automatically puts the word *home* in the field for you. On the occasions when the new entry is a work contact, then you just type 'work' into the field instead.

When are numbers not numbers?

The database thinks of numbers as things that it can do calculations with, like the number of products in an order or the price of an item. Numbers like house numbers, postcodes, or telephone numbers are there just to be read, so set these fields as text Fields.

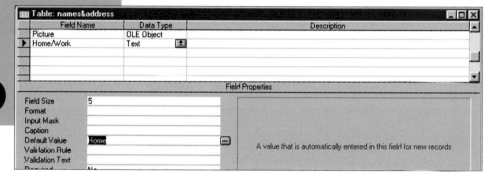

Add more details

Your brother has just put in a separate fax line as well as his phone and mobile, so where do you put the new number? Fortunately, you can reformat your tables. Even when the database has already been set up, you can go back to the original table and add more fields. You will have to remember to change the layout of the entry forms and any reports that may need to use the information.

Now that the database table is complete, you can save it with a suitable title.

Then and start entering data – the names and addresses.

57 varieties

Although you can enter everything into the database as words, things like dates, numbers and values really need to be entered in such a way that you can do things with the information later. You may want to use values and quantities for further calculations or move dates around. Your database program has special ways of making the most of numbers, dates and values, so choose the right field type.

● **Yes/no boxes**
Sometimes you just need to say Yes or No in a box. For example, Christmas card sent? Yes/No. It looks neater and saves typing in more words when you are entering information.

● **The open-ended field**
Often you need more space in an entry to put in additional comments. Unlike the other fields, which you have set to a fixed length, Memo is an automatically adjusting field. It expands if you are putting in several lines of comments and reduces the field to nothing if the comments field is empty.

● **OLE for extras**
The OLE (Object Linking and Embedding) field can be used to add in information from another software program. This can be anything from a graph to a picture or a sound clip.

What's in a name?

- ● **Database** A collection of data that you can store in one, or several, files called tables.
- ● **Tables** These store the data about a topic or part of the database. Contain lots of separate entries, or records.
- ● **Entries** These contain all the information you are storing on one person or item, just like a card in a card index.
- ● **Fields** Each separate piece of information in the entry is given its own particular box.

Studying the

There are two ways of viewing or working with your database. You can look at the full table with all the information in columns and rows, or you can look at each entry in turn, in a way that looks like a form.

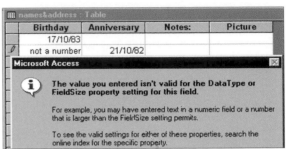

Using the table layout to enter your data, you just type the data into the field box, press Tab to go to the next field, and so on. If you make a mistake, you simply go back to the field and either edit the entry or type over it. The database will also check that you are entering the right type of information. If you try to put letters into a number or date field, it will tell you that you're doing something wrong (see above).

Using forms

Using tables makes it hard to see what you are doing and whether you have filled in all the fields correctly. The best way is to use the on-screen form below (left) that shows you the fields laid out, so you see them all at once.

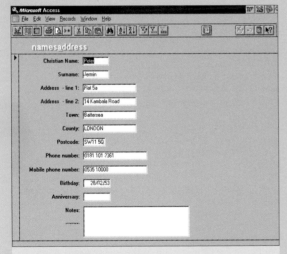

Even the most *basic layouts* are considerably easier to use than the table, and these can often be created automatically for you by your database program.

After it has been created, you can change the layout by dragging and dropping the *fields* into the best place.

Make the form more *compact* so that you can see everything in a smaller area of the screen.

Getting in and out

If you have already created useful lists of information using your word processor or a spreadsheet, many software systems will let you move, or export, these lists directly into a database software with only a small amount of extra work. Check with your software's Import and Export functions in the File menu because directly transferring the data not only saves a lot of time retyping it all but reduces the possibility of errors creeping in.

form

Moving around the form window

Form windows have a similar layout in most database programs.

The form's *information*, laid out to suit your needs.

Tells you there are 21 records in this *list*.

This is the fourth *record* in the list.

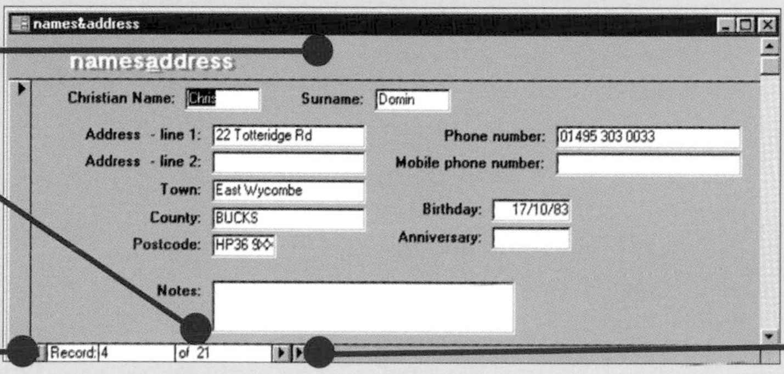

Click on the *arrows* to move backwards or forwards to the next record or to the beginning or end of the list.

In the picture

It would be very boring if your database could only work with text and numbers. The latest databases now fully support OLE (Object Linking and Embedding), the system Windows uses to let one program access text, graphs, images and even sounds from other unrelated software programs.

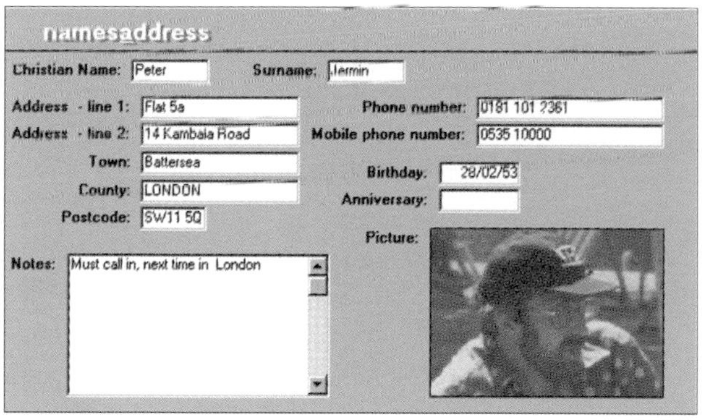

When you create a new table, instead of just putting in text, number and date fields, you can also add in a picture or sound field. When you design the form, make sure there is enough space for the picture. You can then switch over to your normal painting or recording programs and use them to create a picture or sound clip. Then simply copy it using the Edit Copy command and paste it into the space in your database form. This can be handy not just for pictures of people, but places, drawings, graphs, and all sorts of objects, from the contents of a home to a fisherman's prize catch.

Keep a record of your home and its contents

Both for interest and also for insurance purposes, why not make a database of your home and its contents? Create fields with the item, its purchase price and when it was bought. If you have a scanner, you can add a photo of it, too.

Sort it out

Now you have a database all set up and running, you can start moving, sorting and extracting all sorts of useful information and printouts. It doesn't matter in what order you enter the information into your table; the first job you can do is to organise the data with Sort. Using Sort, you can go to the table and look down a specific column and then rearrange the entries so that they appear in alphabetical order. The column or Field your database uses for the sorting is called the Key column. Your database will automatically choose the first column as its sorting Key, unless you tell it to use a different one. Note that you can sort your information using any field as your Key column.

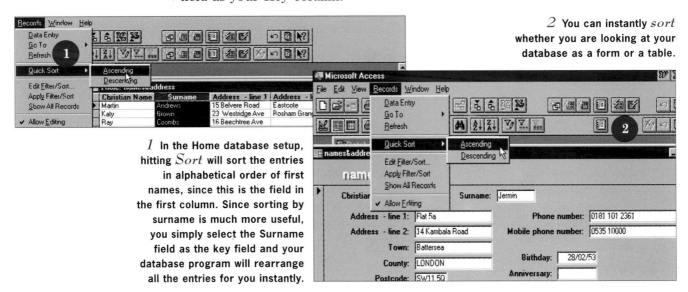

2 **You can instantly** *sort* **whether you are looking at your database as a form or a table.**

1 **In the Home database setup, hitting** *Sort* **will sort the entries in alphabetical order of first names, since this is the field in the first column. Since sorting by surname is much more useful, you simply select the Surname field as the key field and your database program will rearrange all the entries for you instantly.**

Super-organise

You can use more than one key column to sort your database. If you use surnames as the main key and first names as the second, then your system will first sort out the entries in alphabetical order of surname. When it finds several entries for a family sharing the same surname, it will sort those surname entries into alphabetical order by first name.

Searching and finding

Now you've got all your friends and contacts listed and you can see them in alphabetical order in the table. If you need to look someone up, you can just run down the table to find them. But why not let the database program do the work for you? It can find things quicker than you can.

Searches can be as simple as looking up someone's address or phone

number. After highlighting the relevant field, you just type in the name, word or value you are looking for into the Find menu box and your PC will instantly show the first entry it finds in the database that matches. If there's more than one match, pressing Find Next will display the next record that matches.

Find it even if you can't remember it

While Find is the most basic search function in your database, it is also one of the most commonly used, since you can find an entry even if you can only remember one piece of information. Can't remember the surname but you know the first name is Katy? Then use Find to locate all the Katies.

Filter tips

Finding a single name is handy on a day-to-day basis, but the database system really comes into its own when you want to start making lists. If you are always forgetting birthdays, you can get your database to list them all for you by simply entering the month into the Birthdays field.

Entering a specific requirement for a match in one of the fields is called filtering. The database looks at what you've typed in and uses the information to filter out all the records that match. It then displays them as a table, or you can go through them one by one.

Go wild!

To sort birthdays that match a particular month, you need to use a wild card symbol. You may already be familiar with the asterisk as a wild card when you look for files on your hard disk. In any search, typing in *.txt will locate files with the .txt extension. So if you type */09/* in the birthdays field, then the program will search for any September birthday (which all have 09/ in the middle of their date entry). The asterisks tell it not to bother checking the day or the year.

Merging mails

Databases are great for producing individualised letters. They print an individual's name and address and other details into a standard letter. This is called mail merging, and the standard mail-merge letter has gaps ready for the details to be loaded automatically. Some databases have this facility built in. Others use what's called DDE (Dynamic Data Exchange) to send the details to a word processor.

Printing

There are many ways of printing out database information. If you just want to print the data you have collected, you can print out the table, but be sure to set your printer to landscape so it can fit it all in. Alternatively, whatever you can sort, you can also print. So, having got your database to produce a sorted list of people, you can then get it to print their names and addresses on labels or envelopes. You can even use it to print out personalised letters.

Wild cards

★ Will stand in for any character or number of characters. So */93 will find 1/93 and 23/08/93.

? Stands in for a single character only, so ?/93 will only find 1/93.

Does for numbers what ? does for all characters.

Business

If you are running a small business, database management systems are essential. You need to keep lists of clients, products, costs, selling prices, stock, and so on. It can all be done in a database: either a general database or one designed specifically for a particular job, such as balancing your accounts.

When you are using database management software for your business, then you will be able to create a huge variety of reports from the information you enter. From a single set of database tables, you can create and print out reports that keep you updated on what has been sold, to whom, when and for how much. The database reports can mix and match the same information in hundreds of different ways. So you can look at what business has been done with individual customers or look at what has been happening month by month. It all comes from the same set of tables, but the database management software extracts just the information you need and shows it to you in a way that makes it easy to see what is going on.

This _query_ is asking the PC to show all the sales, listed by product, and display the date sold and the value.

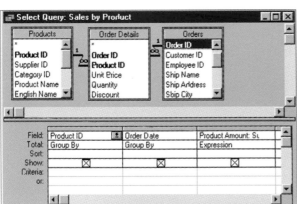

What's your query?

Businesses will want to question the database to find out how sales are going, who has bought what, or what the current stock level is. These sorts of questions are called queries, and you can set up a lot of different regularly used query forms, which you can call up to give you the up-to-date information you need. Each database will have its own way of creating queries, but generally you tell the system which fields are to be used and how they are to sort themselves out into a new table that will contain the results of the query.

Automation

Many business database jobs, such as sales reports, need to be done regularly. So instead of going through the whole procedure of opening up the database files, comparing them, choosing reports and then printing them each time, the whole process can be automated using a macro.

A macro is a short computer program that controls the database functions for you (see below). A word of warning, though: you really need to study the special language that is used for macros. It can be a complicated, but often very rewarding, task to get one to do exactly what you want. As an alternative, many database programs supply templates for the more common business databases and reports.

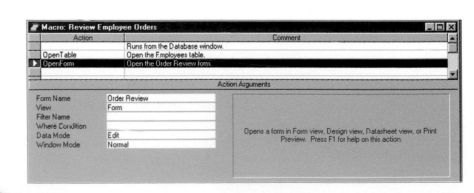

6

SPREADSHEETS

Spread out

The introduction of the spreadsheet was one of the most important developments in PC computer software. It was the spreadsheet, and the power it brought to business accounts, that prompted the first big burst of PC buying. Remember, this was in the days when there was no Windows and if you wanted to use a computer for letter writing, you bought a dedicated word-processor unit.

Spreadsheets are important because they do the one thing that computers do exceptionally well and that people take forever to do: lots and lots of simple repetitive calculations. At the heart of any spreadsheet is a column of information, such as a set of prices, that needs to have something done to it, such as adding tax. Before spreadsheets existed, someone would have to look up the prices, do the calculation by hand with a calculator, and then write down the result. Apart from all the time it takes, doing it manually introduces the possibility of mistakes.

The PC spreadsheet, on the other hand, will do all the calculations in a split second and print out the results the way you want, with no extra effort and virtually no chance of errors. And if the calculation has to change – say, the tax rate goes up – then half a dozen keystrokes later, you have all the new figures printed out for you.

Business loved it, and then, as spreadsheets teamed up with good graphing software, anyone who wanted to analyse and display information of any kind soon found that the spreadsheet was an ideal tool. Now spreadsheets are finding uses everywhere: in the home, in the classroom and in big and small businesses alike.

The blank spreadsheet grid may seem a bit awesome, and some of the calculations more than a little complicated, but spreadsheets are easy to master. They can help you out with any project that involves lots of addition, other calculations or storing information. And once you've got it going, you'll be surprised how quickly you can do complex calculation jobs. ●

The basics

What you need

Spreadsheets are not particularly demanding on your PC, and any PC that can handle Windows 95 will be able to handle them. A fast processor and lots of RAM will help speed up the calculations.

Most home PC users will buy spreadsheet software as part of a suite of programs, such as Microsoft Works or Office. If you have yet to buy your PC, look for one that comes with a software suite.

Spreadsheets are the most effective way of dealing with lists of information that need to have some sort of calculation done to them. In the home, this could be something as simple as a shopping list with prices, while a wedding list and an inventory of your household belongings are other examples of household spreadsheets. There are also spreadsheet programs within other packages. Home-finance software is just a spreadsheet that has been tailored to one particular application. You can set up these types of applications yourself using a general spreadsheet package like Microsoft Excel.

Spreadsheets and the worksheets used by databases have a lot in common. The rows in each represent all the information about a single entry, while the columns group together particular information about all the entries.

Formulas are a set of calculations, sometimes as simple as adding up a row of entries, that produce the spreadsheet results you want to see.

Current cell number tells you which cell you are in.

Cells are individual boxes for your data and formulas.

Rows go across the screen and contain all the information.

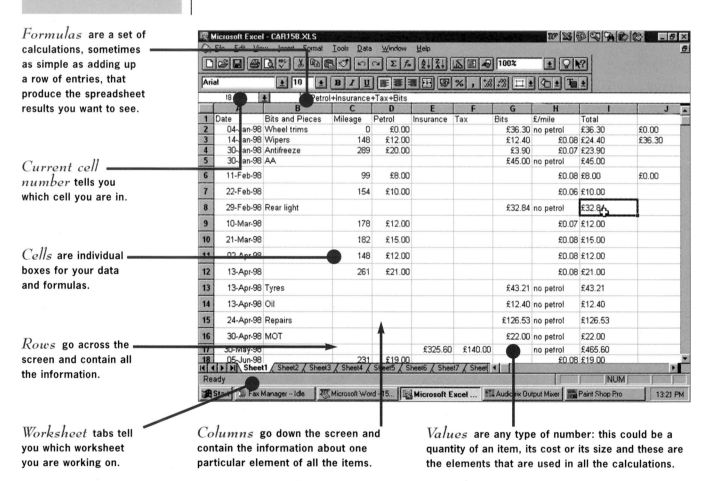

Worksheet tabs tell you which worksheet you are working on.

Columns go down the screen and contain the information about one particular element of all the items.

Values are any type of number: this could be a quantity of an item, its cost or its size and these are the elements that are used in all the calculations.

What does it mean?

- **Worksheet** The large sheet that contains all the data and formulas.
- **Workbooks** A set of worksheets for a complete project.
- **Cells** The boxes that contain pieces of data or calculations.
- **Labels** A text entry in a cell.
- **Value** A number entry in a cell.
- **Formula** A calculation in a cell.
- **Cell address** Identifies a specific cell. Cell addresses work just like map references: cell C24 would be in column C, row 24.

Types of data

There are three separate kinds of information that you can put into a cell: a name or title, called a label; a number or value; and a calculation or formula. In a spreadsheet words are used for the names of the items you are entering and for things such as months and category headings. Your spreadsheet can use words to search, sort and calculate.

Moving around the spreadsheet

Spreadsheets require a lot of simple entering of words and numbers, each into its own cell. Since they are so full of numbers and words, your mouse hand would be falling off if you had to use the mouse to change cells for every entry. Instead, all spreadsheets make use of those arrow keys on your keyboard that hardly ever get used for anything else. Of course, the mouse is essential for moving around to different parts of the spreadsheet.

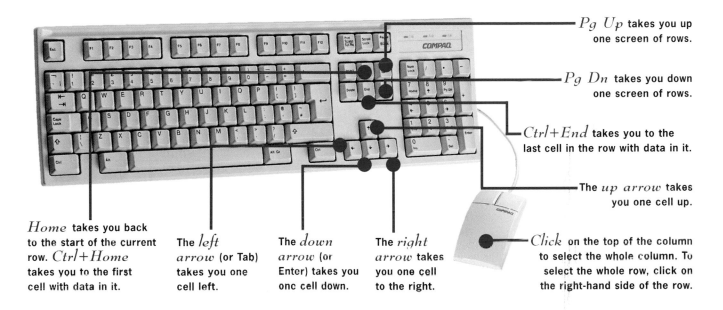

Pg Up takes you up one screen of rows.

Pg Dn takes you down one screen of rows.

Ctrl+End takes you to the last cell in the row with data in it.

The *up arrow* takes you one cell up.

Home takes you back to the start of the current row. *Ctrl+Home* takes you to the first cell with data in it.

The *left arrow* (or Tab) takes you one cell left.

The *down arrow* (or Enter) takes you one cell down.

The *right arrow* takes you one cell to the right.

Click on the top of the column to select the whole column. To select the whole row, click on the right-hand side of the row.

Adding columns and rows

Spreadsheets grow as you enter more information, and you might want to add a new line in the middle or decide you need a new column of information. Highlight the row below or to the left of where you want to put in a new row or column and use Insert Row or Insert Column. The new line will appear and everything will be shifted down or along one. If you want to remove columns or rows, you can do the same with the Delete Row/Column option.

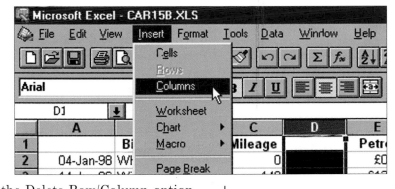

Getting the boxes to fit

When you open your spreadsheet, the boxes are usually big enough to hold about a dozen characters. While this is easily big enough for most number entries, you may run out of space when it comes to putting in text. When the text entry is too long, some spreadsheets grow taller or the end of the text disappears under the cell next to it. You can alter the width of all the cells in a column by dragging the right-hand side of the column until there is enough space for all the words to fit on one line.

If the number is too big to fit into the cell, you will get something like this. Just *enlarge* the cell and you'll see the complete number.

	A	C	D	E
1	Short	column	Wider	column
2	New Engin	######	New Engine	£598.67
3				

Get started

There are many applications that you can use your spreadsheet for, from doing the accounts for your local club or association to charting your children's heights as they grow. Here we'll try something close to home: a spreadsheet to see how your car costs spread over the year.

The first job is to set up the spreadsheet with the headings you are going to use and then format the columns for the sort of information that is going to be entered into them.

Date when the expense was made.

Text to say what the miscellaneous items are.

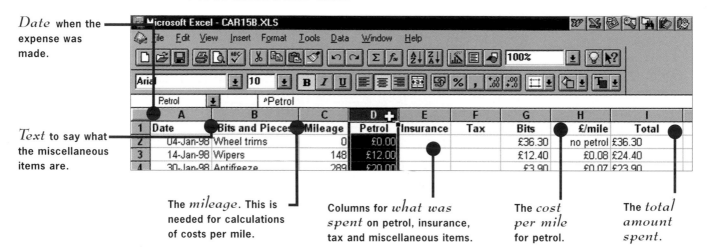

The *mileage*. This is needed for calculations of costs per mile.

Columns for *what was spent* on petrol, insurance, tax and miscellaneous items.

The *cost per mile* for petrol.

The *total amount spent*.

Formatting a column tells your spreadsheet that it contains a specific type of data that should be displayed as you want. You can choose whether you want decimal places or not, what format to display dates in, and whether to display pounds or pounds and pence.

I name this column...

Most spreadsheets let you give each column a name, rather than just a reference letter. For instance, Petrol (above) tells you more about what is in the column than just Column D. Type the name in the column-title section and type it in the top cell. Naming columns and rows also makes life a lot easier when it comes to doing calculations, as you can write formulas in English. Petrol + Insurance + Tax + Bits. is much clearer than D5 + E5 + F5 + G5.

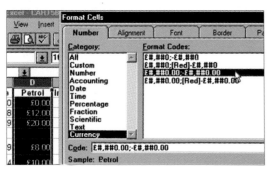

Loads of values

If you thought a value was simply a number, then think again. In spreadsheets there are all sorts of values that you can work with: money, dates, percentages or fractions. Each has its particular usefulness, and spreadsheets have special tricks so that they can handle each in a way that makes sense.

Enter the information

Although for some spreadsheet projects you can enter all the data at once, most of the time the spreadsheet is constantly being updated. You can add more information at any time you like, and when you do, all the totals and other calculations are automatically updated.

Calculating

Formulas and calculations are at the heart of any spreadsheet. Now that you've put in some data, you can order your spreadsheet to do some calculating. Formulas are sets of instructions that tell the spreadsheet to take the values from specified cells, put them through a calculation, and show the answer.

First you need to find an empty cell to put the calculation in, usually at the end of a row or column. You have to tell the spreadsheet that what you are about to type is a formula, not a word or a number. In some spreadsheets, you do this by typing the @ sign. In Excel you use the = sign.

A typical formula

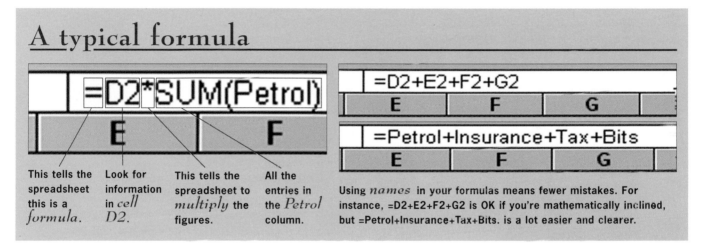

This tells the spreadsheet this is a *formula*.

Look for information in *cell* D2.

This tells the spreadsheet to *multiply* the figures.

All the entries in the *Petrol* column.

Using *names* in your formulas means fewer mistakes. For instance, =D2+E2+F2+G2 is OK if you're mathematically inclined, but =Petrol+Insurance+Tax+Bits. is a lot easier and clearer.

Spread the news

Once you've done one formula and it works, spread the good news down the column. All spreadsheets have a Copy and Fill option (right), which copies the formula all the way down a column so the totals automatically appear at the end of each row. You can see how the spreadsheet can handle a huge number of rows with no more effort than working on a single row.

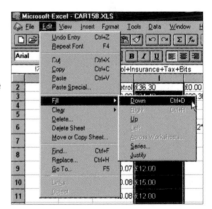

Working with formulas

When you copy a formula down a column, your spreadsheet uses it to work with each row. This is because the formula is relative. It is telling your PC to look down the row and repeat the calculation using the values from relevant cells. When you copy the formula to the end of another row, it will look at the cells in that row and work on those.

Sometimes, however, you'll want to put in a formula that stays the same whatever you do. You need to turn these into absolute formulas so that the formula always looks *only* at the cells you originally specified.

Different spreadsheets use different signs to make a formula absolute. In an Excel or Works spreadsheet, you type the dollar sign in front of any part of the cell address you want to make absolute.

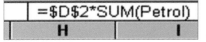

Calculations upon calculations

Now that you've worked out the totals for each item, you can use another formula to add up the results of all the other formulas to give an overall total. The spreadsheet will quickly tell you if you've typed a formula that doesn't make sense.

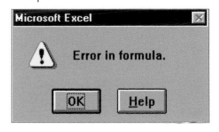

More features

Most spreadsheets give you quick ways to add rows or columns of numbers. You highlight the column and one empty cell at the end and click on the auto-add button. Everything in the column is added together, and the result is inserted into the bottom cell (right).

Inside the Brackets

Often you will want to use a more complicated mathematical formula, in which you group a couple of mathematical functions together in a particular order. Use brackets to make sure everything is done in the right order. Totals inside the brackets are calculated together, before anything else in the formula is worked on.

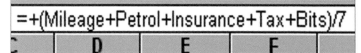

`=+(Mileage+Petrol+Insurance+Tax+Bits)/7`

The spreadsheet will first add the *subtotals* (Mileage+ Petrol+Insurance+Tax+Bits.) together and then divide that total by 7.

	C	D	E
es	Mileage	Petrol	Insuran
	0	£0.00	
	148	£12.00	
	289	£20.00	
	99	£8.00	
	154	£10.00	
	TOTAL	£50.00	

Hundreds of functions

As well as simple arithmetic, spreadsheets offer hundreds of special functions to help you analyse your information. These can do clever tricks with dates and values, statistical functions, functions that can find words or turn text into numbers and back again, and logical functions that can look at a cell and do different things depending on what is in the cell.

No one will pretend that these functions are all simple to use. In fact, some are quite complicated, and you'll need a good understanding of statistics or accounting. But spreadsheets are professional work tools and need these sophisticated functions to meet the needs of businesses as well as the home.

Logical functions in action

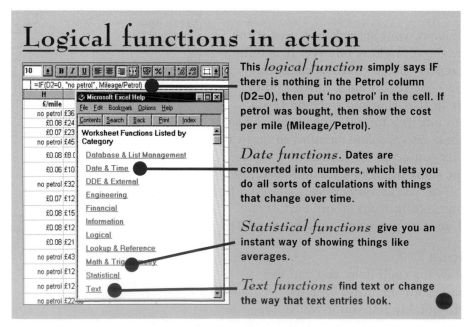

`=IF(D2=0, "no petrol", Mileage/Petrol)`

H	
£/mile	
no petrol	£36
£0.08	£24
£0.07	£23
no petrol	£45
£0.08	£8.0
£0.06	£10
no petrol	£32
£0.07	£12
£0.08	£15
£0.08	£12
£0.08	£21
no petrol	£43
no petrol	£12
no petrol	£12
no petrol	£22

Worksheet Functions Listed by Category

Database & List Management
Date & Time
DDE & External
Engineering
Financial
Information
Logical
Lookup & Reference
Math & Trig
Statistical
Text

This *logical function* simply says IF there is nothing in the Petrol column (D2=0), then put 'no petrol' in the cell. If petrol was bought, then show the cost per mile (Mileage/Petrol).

Date functions. Dates are converted into numbers, which lets you do all sorts of calculations with things that change over time.

Statistical functions give you an instant way of showing things like averages.

Text functions find text or change the way that text entries look.

Multiple spreads

Sophisticated 3-D spreadsheets let you work on several worksheets at once. These can pass information from one sheet to another and calculations spread across several sheets as easily as working in different areas of a single large sheet.

Double-check

Double-check a sample result along a couple of rows with a calculator. This will confirm that your formula is working with the right cells and the calculations you've typed in are correct.

Looking good

Now that you've got the spreadsheet working well and showing the right information, it could use some fixing up. When you type text into a cell, it is normally aligned left. Numbers are aligned to the right. But you can choose how you want your columns to look. Highlight the whole column and use the Align button (or Align menu) to align the entries differently. There are no rules: some alignments will simply look better in different situations.

	A	B	C	D	E	F	G	H	I
1	Date	Bits and Pieces	Mileage	Petrol	Insurance	Tax	Bits	£/mile	Total
2	04-Jan-98	Wheel trims	0	£0.00			£36.30	no petrol	£36.30
3	14-Jan-98	Wipers	148	£12.00			£12.40	£0.08	£24.40
4	30-Jan-98	Antifreeze	289	£20.00			£3.90	£0.07	£23.90
5	30-Jan-98	AA					£45.00	no petrol	£45.00
6	11-Feb-98		99	£8.00				£0.08	£8.00
7	22-Feb-98		154	£10.00				£0.06	£10.00
8	29-Feb-98	Rear light					£32.84	no petrol	£32.84
9	10-Mar-98		178	£12.00				£0.07	£12.00

Keep it simple
When you are working with long lists of numbers and names, you need to make them as clear as possible. Although you can choose any typeface that comes with Windows, it is best to stick to Times or Arial for clarity. Use bold letters to highlight titles, headings, totals, columns or rows containing the most important information.

Reporting in
Even with the totals and subtotals put in bold, it is still difficult to separate the answers from the mass of numbers and words. And when it comes to printing out the results, you don't want to print pages and pages of spreadsheet data just so you can see the totals at the end of the columns and rows. It makes more sense to put all the results you want to see all in one place as a report, which you can either look at on screen or print out on a single page.

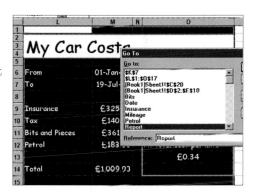

All spreadsheets let you give a block of cells a *name* so you can jump to the area of the spreadsheet where you have put your report information. This means you don't have to page through all your spreadsheet data to get there.

Report on the side

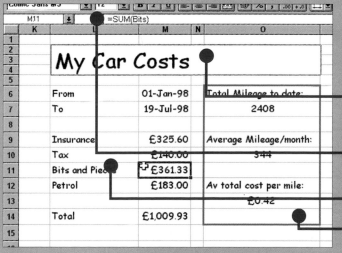

Even if you have a huge amount of data, there will still be plenty of space left on your spreadsheet to use a separate area to make up a report section. With 3-D spreadsheets, use a separate worksheet for your results. You can select the range of cells that you have placed your report into and print it out.

- Insert a *text box* or make this cell large enough for your heading. You can now use some bolder and more interesting typefaces.

- Add the *formula* that pulls in the totals you want from the main spreadsheet area.

- Put the *category heading* in a cell.

- Create *boxes* to surround different sections to separate them from the main data.

Graphs

There are few spreadsheet reports that can't be made clearer and easier to read by the inclusion of a graph or two. Graphs may not give you detail down to the last fraction, but they do show you what is happening in general and highlight trends. Most spreadsheets have good graphing facilities built in, so it is a simple job to turn your data into a graph. You can place your graph in the spreadsheet or copy it over to a word processor to liven it up.

All sorts of graphs

There are a dozen or so types of graphs that you can choose from. But the most important are bar graphs and pie charts. Bar graphs convert each entry into a vertical or horizontal column and are good at showing trends and how things change from one entry to the next. You can also stack several related pieces of information side by side to see how different categories compare. Pie charts are best at showing how one particular item is split up. You can see how big each section is and which are the most, or least, important elements.

Flat or 3-D

If you want a very simple graph, bar and pie charts can be shown completely flat. This is useful if there are a lot of columns and slices in the graph, or where a clear image is important, such as when you are creating graphs for display on an overhead projector. But if your graph is going to be seen on screen or printed out in a report, the 3-D graph looks more interesting. You may have the option to change the viewing angle to make the graph more impressive.

Fine-tuning

Don't feel you are stuck with the text and colour scheme that your spreadsheet uses. You can get back into the graph and change the colour scheme and the text style and size to whatever you feel looks best.

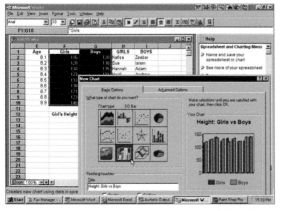

Select the ranges of data you want to show in your *graph* and select the type of graph you want to use. Add the title and the names of the horizontal axis and the vertical axis. Press Done and you'll have your graph.

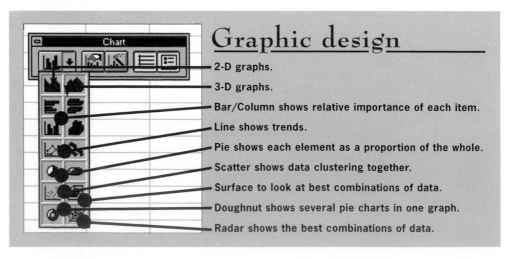

Graphic design

- 2-D graphs.
- 3-D graphs.
- Bar/Column shows relative importance of each item.
- Line shows trends.
- Pie shows each element as a proportion of the whole.
- Scatter shows data clustering together.
- Surface to look at best combinations of data.
- Doughnut shows several pie charts in one graph.
- Radar shows the best combinations of data.

Doing more

You'll be glad to know that most spreadsheets do not leave you on your own. Most offer all sorts of ready-made files for the most common spreadsheet applications. You can open one up and get going immediately, knowing that all the essential formulas have already been developed for you.

There are additional tools – Microsoft calls its tools Wizards – that will help you make your own spreadsheets and reports. As long as you know roughly what you want to do, the Wizard will take you through the options and start putting in the right columns, rows, formulas and reports.

Working backwards

The natural way of working with a spreadsheet is to put in all the data and then calculate a result. This is fine to see how things are now, but it doesn't help you see how things could be. To do that, you need to work backwards: start with the result and calculate what the data should be to get that result.

What if?

What if you think you can afford to spend a little more on a car. You know how much the purchase price is, but what combination of insurance, miles per gallon and everything else will that allow? You can take the data you have already on mileage and how your existing costs spread over the year, and then enter some totals for petrol, insurance and mileage. The spreadsheet will work back from the totals and fill in the blank data cells. You'll then be able to look at several different sets of options to show what miles per gallon and depreciation and insurance levels you can afford, and how those costs are likely to be spread over the year.

Moving data around

If you want to go beyond the simple database functions of your spreadsheet, you can export the sheet into a database program. Databases work from the same type of worksheet as spreadsheets, so you will be able to start working on your data almost immediately. Software suites like Works and Office ensure that data can move from one type of program to another without problems.

You can incorporate *spreadsheet results* into word-processor documents.

To and from a word processor

Your spreadsheet results can be easily added into a report written in your word processor. If it is a single report, use Copy to place the information on your word-processor page and it will appear as a table.

If the spreadsheet information forms part of a regular monthly report, use your word processor's Special Paste function to link the spreadsheet information directly to your report document. Each time you update your spreadsheet, the table or graph in your report document is automatically updated, too.

You can, of course, work the other way around, and bring in information from a database or a table in a word-processor document and feed it directly into your spreadsheet.

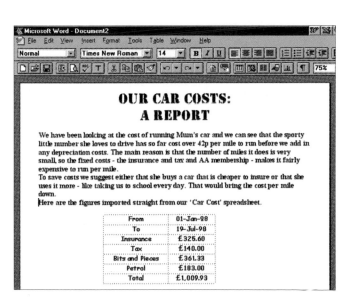

Fun and profit

Although you are not going to be using a spreadsheet as much as your word processor, it is still an important and useful tool whenever you need to do some number crunching. Very few businesses get by without using a spreadsheet of one variety or another, and it will help you manage clubs and associations as well as any other small project that involves lists of things that you have to keep track of and calculate in some way.

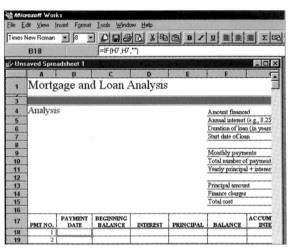

Spreadsheets for finances

Spreadsheets started life as a tool for accountants in large companies, and they have become an essential tool for every company. Now that PCs are available to everyone, and spreadsheet programs have been made much simpler to understand and operate, they can be just as useful for small businesses, the self-employed or anyone helping to run a small club or association.

They will help you keep track of all your financial activities and can be used to create invoices, bills and receipts. Since most businesses or associations need the same sort of spreadsheet layouts and reports, you'll find your software comes with a range of ready-made business sheets that you can simply open up and start entering your finances into.

Home finances

In our next chapter, we will be talking about home-finance software that can keep track of your bank accounts, income and expenses. These are basically spreadsheets, although they don't always look like them. In your spreadsheet software, you'll find ready-made spreadsheets that will cover most home-finance issues, such as making a home inventory.

Spreadsheets at school

Spreadsheets may be new to you, but from primary school on, children are getting used to entering data and looking at the results. Spreadsheets form an important part of information-technology teaching, using projects such as looking at the variation in height among the children in a class. The children can put in information about their own height. Then they can start looking at how many variations there are, what averages are and how one measurement is related to another.

Spreadsheet or not to spreadsheet?

For some jobs, such as home finances, you may be more comfortable using a dedicated system rather than the functions in a spreadsheet. If you have a software suite, you might choose to use a spreadsheet instead of a database, as a spreadsheet will also have database and search functions built in to handle the simple requirements of looking for information. For example, a simple list of people and phone numbers can be put into a spreadsheet and sorted alphabetically so it's easy to find a name and number. If you want to do more with the information, you can always export the data into a real database.

7

HOME FINANCE

Easy money

When asked what they would like their PC to do for them, most people reply: 'Anything to get their home finances in order.' A household can have several different bank accounts, credit-card accounts and credit purchases. This is complicated by the usual expenses: the rent or the mortgage, insurance policies, car costs, electricity, telephone bills and the regular income from work and investments. Accounting for the pennies so the pounds can take care of themselves is not always straightforward. And keeping track of exactly what comes in and what goes out requires a juggling act that is beyond most people. So no wonder the computer, with its history of being used for big company accounts, is seen as a boon for helping to keep the household accounts straight.

Accounts packages have been around for a long time. But they didn't become popular until now because most of them were designed purely for business accounting. Even if they could handle household accounts, people still needed the skills of an accountant to understand how to use them.

But things are changing. Software systems like Microsoft Money and Intuit Quicken have moved away from the business approach. They have become more like multimedia programs, with easy-to-use and attractive interfaces that make accounts much less boring and difficult. The idea is to make them so simple to use that you don't avoid putting your weekly accounts into your PC.

Once you are in the habit of putting your finances into your PC, you can get two types of useful information out of your home-accounts package. The first is an accurate view of what is coming in and going out of the household budget. You can check the accuracy of your bank statements and start looking at where the money goes. Once the information is in the PC, it can be sifted and sorted in different ways so you can check what is going on.

And looking into the future and planning your finances is just as important. Can you afford that new car – or even that new computer? What would happen if you paid in one lump sum or used one of the many credit purchase agreements available? Home-finance packages let you look into your crystal ball and see what the best options are and what impact your choices will have. ●

Accounts

Home-finance programs like Microsoft Money and Intuit Quicken are aimed at helping you with your personal finances. They make it easy for you to keep track of your money. They can handle anything that involves your income, so you know exactly the state of your financial health at any time.

When you are looking for a home-finance package, you should be sure to get one that meets your needs. Your home finances need a different approach from the one you would use for business. You are not going to need the more sophisticated functions included in business-accounts software.

Even if you have a small business or are the treasurer of a club, you may find some of the home-finance packages are more than adequate.

Accounts for small businesses

If your business or club accounts involve more complex functions, such as stock control, it may be worth considering a business-accounts package. In the past, business-accounts packages were expensive and assumed the person using them was an accountant. The increased interest by small businesses and the self-employed in using PCs has created a new generation of accounts software. This combines the business functions of the bigger packages with the ease of use of the home systems.

VAT's the way to do it

A good home-finance package can handle the essential elements of VAT. If you, your business or your club are VAT registered, you have to tell the VAT office the difference between what you have paid in VAT on buying goods and services and the VAT you have charged your customers.

The theory is simple, but the reality can be a headache. Your PC can take the hassle out of preparing VAT accounts. It will calculate the VAT on any transaction and store this as a separate account. When it comes to working out the accounts, your PC will total all the invoices with and without the VAT, show the amount of VAT that has been paid and charged, and generally do all the hard work for you.

Organising accounts

Once you have installed your software, the first thing you will be asked to do is enter all the accounts that make up your finances. A typical family may have quite an array of accounts. First, there are bank accounts, which may include a current account, an interest-paying savings account, and even a building society account. There may also be investments that are treated as separate accounts, since your home-finance package has special tools to keep track of the ups and downs of an investment portfolio.

Then there are the accounts for credit cards and loans. These may include your credit card bill, your mortgage, a car loan, or the credit payments on a TV.

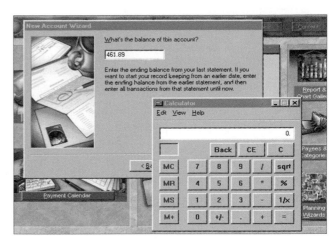

Virtual accounts

Not every account on your PC has to have a matching bank account, so you can also set up virtual accounts. If you want to save for a holiday, you will need to keep track of how those monthly amounts you are putting aside are mounting up. A Savings Goal account will keep track of what you are putting aside for that special week in the sun and show you how close you are to reaching your target, even though, in reality, the money is going into the savings account alongside other payments and withdrawals.

Setting up

You can enter all sorts of information about each account, such as contact names and numbers, and whether it pays interest. Your PC will be able to calculate the interest due automatically at any point in time.

When you are setting up your accounts, you can decide whether or not you need to separate out the VAT. For most home users, this should be set to No VAT across the board. But if one particular account relates to a VAT-registered business, you can get the software to calculate the VAT automatically every time a new entry is made.

As with nearly all the functions in a good home-finance software package, you don't have to go through a complex setting-up procedure. When you set up a new account, your PC will ask you all the necessary questions, one at a time. You'll just have to type in the answers.

The current state of affairs

Once you have the framework, it's time to enter your current state of affairs. The important thing is to get your home accounts and the bank accounts synchronised so that your computer's monthly report can be checked against your bank statement.

The starting point for this is to use your most recent statement for each account. The system will ask you to enter the last balance and its date. When you've entered these simple details, your PC has a starting point that matches your printed statements. It will use this as the starting point for all future calculations.

Setting up **an account is easy. The software asks simple questions. You even get an on-screen calculator to help out.**

Gather those papers

It is a good idea before you start to get hold of as many of your financial papers as possible and sort them into categories and accounts. If things are missing, don't worry, because you can always add another account or other details later. As well as your financial history, you should also think about any savings goals you might want to work towards in the future. It can be very modest, maybe just £5 a month for a special treat at the end of the year. Set up a Savings Goal and your computer will remind you to put the money in the bank each month and keep track of how your savings towards that specific target are progressing.

There are lots of different accounts *options* you can use.

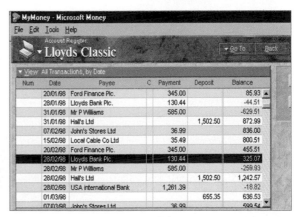

You can look through all the *entries* in any account. There will be a display showing you the current balance, too.

Transactions

Your home-finance program coordinates everything you enter into it, using one large spreadsheet. A spreadsheet is like a large piece of paper with lines and columns. Each new entry or transaction is put on a new line, and the amounts involved are put into a column that corresponds to that particular account. There are separate columns for every account and type of transaction and columns for notes about each entry. Printed out in its raw state, this would be a very complex piece of paper.

But you never have to look at the whole sheet. When you need to enter or look at information, the program sorts the relevant entries for that particular job and shows you just what you need to see. With all your accounts centralised in this way, your computer can extract information in all sorts of ways. If you want to look at your current account, the program will take only the entries in the Transaction Sheet that relate to the current account and show you those, with all the totals and subtotals you might need. You may want to look at everything that has been paid in over the past month. Your PC will look at the entries across all the accounts and collate everything that happened over the previous month for you to see. It is this flexibility that makes home-finance packages so useful.

Once the accounts are set up, you can start entering your transactions. Rather than try to describe every different type of entry that your home-finance program can deal with, they are all given the general name Transactions. A transaction could be money going into an account or money going out—or even money moving from one account to another.

When you write a cheque or deposit money in an account, you should record it on the PC. As you enter the information, the PC will update the account's balance according to your cheque or paying-in slip.

Entering transactions is no more complex than writing a cheque or a paying-in slip. Your PC asks you more or less for the same information that the bank does: the date, who the money is going to or coming from, and the amount involved. Some programs even display an on-screen cheque for you to fill in and transfer the information directly into the Transaction Sheet. You also have space to type in other notes about the transaction, just as you have on the cheque stub.

You do this when you get a bill to pay or deposit money into an account. Most of the information about the account is already loaded, so this takes only a few seconds. The only other information to add is the transaction's category.

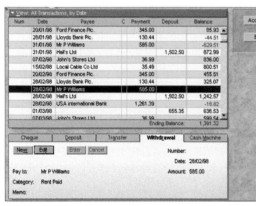

Fill in the *on-screen cheque* and all the information is automatically loaded into the transaction sheet.

Categorise accounts

Every transaction can be linked to any other transaction throughout the year. And you can group money spent on similar things or income coming from the same source.

On the expenses side, groups that will be regularly used will include home

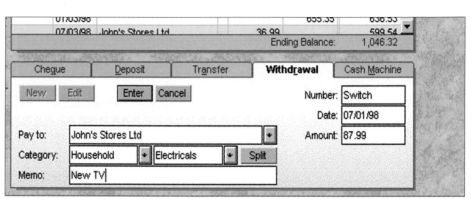

repairs, petrol, holidays, the garden and property taxes. Different sources of income can be grouped together into categories, such as salary, child benefit or interest on savings.

The advantage of categorising all of your transactions is that your PC can start grouping them together. Then you can see how much was spent over the year on a particular activity or how much income came into the household from, say, a part-time job. Your program will have a comprehensive list of categories built into it, and you can always add your own.

There are lots of *categories* that you can assign a payment or receipt to. Or you can create your own.

Groups and supergroups

Once you've grouped a set of payments into a single category, you may then find it useful to group a set of categories together into a supergroup. Take the cost of running a car, for example. You would put your fuel costs into the Petrol category, repairs into the Car Service category, and tax and insurance into the Tax/Insurance category. Having done that, you can get your program to tell you how much you have spent in each category, and when.

But you can't find out from this the total amount you have spent on the car. To do that, you have to set up a supergroup, called Car, which groups together the Petrol, Car Service, and Tax/Insurance categories. Now you can see both the overall amount of money spent on the car and individual categories. Regularly used supergroups are those that group all household expenses, income, social security payments, and car expenses together.

You can create larger *supergroups* to tell you the overall costs, or income, from a group of related categories, such as household expenses.

Self-sorting dates

Everything in the Transaction Sheet is listed in date order. It doesn't matter if you don't get around to entering a transaction until a few weeks after it happened. Your PC will automatically slot it into its rightful place in the listings.

Cash flow

You'd be surprised how many transactions you know about a long time before they happen. There is the rent or mortgage, standing orders and credit-card payments. There are car tax and insurance, membership dues and paydays. There are also one-off payments that you get to know about in advance, such as the balance of a holiday payment.

Even if you don't know the exact amounts that are going to be involved, you can enter these future transactions into a financial calendar that keeps track of them. This allows you to see what your accounts are going to look like in a few months' time. For regular transactions such as standing orders, you only have to enter the details once. Then it is a simple matter of clicking on the due days each month.

Your PC always knows the date from its internal clock. When you load your home-finance system, the first thing it does is look at the calendar and check for any transactions that are due, or overdue. The system will then tell you what should be dealt with.

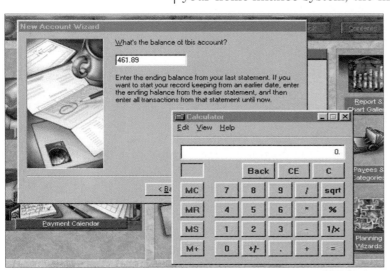

Use the *calendar* to put in details of regular payments and income. If the payments fall on the same day every month, you only have to enter details once and the system will do the rest for you.

Instant transfer

Some transactions will appear in two parts of your system. When you pay a phone bill, the bill will appear in the telephone account, and the payment details will be added when you pay it. Back in your cheque account, which is being used to pay the bill, the details of the payment also have to be entered. In theory, this means several sets of entries. But to save you having to move from one part of the system to another, the software will do this automatically. When it comes to paying the phone bill, you go to the cheque account, which will already have the phone company's details in it. Click on the phone company, and if you have already entered the invoice details, most finance programs will take that information and automatically debit your cheque account while updating all the necessary details. This also works when you transfer money from one account to another. Once you have told the system where the money is coming from and going to, it will do the rest.

Balancing

After you have entered your transactions, at the end of each month you need to reconcile where you think you are with where your bank, building society or credit-card company thinks you are. This is called balancing your accounts. Many people already do this each month by checking the bank-statement entries. This is its simplest form. You just check that each item on

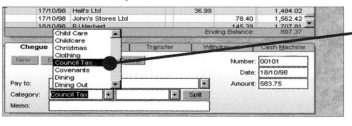

You know the amount, but where is it? Use the *Find* command to sort out those queries.

Matching **your PC's records up with your statements is simple. Click the mouse on each entry that is on your statement and you know exactly the state of your finances.**

your bank statement matches the cheque stubs and paying-in slips.

Balancing your accounts on the PC takes no more time than doing it manually. And it should be quicker because all the information about payments and receipts is at hand. The program shows you the payments and receipts you have entered into your PC. If they are on your bank statement, you check them off by clicking on them. At the bottom of the screen, you can see the current bank balance, the value of items that have not cleared and what the difference is. If everything that you've written has gone through the account, you'll get a satisfying zero in the difference column.

Some cheques written near or after the date of the statement won't have cleared. So in the real world, there will nearly always be some amount in the difference column. While this is normal, it shouldn't stop you from looking through the uncleared entries to verify that nothing is amiss. If a cheque hasn't cleared for a couple of months, you can check with the payee that it was received. It is helpful to keep a little more in your account so that it is not overdrawn when a late cheque finally comes through for payment.

Hide-and-seek

In this imperfect world, paperwork has a tendency to be misplaced. Dates, names and amounts are all needed to be certain that a payment matches an entry in your accounts, but sometimes you may have only one of these pieces of information. This is why the Find function is one of the most useful in your finance package. Whenever there is a problem with payments into or out of your accounts, Find will usually give you the answers.

The command is simple – it just asks you which category you want to search: the name of the payee, the amount or the date. You enter what details you have and the PC will then find entries that match. This is useful with a bank statement that has an entry that you can't figure out. Put in the amount and the program will find the matching entry in your transactions.

The match doesn't have to be exact. If it is a credit-card payment for a small amount that includes an unknown extra (such as a postage payment for something you bought mail order), you can ask the system to Find all transactions below a certain amount. This will help you narrow down the search and make it easier to find the entry.

When you enter a *group* here, the payment will be automatically registered in the Gas account section so you don't have to enter it twice.

Home inventory

A s well as keeping track of the cash that is coming into and going out of the house, you can have a complete inventory of its contents. If you can't see the immediate advantage, you may well find that your insurance company will. The best reason for having an accurate inventory of your home and all its contents is to get an accurate value for insurance purposes. Insurance companies say people under-insure their household contents. People always remember the big expensive items – such as the TV, the microwave, the chairs and tables – but not the plants, bed linens, CDs or cutlery. That's where the home inventory comes in. Since you would naturally list things by room, so does the home inventory. It takes you through each room, suggesting the sort of things you should be listing.

What's it worth?

When you enter a value, you have two options: its resale value or its replacement value. Some insurance policies will replace old items with new ones. In this case you will need to enter the current cost of a replacement. Other policies will pay the secondhand value of the items.

In the inventory you can list either value or both. Another option is to enter the purchase price. The inventory will work out the secondhand cost using a percentage of the original price.

As well as an item's value, you can also include a description and other important information, such as serial numbers, date of purchase, original price, and when the warranty expires.

Holiday time

There are all sorts of things you might find the inventory useful for. You could use it for your holidays, for example. There are always things you'll forget to take. Set up a holiday inventory, and when you get back you can update it. When it comes around to holiday time again, you just print out your inventory and everything is listed. The list is also handy to take with you in case you need to claim loss or damage during your trip.

Mix and match

A home inventory can rearrange its information in lots of different ways. You can list everything by room or by category. You can have a listing of everything in the living room or produce a complete breakdown of all your sports gear, no matter where it is in the house. These different ways of listing things can be important when you have separate insurance policies for the car and its contents, a policy for the contents of the house, and one for the building and fixtures. The separate lists can tell you the necessary insurance value for each policy.

Each room is waiting for you to list its *contents*. We are starting in the living room.

The *items* you are likely to find in the living room are listed. Just click on the ones you have.

You can accept the computer's *estimate* of the items' value or enter your own.

Everything you need to know about your *property* can be included.

Even as the information is being entered, it is already being categorised into *separate groups*.

8 PRINTING

Press on!

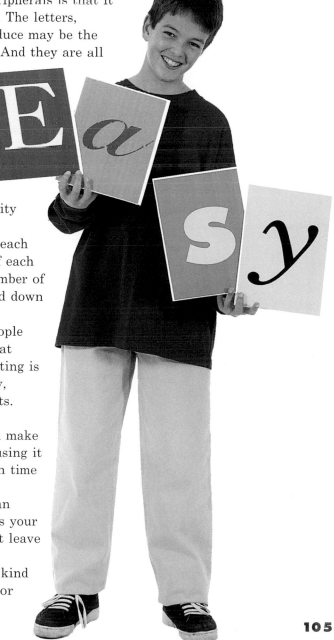

After the screen, keyboard and mouse, the most important device to connect to your computer is a printer. The big difference between a printer and other peripherals is that it affects the way that others see your work. The letters, reports, pictures and graphs that you produce may be the only thing you do on your computer that others will see. And they are all delivered via your printer.

Unlike keyboards or mice, which work in much the same way and differ little in use, there are many kinds of printers. This chapter explores all the options.

There are three main types of printer: dot-matrix, inkjet or bubblejet, and laser. While they all create an image by printing dots on paper, the cost and quality of each type varies enormously. Some produce better-quality prints than others, but may not be within your budget.

When choosing a printer, it is important to know what each type of printer will let you do and what the limitations of each are. Once you've looked at the options, you'll find the number of models that really meet your requirements can be whittled down from the many available to just a manageable handful.

Printing in black and white has been standard since people first started to use PCs, when the idea of colour printing at home would have been just a dream. But now colour printing is no longer a luxury. You can easily, and relatively cheaply, include great-looking, full-colour pictures in your printouts.

Many of you will, of course, already have a printer. Understanding your printer and how it works will let you make the most of it, and it will help you to learn how to keep using it without running up big bills to refill the ink or toner each time it runs out.

And don't forget the paper. The right choice of paper can make as much difference to the quality of your printing as your choice of printer. Using cheap paper for work that doesn't leave your house or office saves money. And it can help the environment if you opt for recycled paper. Find out what kind of paper will make an impression on your friends, clients or anyone who reads your printed paperwork. ●

Your printer

There is a bewildering range of printers available that vary hugely in price. You have to choose one that is going to suit your particular needs and finances. First, you need to decide which category is best for you and then look to see which printer in that category is ideal. There are three main types of printer available: dot-matrix, inkjet and laser. Each has its own pros and cons.

Dot-matrix: cheap but noisy

A dot-matrix printer works by firing tiny pins through a typewriter-like ribbon. The dots formed by each pin make up the letters and graphics on the paper. Dot-matrix printers come in two varieties: 9-pin and 24-pin. This tells you how many pins are placed in a row in the printer head. The pins on a 9-pin printer are spaced widely apart, and you can see the dots that make up each letter. A 24-pin printer makes a better impression, and it is difficult to see the dots that make up the image on the page.

The dot-matrix printer has the advantage of being relatively cheap to buy and cheap to run. The printer ribbons you need to use with them last long enough to print out thousands of pages and are very cheap. Dot-matrix printers are also fairly compact and won't take up a lot of room.

They also have a few advantages over both inkjet and laser printers, although these are mainly things that are only an advantage if you are using the printer at work. A dot-matrix printer works with a continuous fanfold of paper, rather than just one sheet at a time, using a system called tractor feeding. This is useful when a lot of work is printed – say, hundreds of pages of something like a long stock report. The tractor's cogs lock on to the sprocket holes on the side of the continuous fanfold of paper, and just keep feeding the printer until the job is finished.

The other advantage is that a dot-matrix printer can work with multilayer, self-carbonated paper. If you want to run off multicopy invoices, receipts, or those clever wage slips which are totally sealed with the wage details printed through the outer layer on the inside wage slip, you've got to use a dot-matrix printer.

Although the quality produced by a 24-pin dot-matrix printer isn't perfect, it is quite acceptable for most work, and it is fast enough if you are using one at home just to print out letters and other documents. But the thing that deters most people from buying a dot-matrix printer is the noise it makes. The loud metallic buzzing sound that the pins make as they strike the paper will go all through the house, and although you can get cases that cover the whole printer, you can never make it operate anywhere near silently.

All desktop printing is produced by putting *dots* on the paper.

Inkjets: best of both worlds

Inkjet printers – or bubblejets, as some of them are called – work by spraying ink on to the paper from tiny nozzles in the printer cartridge.

For many, inkjets are the ideal solution since they are relatively cheap to buy and can produce very good results. The fact that inkjets are almost silent when printing makes them worth the investment – your computer's fan is likely to be noisier than an inkjet in operation. Typical inkjet printers are fairly compact. And there are several ultra-slim inkjets available that can be used when space is very limited.

Inkjets can handle varying sizes of paper and envelopes. You stack the blank paper in a paper tray, and it is automatically fed into the printer. Although an inkjet printer can be used with a variety of papers, for the best results, paper especially made for inkjet printers should be used.

The printing work is done by the inkjet's printer head, which is part of the ink-refill cartridge. So when the ink runs out, you replace both the ink and the printer head using one small cartridge. This is good because the printer head is the one part that can clog up. It is replaced on a regular basis, each time you change the ink cartridge. The bad news is that this pushes up the cost of the ink cartridge and makes the inkjet the most expensive to operate of the three types of printer, with the highest cost per page printed.

There is one important thing that an inkjet can do well that is not really practical with either a dot-matrix or a laser printer: full-colour printing. Inkjet manufacturers have found that if they use a specially designed three-colour ink cartridge/printer head, there is little else they have to change to turn an ordinary inkjet into a full-colour printer. So nearly all but the lowest-priced inkjet printers have colour capability. An inkjet uses a lot more ink when it is working in colour, so the operating cost goes up. But when you are printing out black-and-white pages only, you can revert to using just the black ink cartridge, which brings the cost per page back to a normal level.

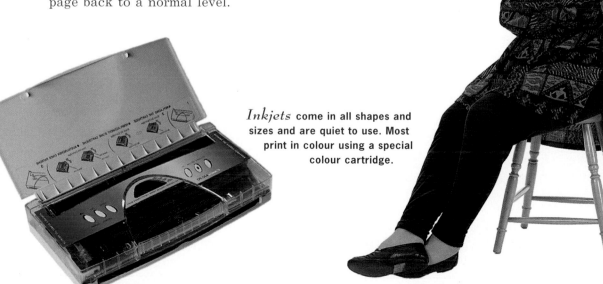

Inkjets come in all shapes and sizes and are quiet to use. Most print in colour using a special colour cartridge.

Lasers: quality at an affordable price

Laser printers create their copies in a way similar to that of a photocopier. A tiny laser beams the image on to a special photosensitive drum, where the image's black areas become charged with static electricity. The statically charged areas then pick up toner, which is ink in powder form. This black-powder image is then rolled on to the paper, and a heating element melts the powder, fusing it on to the page.

Because of their complexity, lasers have traditionally been at the luxury end of the printer range and could cost as much or more than your PC itself. But since more manufacturers have started making them, and more people have started using them, the prices have dropped dramatically. Now there are many laser printers the prices of which are comparable with those of the top-of-the-line inkjets.

Laser printers have many advantages over dot-matrix and inkjet printers. The print quality they offer is excellent because the fused-ink system produces very crisp, clear text and images – better than the best inkjets. They are fast, producing several pages per minute, even at higher quality, and are cheaper to run than inkjet printers. Another advantage is that because the ink is fused on to the page, there is no risk of smudging, and laser-printed pages can be handled as soon as they appear.

But laser printers have a downside, too. Normally, they are a bit bigger than inkjet or dot-matrix printers, and this can be a problem at home if you don't have a lot of space. Also, they are less environmentally friendly, producing ozone as a by-product of the printing process. While laser printers are cheaper to run over a period of time, they can be more expensive to buy than other kinds of printers. Plus, although the toner cartridges last a very long time, when they do run out, you will be faced with a large bill for a new one. Even though the cost per page is low, this can still come as a bit of a shock. Last, although there are some colour laser printers available, they are very expensive. They are not worth considering for use at home unless you need to take advantage of the excellent print quality they offer for business or some other reason.

Laser printers **can be expensive but offer excellent print quality.**

Questions to ask

- **Print quality** How good does the printed page look?
- **Speed** How fast will it print each page?
- **Size** Will it fit on my desk/table?
- **Output** Do I need colour or black-and-white?
- **Purchase price** Can I afford it?
- **Running costs** How much is it going to cost to run each year?
- **Noise** Does it have to be quiet?

What to buy

For nearly everyone, the quality of the printed image is the first thing to look at. All printers make up their images as a series of dots. If the dots are quite big, as in the case of a 9-pin dot-matrix printer, you can see them easily, ruining any illusion of smooth lines and curves. As the dots get smaller and closer together, they merge into one another, creating the look of perfectly straight lines and perfect curved edges. So the quality of a printer is measured primarily in dots per inch – abbreviated to dpi – and the more dots per inch, the better the print quality.

Basic inkjets all produce 600dpi, so a line 25.4mm (1in) long would be made up of 600 dots. This quality – or resolution – is good enough for normal letter writing. The later generations of inkjet and laser printers work at 1,200dpi and more. This gives crisper, clearer letters and also means that the printer can accurately print very small text and the fine details or images and pictures.

Better quality
There is special software that alters the look of the lines and curves just a little, to smooth out the jagged edges that the printer would normally produce. This gives the print quality the appearance of a resolution higher than the printer is actually producing. This is such a good trick that many manufacturers have built the software into their printers so that your printing quality is improved automatically whenever you print anything.

Size
The size of the printer, its width and depth, is called the footprint. If your PC and printer have to sit on one desk, you will probably want the printer to take up as little room as possible, so its footprint has to be small.

Inkjets tend to be medium-sized because you store the paper in the printer. Some inkjets hold the paper up at an angle, so the footprint is reduced, but they are then unable to hold large amounts of blank paper.

Some dot-matrix printers are quite narrow, as they use continuous fanfold paper that can be stored under the desk. If you want to use A4 paper, you will need to add a paper tray, which increases the printer's footprint.

Nearly all laser printers are bigger than inkjet or dot-matrix printers, so you need to reserve more space.

Speed
If you do a fair amount of printing, you will appreciate a printer that produces pages quickly. A printer's speed is measured in pages per minute – abbreviated to ppm. This is calculated using a test page with enough text and images printed on it to cover about 25 per cent. Assessing printer speeds is not an exact science. The less print there is on each page, the faster the page will print, and if you are printing out lots of images, you will not reach the printer's quoted speed. It also takes a while for your PC or the printer to do all the calculations necessary to print out the image, so the first page always takes longer than the following ones.

DOT-MATRIX INKJET LASER

Different types of printers produce different-quality output.

Laser

Laser printers can produce the sharpest printing, even approaching magazine quality in many cases. Because they contain their own powerful processors and memory and also have the necessary font or typeface information already loaded in them, they can do a lot of the page's image-processing work very quickly. This means they can produce the fastest prints.

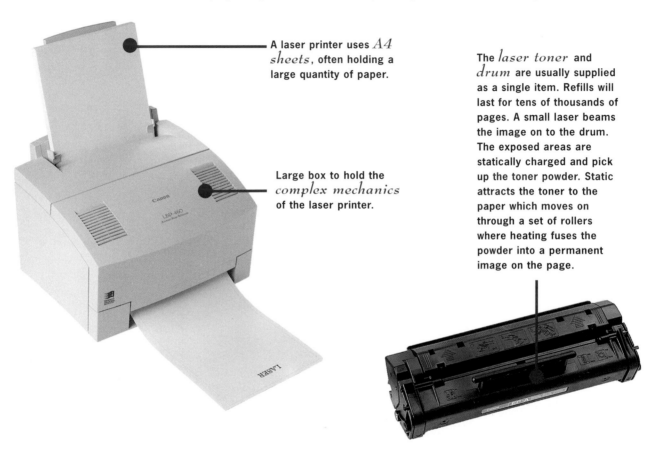

A laser printer uses *A4 sheets*, often holding a large quantity of paper.

Large box to hold the *complex mechanics* of the laser printer.

The *laser toner* and *drum* are usually supplied as a single item. Refills will last for tens of thousands of pages. A small laser beams the image on to the drum. The exposed areas are statically charged and pick up the toner powder. Static attracts the toner to the paper which moves on through a set of rollers where heating fuses the powder into a permanent image on the page.

Inside information

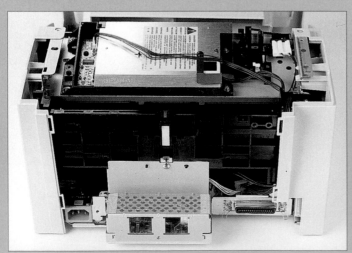

The mechanics inside a laser printer are much more complicated than those inside a dot-matrix or inkjet/bubblejet printer. Laser printers have the details of anywhere between 50 and 100 fonts stored in their memory chips. This means that it can work directly with the fonts, thus speeding up the print process.

Large amounts of memory help speed up the laser-printing process further. Laser printers have anywhere between 2Mb and 50Mb of RAM installed. And a high-power processor handles the complex task of creating high-quality text images, rather than letting the PC do all the work.

As well as the usual connections, some laser printers also have sockets for connecting directly to a network system.

Inkjet

Inkjets represent a good compromise for many home-office and small-business users. They deliver remarkably good-quality prints and do not cost too much to buy. Although they are not particularly fast, or the cheapest to run, they offer good-quality colour printing, which is very attractive, especially when it comes to doing business reports or homework projects.

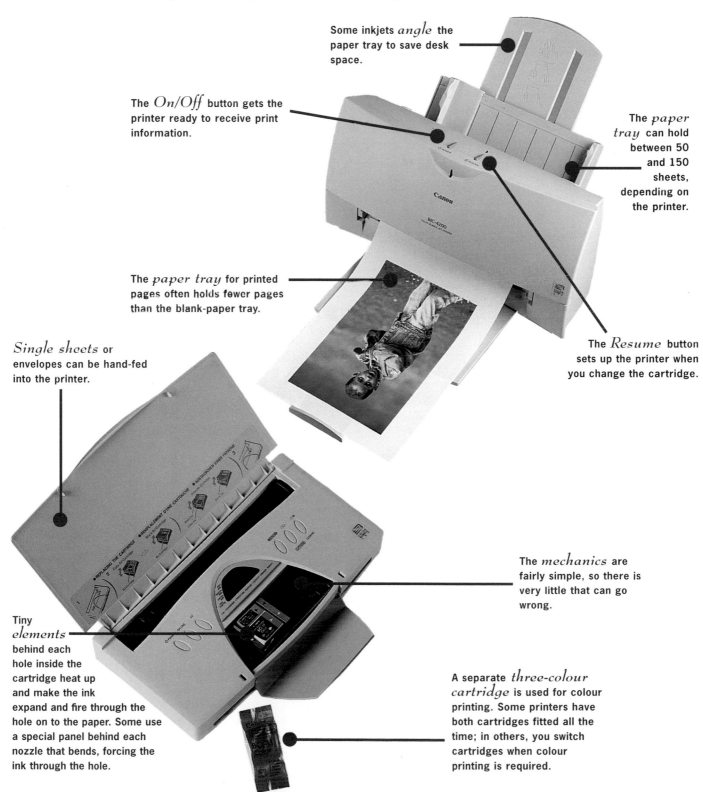

Some inkjets *angle* the paper tray to save desk space.

The *On/Off* button gets the printer ready to receive print information.

The *paper tray* can hold between 50 and 150 sheets, depending on the printer.

The *paper tray* for printed pages often holds fewer pages than the blank-paper tray.

The *Resume* button sets up the printer when you change the cartridge.

Single sheets or envelopes can be hand-fed into the printer.

The *mechanics* are fairly simple, so there is very little that can go wrong.

Tiny *elements* behind each hole inside the cartridge heat up and make the ink expand and fire through the hole on to the paper. Some use a special panel behind each nozzle that bends, forcing the ink through the hole.

A separate *three-colour cartridge* is used for colour printing. Some printers have both cartridges fitted all the time; in others, you switch cartridges when colour printing is required.

Drivers

When you connect your printer to your PC, the connections are standardised and the leads all fit. But it won't print anything from Windows unless you tell Windows what sort of printer you have.

This is because every type of printer uses different software instructions to make it print. Windows has to translate the image you have created into instructions that your printer can follow.

This is the job of the printer driver, a software program that translates the image data for the printer to use. Installing a driver is simple. When you install Windows, you are asked what printer you have. You can choose from over 1,000 printers Windows has drivers for.

If your printer isn't on the list, check its instruction manual, as it may tell you that it works in the same way as another printer. Alternatively, the printer will have come with a disk that contains the right driver for it.

Standards

There are several standards for controlling printers, and your printer will be able to work with some or all of them. The ASCII system sends numbers to the printer, each representing a letter or a function. It is a crude system, but it does its job well. Adobe's PostScript was developed as a much better system to create text and page information. PostScript is excellent but requires a lot of computing power. Windows 95 comes with a translation driver called the graphical device interface, or GDI. To use this you will need a printer that supports GDI.

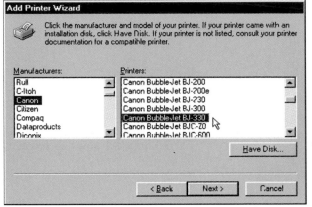

Who does the processing?

Many printers now come with their own processors and memory. Many laser printers and some inkjet printers also have details of all the common Windows typefaces built into them. So, instead of your computer having to do all the work in creating the page, it simply does some preliminary calculations and then sends off a simple set of instructions. The printer's processor will do the rest. This is just like having two computers working on your print job rather than one and will considerably increase the printing speed as well as allow your PC to move on to the next function.

Faster prints

Your computer system needs a lot of memory to store the page image that is being created and sent to the printer. If your PC or your laser printer doesn't have enough RAM, the job will be temporarily stored on your hard disk, which will slow things up considerably. If you add more memory to your PC or laser printer, it will noticeably speed up the printing process.

Printer control

Printing is a background operation, which means that, behind the scenes, your computer does all the calculations involved in creating the images and sending them to the printer so you can get on with other things.

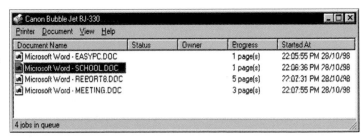

You don't even have to wait for one print run to finish before you tell your computer about the next. If there are several documents to print, Windows creates a line of print jobs, and as each job is finished, the next is sent off to the printer automatically.

Windows controls it all through the Printer menu. As soon as you click on Print, a printer icon will appear in the bottom right-hand corner of the screen. If you want to see how a particular printing job is progressing, or want to pause or change the order of the print line, just click on this icon.

Connecting

A printer is one of the easiest things to connect to your computer. All printers have at least a parallel connector to go to the printer port on your PC – the one marked LPT1 or Printer. The lead you will have will be a little thicker than those used when connecting to the communications ports. This is because the printer port is a parallel connection. This means different information is sent down several wires at the same time. The serial connection used by the mouse or external modem sends digital information in little blocks, one after another, down the same wire. Your printer may well have a connector for a serial (communications) port but this is mainly for connecting to non-PC computers.

The connector that goes into the printer is also different from those used on your PC. It is called a Centronics connector and is standard among most printers. This connector passes information in both directions. The print instructions are sent from the computer to the printer on this lead, and the printer sends back information about itself. It will tell you whether it's ready for printing or not, whether there is paper in the tray or if the printer is jammed for any reason. Armed with this information, your computer can tell you exactly what is going on with any print job and also if there is a problem that needs to be dealt with.

As well as the connector lead to the PC, the printer also needs to be connected separately to a power supply. The easiest and safest way is to use a multi-outlet power strip or surge protector, which can be used to switch on or off the power to both the computer and all its peripherals.

The printer is connected to the computer via a cable with a *Centronics connector* at the printer end and a *D-25 plug*, shown here, at the computer end.

All together now

It can be useful to have two printers for different types of work. By connecting computers together in a network, they can all share the same printer. When you click on Print on your screen, the instructions are sent around the network to the printer. Your particular job then joins the line behind print jobs already asked for by other people on the same network. Higher-quality laser printers have special connectors so that they can be hooked directly into the network system.

But you don't have to use a network to share a printer. If you have two or three computers and want to use one high-quality laser printer, then you can use a switch-box. The computers plug into a small box that has a switch that allows you to select which computer is going to work with the printer. This is a crude but effective way of sharing a printer.

The switch-box idea can also be used to feed the output of one computer to a selection of different printers, where you may want to use a laser printer for its quality and a dot-matrix printer for a large run of invoices.

Two printers may seem like a luxury, but if you are moving up to an inkjet or laser printer, you may find your existing printer still comes in handy.

Portables

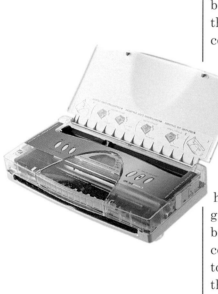

Even if you are on the move, you can still take a printer with you. There are several very effective portable printers that can slip easily into your briefcase. Portable printers work just like ordinary printers and connect in the same way to the laptop computer's serial or parallel ports. Because the printer has to be wide enough to handle an A4 piece of paper, they are around 3cm (1ft) long. Still, they are usually very slim and range from around 127mm (5in) to as little as a half that size wide and deep, so they take up the minimum amount of space.

Some portable printers are more portable than others. Some have internal batteries, while others use an external battery power pack that plugs into the printer and takes up a little more space. All offer the option of connecting to an outlet, often using an external adapter.

When you look at a portable, you should decide how portable you need it to be. If you are travelling to a hotel and just want the ability to print out documents, it is the size of the printer, rather than the ability to work from battery power, that is most important.

Some business users, however, want to be able to visit customers, work on projects on their laptop, and then print out the results on the spot. Obviously, turning someone else's office or home upside down looking for an outlet doesn't give the right impression, so in these circumstances battery power is an essential feature. The computer and printer can be quickly connected together and the hard copy printout produced there and then.

Quality

Because the printer is small it doesn't mean it is going to perform significantly worse than a full-size desktop printer. The resolution of most portables is at least 600dpi, with many capable of working at 1,200dpi resolution. There are no compromises on speed, either. You can easily get four pages per minute out of an inkjet portable. While most portables use black ink only, there are some that will work in full colour, so even that option is there if you need it.

The only real limitation on the portable printer is its lack of input and output paper trays. Adding a reasonably large paper tray would make the printer too big, so most allow you either to feed in individual sheets or to use a small paper feeder. The fact that ink capacities are often smaller than with desktop printers, and the fact that the batteries will last only for a few dozen pages, makes the portable suitable for occasional print jobs rather than for running off large reports.

Printing with no printer

Away from home and desperately need a hard copy of something you have done on your laptop? Provided your computer has a fax/modem, you can get it printed even if you don't have a printer with you. Simply fax the document to anyone with a fax machine and you have an instant hard copy of what you have done.

DIY refills

E ach time the ink runs out, you can save money by buying
alternatives to brand-new ribbons, inkjet cartridges or laser
toner cartridges. For dot-matrix printers there are
ribbon re-inkers, which wind the ribbon through an
inked pad to recharge it. Because ribbons are
not that expensive and last so long, the saving
involved is relatively small. Unless you are
using your printer very heavily, this alternative
is probably not worth the effort. Not all printer
manufacturers recommend using such
alternatives, and it is worth checking that using
them does not affect the warranty on your printer.

Inkjet cartridges

When you replace an empty inkjet cartridge, you are paying at least as much
for the new cartridge itself as for the ink it contains. So re-using an empty
cartridge by filling it with ink can save money.

Many companies produce inkjet refill packs that contain a bottle of ink, a
syringe or filler bottle, and a seal to put over the filler hole on the cartridge.

Although refilling an inkjet cartridge is a simple job, it can be a messy
one, too, and many kits come with light plastic gloves to protect you from
accidentally staining your hands with the ink.

New *inkjet cartridges* (1),
dot-matrix ribbons (2) and
laser toner cartridges (3)
should all be simple enough for
you to install at home, but
make sure that doing so does
not affect your warranty.

Refuelling your inkjet

Remove the filler-hole seal and refill the cartridge to around half to three-
quarters full. Then seal the filler hole again with the sealing pin or adhesive
foil. The cartridge must be left to settle for an hour so the ink can find its way
fully into the cartridge nozzle. While this is happening, some ink will drip out
of the nozzles. You can save around a third to half the cost of a cartridge by
refilling it, and you can refill cartridges several times. The print quality will
deteriorate just a little, and sooner or later the cartridge nozzle will clog up and
need replacing, so have a spare cartridge handy as well as the refill kit.

Laser toners

When your laser printer's toner is all gone, you
usually have to buy a combined toner
cartridge/printer drum unit. This is considerably
more expensive than just buying the toner. But as
these are sealed units that cannot be refilled at
home, several companies will refill and refurbish
used drum/toner units so they are almost as good
as new. Buying a refurbished and refilled
toner/drum cartridge will save around a third of
the cost of a brand-new unit, although the
performance may not be quite up to the standard of
a new one. A few laser printers have long-life drums and
are designed to be refilled with toner. This will save a
reasonable amount of money, especially if the printer is being used a lot. But
as toner powder has a tendency to get everywhere, handle with care.

Paper

The paper you use can make a big difference to the overall look of your documents. If you are interested enough to choose your printer carefully, you should also spend some time finding the right paper. When you send any document out to other people, whether it's for business, for school or for the bank manager, you will want your document to look and feel good.

This is the first area of choice regarding your paper: how good you want it to feel. Photocopy paper is the cheapest you can buy. Although it does the job, it will not provide the quality feel of better paper. But the choice isn't just about the quality you would like to have. The clarity of your print depends on the paper working well with the print process you are using.

One point in favour of dot-matrix printers is that they care little about the type of paper being used and will give more or less the same print quality to every type of paper. If the paper is too absorbent for inkjet printers, the ink being sprayed on to the paper will spread, making the edges of the letters slightly fuzzy. So paper makers have come up with papers designed to absorb the ink uniformly and give your printing a cleaner look. This is even more important when printing colour pictures. If you really want these to stand out, you should use specially coated inkjet paper. Coated paper produces really clear colour images but costs much more than ordinary inkjet paper.

Laser printing, in which the ink powder is fused into the paper, also works better if you use paper that has been developed especially for it. Because laser printers are usually associated with the highest quality, you will find that there is also a wide range of luxury papers available for this type of printer. Wove, linen and laid paper finishes are all available to really enhance the look of your documents and make the right impression.

Buying paper

It used to be quite difficult to find paper for computer printers, but now office-supply stores offer a wide range of paper, usually packed in reams of 500 sheets.

You may find that stationery, office or computer supply companies that work by mail order offer a wider range of specialised papers, as well as slightly lower prices, provided you buy in large enough quantities.

Put on some weight

The thickness of paper is measured in grams per square meter (gsm). The heavier the paper's weight rating, the thicker and firmer the paper.

gsm	70	80	90	100	150	200	250
Basic photocopy	☺	☺	☺	☺			
Good-quality			☺	☺	☺	☺	☺ ☺ ☺ ☺
Card						☺	☺ ☺ ☺

Storage

Your printer cannot hold a whole ream of paper, so the rest has to be stored. Paper should be kept flat, out of the light, and in a box so the edges don't get damaged. Make sure the storage area is dry, as paper will quickly absorb dampness in the atmosphere, and this produces a blotting effect.

Fonts & images

All text is printed as fonts, and fonts are stored in your computer not as pictures of letters but as a set of equations that say where the lines and curves should be and how thick each part of the letter is. There are several standards for fonts, the most common being TrueType and PostScript. With most lower-cost printers, the font information is stored only in your PC. When you want to print out a document, your PC will pull out the relevant fonts' equations and create the page ready for printing.

Some printers have extra memory and processing power built into them. These printers can store fonts or take over some of the processing work needed to create the page. Whenever you use these fonts, the printer takes over the calculating function, thus speeding up the printing process. Many such printers also let you load your own regularly used fonts into their internal memory so they can be used by the printer, too.

Grey from black-and-white

While hard-edged black-and-white is ideal for letters, you need to have lots of different shades of grey or colour for pictures. Although your printer can only produce black dots on white paper, it can still give the illusion of printing lots of shades of grey by using halftoning. This converts the photo into a pattern of dots that give the illusion of lots of degrees of grey.

In magazine printing, halftoning is done by making the dot size bigger or smaller. A large dot with no white space around it will create a dark grey area, whereas a small dot with lots of white space looks light grey. Printers cannot change the size of the dots, so they split the image into little squares of 2x2 dots or 4x4 dots and make those darker or lighter by printing more of the dots, or pixels, in the square. The more dots that are black in each square, the darker the little square appears. If you use a 4x4-dots square, then you have up to 16 possible shades of grey. To get a nearly realistic level of 256 shades of grey, you need a 16x16 square. But if you split the picture into large squares rather than single dots, the resolution –the ability to print fine detail – is reduced. A printer that produces 600dpi on text will only perform to 150dpi on pictures with 16 shades of grey. On 256 shades, it will be about 37dpi.

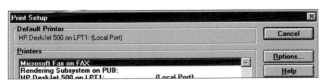

Print a fax

If you have a fax/modem, you can send faxes by calling up dedicated fax software, like Microsoft Fax, or you can treat the fax/modem as though it were a printer.

When you install your fax, you can load the fax system as a Printer driver. When you want to send a fax, you simply click on Print and select the fax/modem as the printer, and this will send the page to your fax software. This is a quicker and simpler way of sending faxes.

Printing to disk

If you want your pages printed professionally, you need to be able to put your file on a disk to take to a bureau. If you are using well-known desktop-publishing or word-processing software, it is possible the bureau will have the same software and you can take just the desktop-publishing or word-processor file. If not, you can use one of the PostScript printer drivers to create the page's image, but instead of sending it to a printer, you can store it on disk. The bureau's printer will take that image and print it out directly on to its system.

Colour

If you want to print in colour, you will probably be working with an inkjet printer. But how do you get a full-colour image from a printer that has only three ink colours? When you were at school mixing paints, the primary colours were easy: red, blue and yellow. You could make green, orange and purple from those, and then all the other colours by mixing the primary colours with one of the secondary colours.

Colour separations

It gets a little more complicated when it comes to printing. The white light from a light bulb or the sun hits the printing ink on the page, which absorbs all the light except for the colour the ink represents. So you are taking light away to get the colour. This is called a subtractive process. The subtractive primary colours are magenta (red), yellow and cyan (blue).

The printer's software takes the image of the page to be printed and creates three separate images using an electronic colour filter. One is for the cyan content of the page and its pictures; one is for the magenta; and one is for the yellow. These are called colour separations and all colour printing, whether it is done at home on your inkjet printer or by a large magazine or newspaper printer, uses separations to create a colour image.

The inkjet printer's software sends the three images to the three separate sets of inkjet nozzles that are built into the colour inkjet cartridge. The cyan image is sprayed on to the page by the cyan nozzle and at the same time the yellow and magenta images are being placed on the page. So you end up with the full-colour image you started with, made up from just three sets of different coloured dots.

A touch of black

In magazine printing the image is split into four different filtered images, the fourth being the black, or the key, image. Although adding CMY (cyan, yellow and magenta) together will produce black, it will not be as pure and crisp as using CMYK (cyan, magenta, yellow, key) printing, which uses black ink for the key outlines and shadows. For the best-looking pictures you should consider a CMYK inkjet rather than the CMY types.

Using CMYK printing, which adds the black *key lines* to cyan, magenta and yellow, gives the picture stronger definition.

SENDING FAXES

Face fax

Time was when a fax was an amazing new gadget that up-to-date companies showed off in their front offices and reception areas. Now the fax has become one of the most common and useful ways of sending documents. Official letters or quick notes scribbled on a piece of paper can get to their destination within seconds of leaving your hand.

In the home, fax machines haven't proved quite so popular. Their size has deterred people, and the cost of a fax machine had to be evaluated, especially if it was not going to be used very often. Enter the fax/modem. If you have a PC, then you probably have a modem. With the power of your PC behind it, your modem can double as a fax machine that sends anything you are working on straight from your PC to a fax thousands of miles away.

With the modem doing all the transmitting and fax software included in both Windows and in the software you get with the modem, you essentially get a fax machine for free. The fax/modem is ideal for anyone working from home, part-time or full-time, but it is also a way to send faxes to friends and relatives. As PCs are becoming more common in homes, so is the home-based PC fax. If you forget someone's birthday you can fax a message and follow up with a call. Do you urgently need a copy of the school's activity list for next week? Call another parent and ask them to fax it over. Are you writing a letter of complaint? Fax it for more immediate attention. ●

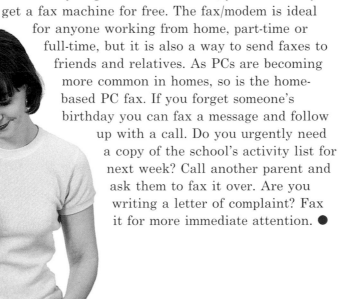

Fax/modems

To send and receive faxes from your computer, all you need is a fax/modem and the fax software that is part of Windows 95 and 98, or that comes free with your modem. Turn to Chapter 11 On-line for all you need to know about modems. If you are only interested in faxing then a basic fax/modem will be fine. However, you may want to use your fax/modem for e-mailing or accessing the World Wide Web, in which case it is worth investing in a high speed fax/modem, since this will do a faster job of connecting to the Internet.

You can buy your fax/modem as an internal card that plugs into one of your computer's expansion sockets or as a stand-alone unit that connects to one of the serial ports. External modems tend to be more expensive than their internal equivalents, but they are slightly easier to install and set up. On the other hand, once an internal fax/modem is installed, it doesn't clutter up your desk and you can almost forget that it is there.

PCMCIA Cards
You can also fax when you are on the move by plugging a fax/modem PCMCIA card into your portable PC; or prepare your faxes on your notebook PC and then send them all at once when you get to a phone.

Plugging in a fax/modem
At the back of the fax/modem is a pair of telephone sockets and it will be supplied with a lead to connect direct to your telephone wall socket. Your normal phone plugs into the other socket at the back of the fax/modem. This arrangement lets you use the phone and the fax on the same line.

Fax/phone switchers
If you are using a single phone line, you may want to buy a fax/phone switch box which has separate connections for your phone and fax/modem. This answers the phone with a short message telling your caller to hold on. It then pauses and if it hears a fax-machine signal it will switch the call to your PC's fax/modem with a ringing signal that

One line or two?
If you receive only a few faxes every now and then, it makes sense to use one telephone line for both fax and telephone calls. If you receive a lot of faxes, then you will probably find it worthwhile to invest in a second phone line just for the fax.

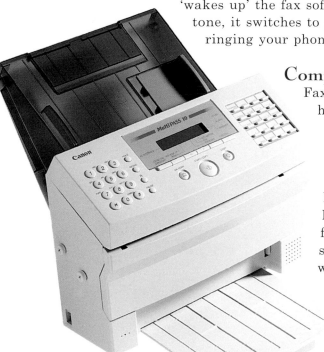

'wakes up' the fax software. If it doesn't hear a fax tone, it switches to your phone line and starts ringing your phone.

Computer fax vs fax machine

Fax machines and fax/modems both have their advantages and disadvantages. If your faxes are generated mainly on your PC, then the fax/modem is cheaper and more convenient. It also has more flexibility and takes up less space. On the other hand, a fax machine has a built-in scanner to handle any document wherever it comes from, and it doesn't require that you leave your computer switched on all the time to receive every fax.

Fax/phone/scanners

There is another way to get a fax up and running with your PC, which combines the best features of the stand-alone fax and the computer fax. These multi-function centres are fax machines that also link up with your PC. You can feed paper into them for quick faxes and paperwork you haven't created on your PC. But the link with your PC means that you can still send faxes directly from your computer and do all the other things you can do with fax software, such as sending faxes to groups of people and storing received faxes on your hard disk. These machines can also function as a black-and-white scanner for your PC, as a printer and as a photocopier.

Quality

If you receive faxes regularly, you'll have noticed a huge variation in their image quality: thick lines down the middle, jagged edges to all the lettering or whole pages fed through askew. What causes these problems is the quality of the fax's scanning section: how well it has been adjusted, how smoothly it feeds the page through and how clean it is.

When you send a fax from your computer, the file information is converted directly into the fax format, so bypassing the scanning operation. You can always recognise a fax that has come from a computer. It looks like it has come straight out of a printer.

Voice-mail modems

You can go one step further with your fax/modem and buy a voice-mail fax/modem that has a microphone and records and plays messages from your hard disk. These add all the facilities of a good answering machine to your PC and are as easy to install as a normal fax/modem card.

Speedy faxes

The slowest fax machines send their fax data out at 2,400 bits (the computer's basic number system) per second, while the fastest fax systems send out data at 14,400bps, which is over five times faster. The faster the transmission rate the quicker the fax is sent and the cheaper it is to do.

Fax basics

When two fax machines are connected via a telephone line, the first thing they do is exchange some basic information about the fax being sent and how quickly the two machines can send and receive the fax information. This process is called handshaking and is what all those funny fax tones are about when you first make a fax connection.

When the handshaking is finished, the fax machine starts feeding the sheet through, scanning lots of thin lines across the page. The scan turns the areas of black and white that make up the text and pictures into a series of computer numbers that are sent down the phone line as warbling tones. The receiving fax machine turns this information into instructions to print the identical black-and-white areas on to its blank fax paper.

Your page is scanned in thin *lines* by the fax machine.

PCs do it differently

Your PC fax works slightly differently. The pages that you have on screen are first converted into a new image and stored in your PC's memory or on the hard disk as a fax file. The fax/modem then dials the number and calls up the fax image, a line at a time, and sends it to the fax machine at the other end to print it out on its fax paper.

When you receive a fax, the PC fax/modem stores the incoming fax on your computer's hard disk as a fax file. From this it recreates a fax image that you can see on screen, print out, or turn into a picture that you can use in any of your applications.

Files or faxes?

Since your PC's fax hardware is based around a modem, your computer can choose to send your fax as a file instead. Say you have used Microsoft Word for Windows to create a letter and your fax/modem to send it to someone else who, as it happens, also has a PC with a fax/modem and uses Word for Windows. Instead of turning everything to and from fax images, your message can be sent simply as a Word for Windows document file that the user at the other end can call up like any other Word file.

Microsoft Fax and some of the other fax-software systems can do this trick using a system called binary transfer. When your fax/modem starts the handshaking process it checks if the other fax is in fact a PC-based fax/modem geared up for binary transfer. If the answer is yes, your PC will send the document as a Word file instead of a fax image. The two PCs can work all this out themselves. You are not aware of anything different except that you have received a perfect word-processor file that you can edit and print out, rather than a fax image that you can only look at.

Setting up

icrosoft Fax (Windows' fax software that comes free with your fax/modem) or other fax software will handle all your basic faxing needs. No matter which software system you decide to use, you first have to set it up with some basic information about you and your phone number. Once you've loaded your fax software, you will be asked a few questions about your system.

Enter your details

Your name and phone number:	This will appear at the top of each fax you send.
Modem details:	What type of fax hardware you have and how it is set up.
Page size:	The same as your usual page size (A4).
Cover page:	Do you usually want to send a cover page?
Resolution:	Do you usually want to send standard quality faxes or high-resolution images that will take twice as long?

The printer fax

When you install your fax/modem, you should check that it has also been included in your list of printers. For everyday faxing, the easiest way to send a fax directly from your word processor, or any other Windows application, is to go to the File/Print menu and send the fax from there.

Locked faxes

Faxes can be kept private by having them placed in personal mailboxes; for extra privacy, they can be encoded and made into a fax file that cannot be read unless you enter the password.

Can I use Mercury?

If you are in the UK, when you set up your fax software, you can also put in your Mercury access information. Then your fax/modem will automatically dial your Mercury number before dialling the fax number you've entered or selected from your fax address list.

See it first

Some PC fax systems let you decide what happens when a fax arrives. You may choose to have it automatically printed out or to display an on-screen message or icon that tells you that a new fax has been received and stored on your PC. Others may show the fax on screen after, or even during fax transmission so you don't have to wait to see what it is all about.

MS Fax, like all fax software, has a *fax viewer* so you can look at a fax on screen without having to print it out first.

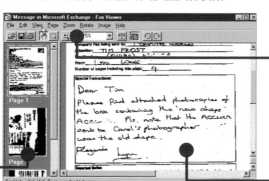

You can *zoom* in on passages that are difficult to read or use *rotate* to turn upside-down faxes the right way up.

All the other pages of the fax are shown as *thumbnails*.

Read your fax *on screen*.

In and out

When it comes to receiving faxes, whenever your PC is switched on, and no matter what you are doing, the fax/modem is always in the background, monitoring the phone line and waiting for it to ring. What it does when the phone rings depends on what you have entered in the Fax Receive options.

If you are in an office, set up the fax to answer after a certain number of rings. The fax/modem answers the phone after the set number of rings, sends out the fax handshaking signal, and waits for a response from the other end. This is the option to use if your PC is connected to a separate fax line.

If you are at home, choose Manual Answer. When the phone rings, pick it up. If it is a fax, you can click on the fax button and your fax/modem will take the call and receive the fax. This is the option you should use if most of your phone calls are from people who want to talk rather than send faxes.

Sending faxes

When you are working on a letter, spreadsheet, image, or any other kind of document you want to send to someone, you don't want to be wasting time saving files, opening up fax software and finding files to convert to fax format before you even start selecting who to send it to. With the fax system set up as a printer, you send faxes just as though you were printing it on your dot-matrix, inkjet or laser printer. But instead of the sheet being printed at your desk, it turns up on a fax machine that can be thousands of miles away.

STEP 2 Choose your fax as your *printer*.

STEPs 4 & 5 Click on *Finish* or *Send* and your PC takes care of the rest as a background operation while you move on to something else.

STEP 1 *Select* what you want to fax. It can be an entire document or a selected area of text.

STEP 3 Your *fax system* will now ask you to whom you want to send the fax.

Broadcasting faxes

Most faxes are messages to be sent to a single person. Occasionally you might want to send the same information to a whole group of people. With an ordinary fax it can be time-consuming feeding the same sheet of paper through the machine over and over again, manually dialling the different numbers.

With your fax/modem you can tick off as many names in your address list as you like. Your PC will go through the list one by one and send the same fax to each of them, with individualised cover sheets. It takes only a little more time to organise sending a fax to 100 people than it does to send a fax to one.

Send now/send later

You'll usually send faxes the minute you've prepared them. But you can also save them and get your PC to send them later. This lets your PC concentrate just on the job of sending faxes, as you will find that faxing in the background still takes up enough of your PC's processing power to slow down whatever else you are doing. Sending faxes after you've finished working on your PC avoids this.

The other advantage is more interesting: it's cheaper to phone in the evening and at weekends, as the cost for national and international calls is significantly reduced. By faxing after hours, you can save quite a lot of money, and you can just leave everything to your PC.

Set it up and sign it

Since you produce most of your faxes using your word processor, it makes a lot of sense to create a standard fax layout to use every time you want to send a fax. Then all you have to do is write what you want to say and send it.

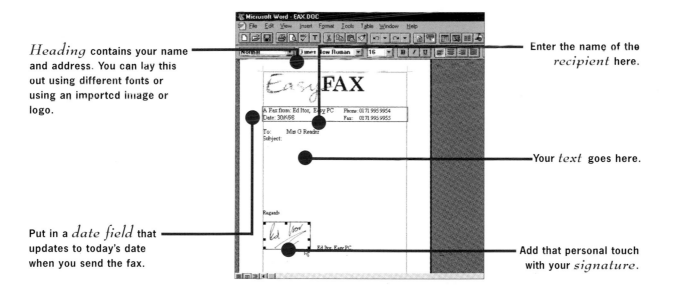

Heading contains your name and address. You can lay this out using different fonts or using an imported image or logo.

Enter the name of the *recipient* here.

Your *text* goes here.

Put in a *date field* that updates to today's date when you send the fax.

Add that personal touch with your *signature*.

Signing off

When you receive a fax, one of the clues that it has been sent from a fax/modem is that it doesn't have a signature at the bottom – this is because you can't type a signature. Yet adding a signature is easy. First, write several signatures on a piece of paper and scan it into your PC. Then use a paint program to select the best one to import into your fax sheet and adjust the image so that it is the right size.

Don't worry if you don't have a scanner. Send the signature to yourself from someone else's fax, preferably set to high resolution. You can now turn that fax into a picture and continue as before.

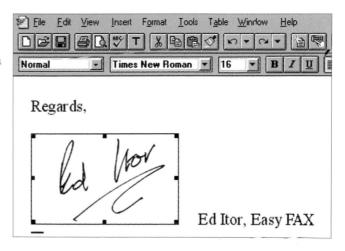

Who's there?

If you want to know who you have sent a fax to, it's easy enough to find out. The fax software keeps a record of every time it sends or receives a fax. You can look up in the fax log exactly what was sent and when. If you are sending faxes when you are away from your PC, the send log will tell you which faxes were successfully sent and which didn't get through.

Get a little help

Although faxes are received and stored as images, what is on the page is usually text, which would be more useful as a word-processor file. There is a magical piece of software called Optical Character Recognition (OCR) that can do the conversion for you, instead of you typing it in.

OCR software, which is included in some fax-software packages, scans the fax and sees if it can read the letters. Provided the fax is clean and the text is not too small, then good OCR software can produce remarkable results. You'll always need to double-check the copy against the original fax image, but usually it is very easy to spot the occasional errors.

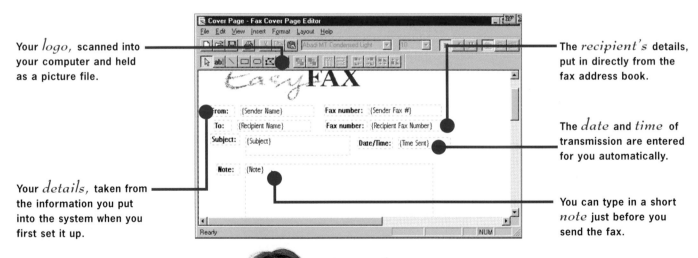

Your *logo,* scanned into your computer and held as a picture file.

Your *details,* taken from the information you put into the system when you first set it up.

The *recipient's* details, put in directly from the fax address book.

The *date* and *time* of transmission are entered for you automatically.

You can type in a short *note* just before you send the fax.

Cover sheets

When you use a fax machine to send a fax, you can add a cover sheet with your own name and number and the recipient's name and number on it. Instead of typing this up each time, your PC fax can do it all for you.

When you enter someone's number in the fax address book, you'll also include their name and the name of their company. When you send a fax, the software takes all of this information, as well as your details and any logos you might want to add, and creates a cover page which is then sent in front of the fax. Every cover page is completely personalised without you even having to think about it.

Clean up!

Spring-cleaning is always a good excuse to go through the house with a fresh eye to tidy up, reorganise and throw out all the things that have accumulated over the year. We don't always do it in spring: the clearing-out is sometimes prompted by an impending visit by a relative or just because you are in the mood.

Well, things are no different with your PC. It has a great capacity to store all sorts of clutter on its hard disk, and it can do with a good clear out from time to time. It may be because it's spring, because you're about to load a big new program, because you're about to make the transition to the latest Windows, or just because you feel like it.

Housekeeping on your PC has a lot of benefits. After you've finished, you'll have more space on your hard disk. You'll also have a PC that works faster, looks better and is tailored a little closer to the way you would like to work.

Even if there isn't too much in the way of things to delete, your computer's files can always benefit from some reorganisation so that you know exactly where everything is.

And, like any house, where things get worn out over time and need some attention, your PC can often do with a bit of repair work. There are all sorts of ways that you can make sure your PC is properly maintained, with very little effort and without taking up too much of your time.

There are many elements of your software that were setup when you first started running your computer and have never been touched since. So you continue to work the same way, not because it suits you and your family best but because you never got around to looking at the alternatives. While you are spring-cleaning, you can also add, remove and change parts of your programs and your PC's general setup to get it to work the way you want to work. And even if you haven't yet bought your PC, looking at the kind of things you may be doing after a few months will prepare you for taking care of it properly. ●

Wash day

Why not take this opportunity to give your whole system a good clean up, starting with the outside? Unplug everything from the mains and then clean the computer and the monitor. Use cleaning cloths sold in computer suppliers or a cloth lightly dampened with a cleaner designed for plastic and metal surfaces. Antistatic wipes will help stop the build-up of dust, especially on your monitor. Watch out for the air vents on top of the monitor and at the rear of the computer and make sure they are clear of dust and fluff.

Remove the mouse ball, check the rollers inside and clean them with a cotton bud. This may also be a good time to replace your mouse mat, or at least clean it. Most material mats can be cleaned by immersing them in warm soapy water, rinsing and letting them dry. But mats are so cheap now that it may make more sense to replace them. And if you haven't already got wrist supports for the mouse and your keyboard, now is a good time to add them to your shopping list.

Give scanners and printers a gentle wipe. Make sure that the scanner's lens or window is clean, as any marks will translate into spots or lines on your scanned copies. If you have a laser printer, run cleaning paper through it to pick up any stray toner dust, but do not try to clean inside any type of printer unless you really know what you are doing.

Both floppy disk and CD-ROM drives need an occasional cleaning. Use a special floppy-disk cleaning kit. These look like floppy disks but have a material surface in place of the magnetic disk. Some of them need dampening with a cleaning solution supplied with the disk, which helps the material clear dirt off the heads inside the drive.

CD-ROM cleaners work in a similar way, with a CD that has a cleaning area on it. CD cleaners designed for hi-fi CD players will work just as well as those specially designed for CD-ROM drives.

Shake it all about

Your keyboard's keys can get quite dirty, so clean them in the same way. Turn the keyboard upside down and gently shake it to remove any debris that may have dropped between the keys. You can also gently use a soft small paintbrush to help clear the spaces between the keys or a small can of compressed air to blow the dust out. ●

Spring-clean shopping list

- Floppy-disk cleaning kit
- CD-ROM cleaning kit
- Mouse mat
- New floppy disks, plus a disk-storage box or two
- Keyboard and wrist supports
- Antistatic screen wipes
- Spare printer ribbons or ink cartridges

Organise

Spring-cleaning includes reorganising what you want to keep and throwing the rest away. Keeping your filing straight is an important job and you should look at your PC's filing to make sure everything is in a logical place. It's not just neatness for its own sake: with so many files on your PC's hard disk, some are going to be almost impossible to find again without good organisation.

Whether you are filing on a PC or in a real filing cabinet, you always use a tree directory system. The directory starts with a main root store which has branches off it. Those branches have branches off them, and so on.

The filing cabinet itself would be a root directory, where everything you are looking for is kept. The drawer marked Letters is the first branch off the root directory; the file section in the drawer marked Customers Letters is the next branch off that; and the A–G compartment is yet another branch. This system has been used for centuries as a very natural way of working, and your PC's hard disk should be organised in a similar way.

Windows 95 and 98 take the filing cabinet idea and call the separate filing areas Folders. Windows 3.1 and DOS call these filing areas Directories. Use Explorer (shown right) or File Manager in Windows 3.1 to look at the way your files are organised. Looking for a file in the thousands on your hard disk is easy provided you have organised your filing properly.

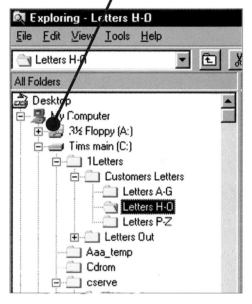

A *folder* containing more branches is marked with a **+**.

Change a name

If you have upgraded from Windows 3.1, you will have used directory names that were a sort of shorthand, since you were restricted to only eight letters. Now that Folders can use longer names you might want to rename some of them to make clearer what they contain.

Click on the Folder's name and then type over it with the new name. Remember, when you use the application or program that generated those files, it will be looking for the folder in the old name. So the next time you run the program, you will have to tell it the new name.

More but smaller folders

Don't be frightened of creating more folders, or directories, to separate your various files into smaller compartments. It is easier to find a file among just five or six others in a small and very specific folder, rather than sifting through 40 or 50 files in a big general folder.

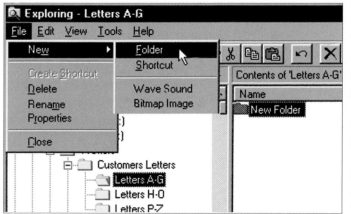

Click on the area where you want the new folder to be, then click New Folder. Now type the name you want to use into the New Folder's title box.

Folders and files

You can Move folders and Delete them in just the same way that you handle individual files. When you drag and drop a folder to a new position, all of its files and subfolders will also be moved automatically.

Disk care

Your hard disk is your computer's library. It is the storehouse for all your files and programs. Like a library it has to be properly maintained if it is going to do its job properly. The best tools for taking care of your library are the utilities supplied with Windows or DOS. We will concentrate on how these systems work in Windows as this is the system you are most likely to be using if you have recently bought a PC.

To find the hard disk maintenance tools, double-click on My Computer (shown left) and use the right mouse button to click on the disk drive that you want to work on. Then click on Properties (1). You'll see the Properties folder which will show you how much disk space you have used and how much is left. Take a note of the amount used so you can see how much space you can create by maintaining the disk.

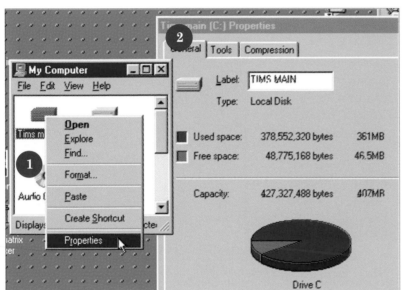

The tools

Click on the Tools tab (2) and you will see the three main hard-disk tools: ScanDisk, Backup, and Defragmenter. Backing up your hard disk is a special function that we cover in depth on pages 59–60.

On the mend

Over the years your hard disk can get damaged. Tiny areas of disk often become unstable. Fortunately, when your PC is writing new data on to your hard disk, it checks what it is doing. If there is a problem, it will mark the

ScanDisk to the rescue

ScanDisk is the repair kit inside Windows 95 that tests your hard disk and will fix any problems it finds.

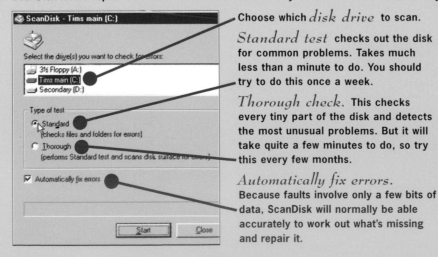

Choose which *disk drive* to scan.

Standard test checks out the disk for common problems. Takes much less than a minute to do. You should try to do this once a week.

Thorough check. This checks every tiny part of the disk and detects the most unusual problems. But it will take quite a few minutes to do, so try this every few months.

Automatically fix errors. Because faults involve only a few bits of data, ScanDisk will normally be able accurately to work out what's missing and repair it.

area as being unusable. Some of the problems your PC finds may not be faults on the disk, but a problem caused by something else – such as someone bumping into the desk while the PC is trying to write a file. So there may be nothing wrong with the area now marked as faulty. After a while you could end up with a hard disk that has perfectly good areas cordoned off as being unusable. Windows 95 and 98 come with their own repair kit called ScanDisk. This will go through your hard disk and test every bit of it, looking for errors.

Even if files on your hard disk are not very fragmented it is still worth *defragmenting*. **Either watch how the defragmentation process is going or click on Details to see the data actually being shifted around.**

Defragmentation

When your hard disk stores a file, it doesn't always put it all in one place. The hard disk has its spaces set out in clusters. Windows looks for the first available space, which could be a gap between two other files, and starts pouring the new file into it. If the gap isn't big enough to hold the complete file,

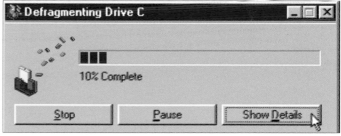

Windows goes off and finds the next available gap and puts the rest of the file in there. A large file may end up spread all over the disk.

Even though the file is split up, your PC can still retrieve it because it creates a special index that tells it where all the fragments of the file are. This fragmentation of your data tends to get worse as fragmented files are deleted, leaving more small gaps for the next file you save. Because it has to keep searching backwards and forwards to get all the parts of the file, a fragmented hard disk slows up the retrieval of files.

Windows comes with a Disk Defragmenter that will go through your disk, find all the files, and then clear space to rerecord each of them so that each one is a continuous run of clusters. The rewriting is almost always perfect, so you don't need to worry that anything will be lost or altered during the defragmentation process.

G et Plus! to do it for you

Microsoft has produced a separate set of facilities called Plus! to work with Windows 95. Plus! includes a Systems Agent that can be set up to run ScanDisk and the Defragmenter automatically for you at regular times each week or month, so that your disk is well maintained. System Agent will constantly monitor your use of your computer. It waits for the first opportunity when you have stopped using it and does its work then. This means you don't even have to interrupt your work to keep your hard disk organised.

If you have Windows 3.1

If you are using Windows 3.1, you will have Defragmenter and probably ScanDisk available as DOS functions. To run them you first exit Windows and go to the DOS directory. Typing scandisk or defrag will start the programs.

Health check

Every now and then a computer virus hits the headlines when a company contracts a nasty one that does a lot of damage to the information on its computers. There are about 10,000 computer viruses floating around, varying from old, easy-to-detect and relatively harmless ones, to some difficult-to-spot examples that can destroy all your data. Although the chances of your PC catching a virus are relatively low, it is still something you need to guard against.

What's a virus?

A virus is a small program designed to hide itself on your PC. It cannot do physical damage, but it can give instructions to your computer to do anything from displaying an unwanted message to totally wiping out your hard disk. A virus can be built into an otherwise innocuous program, or it can hide itself away on a floppy disk. It is called a virus because, like a real virus in the body, it has the ability to replicate and pass itself on. It does this by copying itself on to your PC's hard disk and then back to any floppy disk put into your PC; it then goes on to infect another computer.

Who are the culprits?

People who create viruses fall into two main categories. There are those who just want to prove how clever they are at programming. These people usually produce a benign virus that displays a message on your screen that is often linked to a special occasion. Then there are those who want to prove how clever they are and have an axe to grind against the world in general. They produce the most damaging viruses.

How to protect against a virus

The best way to solve a virus problem is not to catch one in the first place. The most common way of catching a virus is from a floppy disk made on another PC, so try to avoid using disks copied from other PCs. It's also possible to catch viruses from the Internet and e-mail. Invest in virus-protection software that will spot a virus and chase it out of your system.

When you first put a copied disk in your PC, you must run the virus checker before doing anything else. If the disk has a virus, let the virus protector remove it.

Make it a routine

Try to get into the habit, and get your children into the habit, of checking any disks coming into your house for viruses. Explain that it is their software, as much as anything else, that will be destroyed by a virus. You can set anti-virus software to check your PC each time it is switched on. This will mean that there is a longer delay between pressing the On button and having Windows finally loaded, but it guarantees that your PC is checked for intruders before they can do any damage.

Running virus detectors

There are several virus protection software packages around, including those from Norton, and the UK-based Dr Solomon. There are also some good ones available as shareware on disk or via your modem. The only problem with downloading anti-virus programs is that some unsavory characters have created anti-virus programs that actually contain a virus, but these are usually spotted before they spread too far.

Prevention is better than cure

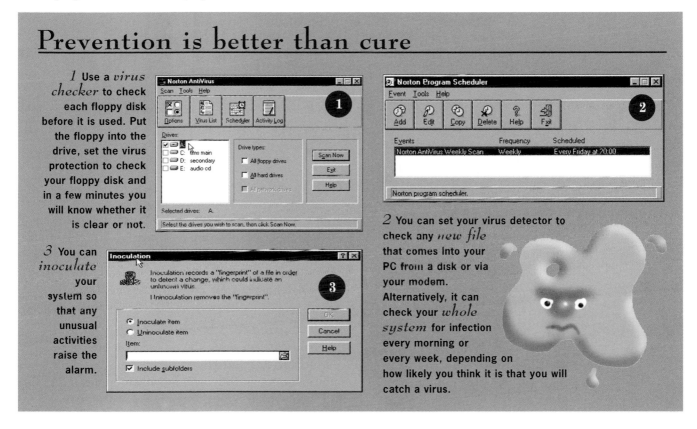

1 Use a *virus checker* to check each floppy disk before it is used. Put the floppy into the drive, set the virus protection to check your floppy disk and in a few minutes you will know whether it is clear or not.

3 You can *inoculate* your system so that any unusual activities raise the alarm.

2 You can set your virus detector to check any *new file* that comes into your PC from a disk or via your modem. Alternatively, it can check your *whole system* for infection every morning or every week, depending on how likely you think it is that you will catch a virus.

How a virus detector works

Virus detectors work in several ways. Like a detective, some will go through all the program files that could carry a virus and check on the number of computer data bits that each uses up. For a program file, this amount should hardly ever alter. But if the program catches a virus, this amount will change.

Some look for the fingerprint evidence. Most viruses give a tell-tale sign of their presence, and some anti-virus programs use lists of fingerprints to identify them. Other systems look for suspiciously acting characters, and investigate anything on your hard disk that is out of the ordinary.

Can my PC catch a virus from commercial software?

The companies that copy commercial software are very careful. Any disk that comes to them to be copied is thoroughly checked, so it is very unlikely that commercial disks, whether floppies or CD-ROMs, will carry a virus.

If you use a commercially produced floppy disk that has been used on another PC, you do have to be careful. The one thing that cannot pick up a virus by being used on another PC is a CD-ROM disc.

Compress

Virtual drives

Virtual hard disk drives are created by Windows software rather than being physical disks that you install. As far as your everyday work is concerned, you treat these drives just like real ones.

Y ou can make better use of your disk space by using file compression. File compression uses a mathematical technique that looks at all the data that you are trying to file away and takes out any unused, duplicate, or spare data. In the end you get a file that is much smaller, but that can be expanded back to its original form. The data compression used on your PC is lossless compression, which means that when the file is read back it is exactly the same as the original. There is no way of telling whether the file has gone through a compression process or not.

When you store files on floppy disks, compressing them means you can fit more on each disk. When you back up your files, the backup software can also compress files so they take up less space. Compression can also be used to reduce the size of a file when you are sending it by modem. Since the file is smaller, it takes less time to transmit, saving everyone money.

There are many different types of file-compression systems, but the most common is PKZIP. You will recognise a PKZIP file because it will have the file extension .zip.

Zip by shareware

There are various software systems designed to zip and unzip files. Nearly all are available in shareware from Web sites on the Internet, or on shareware CD-ROMs and shareware disks in computer stores. Don't forget to register your copy if you use it.

Squeeze a disk

You can get your PC to use compression automatically all the time and create whole compressed hard disks. Windows 95 comes with DriveSpace, which uses file compression effectively to double the size of your hard disk for free. Set up DriveSpace to make your drive seem twice as big (see below). If you have a 400Mb disk that has 50Mb free, you can turn it into an 800Mb disk with around 100Mb free.

Alternatively, you can tell Windows to turn any free space into another virtual drive. So the free 50Mb on Drive C: will be turned into 100Mb of free space in what Windows displays as a new drive, E:.

To make the new drive bigger, archive all the folders that will go into it and then delete them from your hard disk. This way you increase the amount of free space that DriveSpace can compress so it can make a larger virtual drive. Then use Restore to put the files back into the new virtual drive.

Nothing in life is free

It takes your PC a small amount of extra time to compress and decompress the files, so you will find that your computer will work marginally slower when it is reading or writing DriveSpace files on the hard disk. Normally this will not be noticeable, but it might affect some higher-quality audio or video files where the data has to be taken off the hard disk very quickly.

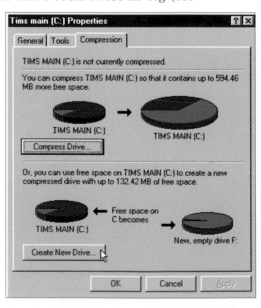

All lined up

There has been an explosion of interest in using computers on-line. *World Wide Web*, *surfing the Net* and the *Information Superhighway* are all mysterious phrases associated with the new worldwide community that has been created by people using their computers and a phone line to talk to each other.

Linking your computer to the outside world by using your telephone is one of the most useful and exciting aspects of home computing. If you have been impressed by the amount of information you can get from CD-ROM encyclopaedias, then just wait and see the limitless possibilities that going on-line offers. If there are others interested in your favourite subject, you'll be able to find them on-line with a crowd of people all pooling their knowledge.

It doesn't really matter where they are in the world. You can leave messages and talk to others using your computer keyboard for a little more than the cost of a local phone call. Australia for a penny a minute? It's possible on-line.

On-line also means more access to the new ways of using the telephone line. With a modem you turn your computer into a fax machine at no extra cost. In the home office, the fax/modem is an essential tool. And as more families go on-line with their PCs, faxing a friend becomes a real possibility.

Console games can also go on-line, so kids can play against others either down the road or on another continent. You can go shopping on-line, order those latest CDs via your computer, and have them delivered by post.

Going on-line turns the home office into a real extension of the workplace, letting you stay in contact using e-mail. Mobile phone systems make it possible to go on-line from anywhere – the middle of a field, a motorway rest stop, or even the beach.

In this chapter, we will take you through all the possibilities that going on-line opens up to you. But on-line also has a dark side – the spread of pornography and extremist political material. This is of real concern, especially to parents. We will show you how difficult it is to come across unsuitable material on-line accidentally and how access to it can be restricted. ●

How to buy

Your phone still works

Most modems have a second socket to plug your telephone into. When your computer is off or the modem is not in answering mode, then your phone will work normally, as though the modem isn't there. If your modem doesn't have an extra socket to connect your telephone into, then you need to get a two-way telephone adapter. This will give you a pair of sockets into which you can plug your modem and your phone.

There are internal and external modems. External modems are about the size of a small paperback book and connect to the computer's serial port. They have small status lights at the front that tell you about the modem link. An internal modem fits into one of the expansion slots inside your computer and becomes part of your PC. Which you go for is a matter of personal choice, as one works as well as the other.

If you are about to buy your first PC, you may well consider one that has a modem and communications system built in. This will save you time and energy in setting up the modem hardware and software. If you are adding a modem, they come in several shapes and sizes from many reputable companies, such as Hayes, the inventor of the first modem standards.

Speed is money

The better the modem, the faster it will transmit the data. The faster the data moves, the less time you need to be connected to the phone to move files and messages around. That means less to pay out in phone bills and on-line charges. For anything more than simple text, you must have a modem that will send the computer data bits – the 1s and 0s that make up all computer information – at the rate of at least 33,600 bits per second (bps). These are now the cheapest modems available. You should be looking for a modem of 56,000bps (often referred to as 56K) for regular Internet access. Most modems also offer what is called V.42bis. This is a software system that compresses the files to make them a quarter of their regular size, without losing any information at all. A V.42bis compressed file will take only a quarter of the time to transmit. Not all service providers support V.42bis, unfortunately.

Nearly all good modems also have the ability to send and receive faxes. It is included, so it's well worth having. You should not have to buy additional modem communications software unless you have very special requirements, such as sophisticated faxing needs. The modem will come with its own, usually very good, communications software.

Internal or external? The pros and cons

Whether you choose an internal or external modem is a matter of preference. There are pluses and minuses to both types.

Internal
GOOD POINTS Takes up no additional space on your desk. Doesn't need to be connected separately to the mains. Leaves your second serial port free.

BAD POINTS Have to take the computer apart to install or repair. Doesn't have status lights to monitor modem activity.

External
GOOD POINTS Can be installed or repaired without taking the lid off the computer. Status lights show what is going on with your modem and fax connections.

BAD POINTS More desk space needed.

a modem

56K Data/Fax Modem

An *external modem* such as this model can be inconspicuously placed behind the computer. An *internal modem* should be considered for use with a portable computer.

The modem is fully compatible with the industry standard AT-commands developed by the modem manufacturer Hayes.

This particular modem was manufactured before the new industry-wide V.90 data transmission standard was agreed upon in February 1998, but manufacturers will ensure that all 56,000bps (56K) modems now available will conform to the new V.90 standard.

Features

All Models

Datacomm
- Fully AT-command compatible.
- DTMF tone detection.
- Dialing features: automatic dialing, redial, repeat dial, dial linking, pulse or tone dialing, and dial pauses.
- Negotiation features: Fallback and return to accommodate line quality, speed detection, plus automatic baud adjustment and data rate selection.
- Nonvolatile memory for, and on-screen display of, modem settings.
- Telephone number storage for automatic dialing.

Fax
- V.17 (14.4K bps) fax.

MT5600ZDX K56flex Data/Fax Modem

Datacomm
- K56flex speeds when calling a fully digital K56flex server. Enhanced V.34 (33.6K bps) speeds from client to client.
- Flash memory for updates to full ITU-standards compliance, when available.

Software
- Includes English-language documentation and Windows®-based datacomm and fax software.

MT2834ZDXb 33.6K bps Data/Fax Modem

Datacomm
- Enhanced V.34 (33.6K bps) speeds.
- Additions: MT2834ZDXb has Help menus and supports remote configuration. It also receives in "Fax only", "data only", or "auto-detect" mode (auto-detect requires "CNG" tone from the sender).

Software
- Includes English-language documentation and Windows-based datacomm and fax software.

MT5600ZDXV K56flex Voice Mail Modem

Voice
- IS-101 AT+V voice commands for Telephone Answering Machine (TAM) operation.

Datacomm
- K56flex speeds when calling a fully digital K56flex server. Enhanced V.34 (33.6K bps) speeds from client to client.
- Flash memory for updates to full ITU-standards compliance, when available.

Software
- Includes Windows 95-based voice mail and telephone answering machine (TAM) operation, datacomm, and faxing software.

MT2834ZDXV 33.6K bps Voice Mail Modem

Voice
- IS-101 AT+V voice commands for Telephone Answering Machine (TAM) operation.

Datacomm
- Enhanced V.34 (33.6K bps) speeds.
- Additions: MT2834ZDXV has Help menus and supports remote configuration. It also receives in "Fax only", "data only", or "auto-detect" mode (auto-detect requires "CNG" tone from the sender).

Software
- Includes Windows 95-based voice mail and telephone answering machine (TAM) operation, datacomm, and faxing software.

MultiTech Systems

The modem is capable of transferring data at 56,000bps (56K) when calling an Internet Service Provider that is compatible with its K56Flex technology, and will work at the enhanced V.34 standard speed of 33,600bps (33.6K).

All the major modem manufacturers supply software with their modems, and this one comes with Windows 95-based data communications and fax software.

Specifications

All Models

Datacomm
Transmission & Control Standards: Enhanced V.34, V.34, V.32bis, V.32, V.22bis, V.22, Bell* 212A, and Bell 103
Data Rates: 33.6K, 31.2K, 28.8K, 26.4K, 24K, 21.6K, 19.2K, 16.8K, 14.4K, 12K, 9.6K, 7.2K, 4.8K, 2.4K, 1.2K, and 0-300 bps
Error Correction Standards: V.42 LAP-M and MNP* Classes 3&4 error correction
Data Compression Standards: MNP 5 (2:1) and V.42bis (4:1)

Fax
Fax Rates: 14.4K, 9600, and 4800 bps
Transmission & Control Standards: V.27ter, V.29, and V.17

Physical / Electrical
Dimensions: 4.3" W x 1" H x 5.6" L
10.8 cm x 2.5 cm x 14.2 cm

Weight: 8 oz. (224 g)
Connectors: DB-25S (EIA RS-232/V.24), 1 RJ11 for PHONE, 1 RJ11 for LINE, and power
LEDs: TD, RD, CD, various data rates, OH, TR, EC, and FX

General
Flow Control: Xon/Xoff or RTS/CTS
Data Format: Serial, binary, async
Operation: Dial-up line only
Accessories: RJ11 phone cable, power transformer with cord, and English-language fax/datacomm software and Owner's manual
Warranty: Ten years
Manufactured in Mounds View, MN, U.S.A.

MT5600ZDX & MT5600ZDXV

Datacomm
Transmission & Control Standards: K56flex, enhanced V.34, V.34, V.32bis, V.32, V.22bis, V.22, Bell 212A, and Bell 103

Data Rates: K56flex speeds plus 33.6K, 31.2K, 28.8K, 26.4K, 24K, 21.6K, 19.2K, 16.8K, 14.4K, 12K, 9.6K, 7.2K, 4.8K, 2.4K, 1.2K, and 0-300 bps

MT5600ZDXV & MT2834ZDXV

Datacomm
Voice Commands: IS-101 AT+V

General
Accessories: Also includes voice mail software

MultiTech Systems

As well as Internet use, the modem can send and receive faxes at speeds of either 9,600bps (9.6K) or 14,400bps (14.4K), according to the maximum speed of the fax machine you are sending to or receiving from.

This modem can receive data at a maximum speed of 56,000bps (56K). Older modems with speeds under 14,400bps (14.4K) are too slow to work on the Internet, but 33,600bps (33.6K) modems are highly effective on domestic telephone lines.

Power for on-line

On-line work is a very undemanding process for your computer. Modems transfer data at a snail's pace compared to the speed that your computer can process it. So even a computer equipped with the most limited Windows setup will work with your modem.

Modem basics

As soon as the computer stopped being something that had to have a room all to itself and became small and cheap enough to be used on a desk in an office, people started looking at ways to get one computer to talk to another. If the computers are in the same building, they can be linked together with cables creating a network of computers that pass information back and forth using a very fast and reliable system.

It's for you

Early PC users soon looked to the phone system as a way of spreading computer links to any house with a phone. But phone lines are designed for people to talk to each other, not computers. When you try to send data signals down the phone it doesn't work. So the modem was developed as a way of making computers seem like people by turning data into electronic speech.

What's in a name?

The modem takes the data and turns it into sound by modulating tones to represent bits of computer data – the 0s and 1s that make up all computer information. The sounds are sent down the phone line and the modem at the other end takes those sounds and demodulates them, turning them back into digital data. The name modem comes from these two functions: MODulator/DEModulator.

This is a great idea in theory, but in practice there are several drawbacks. First, the phone system can't carry much data. Early modems could transmit only 300bps. At that rate it would take over three hours to transmit a full-screen colour image.

Then there is the problem of static and interference on the line. The data that make up a file or a message have to be perfect and a crackle on the line can cause the receiving modem to make a mistake.

Parcel delivery

The modem sends your data in small parcels that include additional bits of information that allow the receiving PC to check whether each parcel of data has been perfectly received. If there has been a problem, it reports back to the modem transmitting the information, telling it to send the data again.

V signs

Modems have become a lot faster. Each new speed is set out in an internationally agreed standard which is given a V number.

- **V.17** Most common fax transmission standard. Up to 14,400bps.
- **V.27 Ter** Older fax standard. Up to 4,800bps.
- **V.29** Older fax standard. Up to 9,600bps.
- **V.32** Data transmission standard. Up to 9,600bps Minimum for good Internet and World Wide Web use.
- **V.32 bis** Data transmission standard. Up to 14,400bps.
- **V.32 Turbo** Data transmission standard. Up to 19,200bps.
- **V.34** Data transmission standard. Up to 28,000bps.
- **V.42** Error correction system for more reliable data transmissions (also known as LAP-M).
- **V.42 bis** Data compression system. Helps to transmit a file in a quarter of the normal time.
- **V.90** Latest data transmission standard for 56,000 bps.

Fitting

I f you don't want to take your computer apart to add a modem, or if you have a laptop PC that doesn't have internal expansion slots, an external modem would be the right choice. They are simple to connect, but you must make certain that you have a spare socket to plug it into.

An external modem is connected to one of the two serial ports at the back of your computer (1). They are the connectors marked serial 1 and serial 2 or com1 and com2. Since the mouse is often already connected to serial 1, the modem usually goes into serial 2 using the cable supplied with it (2) from the DTE interface at the back of the modem.

Then it is simply a matter of connecting your modem to the mains using the power lead (3) and then wiring it to the telephone socket (4). If you have a separate line for your modem, connect the line socket (5) on the modem to your telephone wall socket using the cable supplied (6). However, if you want to use a telephone on the same line as the modem, buy a double connector (7) and plug both the modem and the telephone into it. It is also possible to route the telephone through the modem by plugging it into the phone socket (8) on the modem with the adapter lead supplied (9).

Internal modems

Internal modem cards are almost as simple to fit. Turn the PC off and unscrew the lid. Firmly slide the modem card into a spare expansion slot and replace the computer's lid. The internal modem doesn't need to be connected to a power outlet or additional connector leads; it just has to be connected to the phone socket.

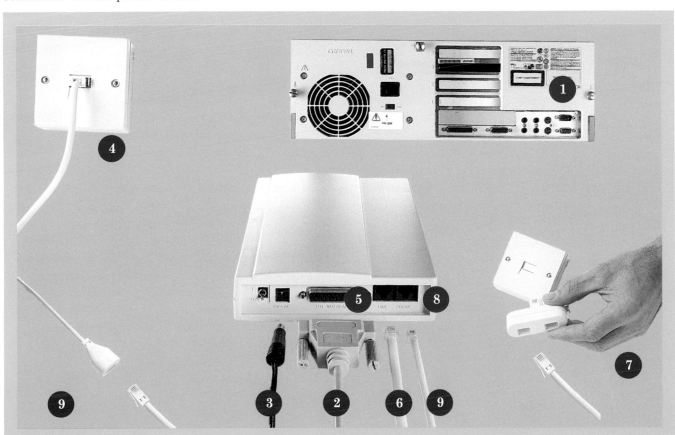

Communications

Y ou can use your modem with several types of communications software. Windows comes with Exchange and HyperTerminal so you can connect to other modems and faxes. It also has a special software system for going on-line with the Microsoft Network (MSN). If you prefer, you can use the software that comes with your modem. This will usually give you general modem connections and fax capability. If you are going on-line with a major on-line service provider such as Microsoft Network, all the software you need to operate the system will be supplied.

Although it might seem confusing, having different software for each modem service makes life easier. If you want to connect to your on-line service, you just have to click on its icon. Your PC will dial the number, make the connection, log on and give you a simple interface so you can get all the on-line functions available at the click of a mouse.

Setting up the software

After you've installed your modem, you'll have to tell your communications software some basic information about it, such as which port it is connected to and its fastest transmission speed. You may also have to check settings for the fax part of the communications software. Many software packages will do this for you. Windows has settings for a range of the most commonly available modems. You only have to call up the right one and Windows will do the rest.

Once you've set up your communications software to work with your modem, you have to set it up to work with the modems at the other end of the telephone. If you are only going to use a service that comes with its own communications software, such as Microsoft Network or CompuServe, all of these details are already preset and you don't have to worry about them at all.

Sort out the settings

The first thing to check is how fast your modem and the modem at the other end can transmit data. Many modems will be able to agree on a suitable transmission speed automatically, but it is always a good idea to set up the software to match speeds.

When you first make a connection between two computers, neither side knows what is about to be sent, at what speed it will be sent, or even which part of the long stream of signals coming through the telephone line represents the important file information. To make certain it all works properly there are systems known as protocols, which put the stream of modem data into a fixed format.

Stop bits and pieces

The data to be sent is packaged into parcels of either seven or eight bits per parcel. Then, at the end of each parcel is an indicator, called a Stop Bit, to say this is the end of the parcel. Parity is one way that modems can check that the data has been received correctly, but not all systems use it. There is also a system for the modems to tell each other that they are ready to transmit or receive. This is called Xon/Xoff.

General	Connection
Connection preferences	
Data bits:	8
Parity:	None
Stop bits:	1

software

Setup details

Different on-line services use different combinations of Stop Bit, Data Length, Parity and Xon/Xoff settings. When you set up your connection to an on-line service you need to set up your communications software so that it will work with the service.

Uploading and downloading

Taking a file from a bulletin board or a service provider is called downloading. You can send a file to the service provider by uploading it. The process is virtually the same when either downloading or uploading.

Kermit makes perfect

A crackle or static may cause the modem to make a mistake. If you are typing a message live to someone, that person can ask you to retype the words. When you are transferring files from one computer to another you need a similar system to ensure that the file is received perfectly.

This is where protocols Kermit, X-modem, Y-modem and Z-modem come in. These automatically check that the data has been received correctly. Each works slightly differently, so you are asked which format you want to use when it is time to transfer a file.

Service providers do it for you

If you are going to use one of the larger service providers for all your on-line work, you need to get hold of its on-line software. Many PCs come bundled with software for America Online, Microsoft Network and CompuServe. Other on-line services will be glad to send you their on-line software so that you can try out their service. The programs are sometimes given away free with computer magazines, or a phone call to the company will usually result in a free copy winging its way to you in the mail.

These systems are loaded on to your computer like any other program. Because they already know what protocols are going to be used for communications and transferring files, the only thing you have to set up is your modem details.

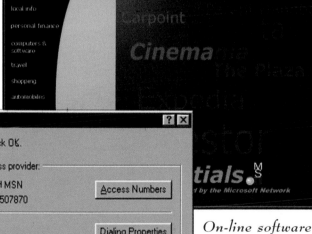
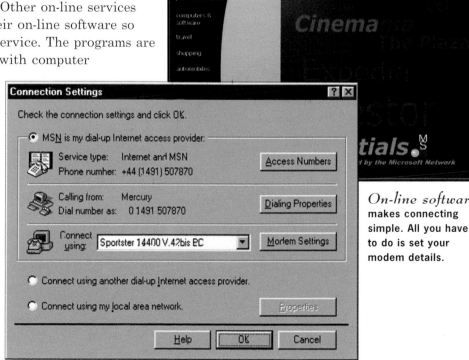

On-line software **makes connecting simple. All you have to do is set your modem details.**

Service providers

Real access to the power of the worldwide network of computer systems comes with joining a service provider and getting firmly on the Internet. Put all the on-line networks together and you have the Internet. It started in 1969 as a way of connecting together three computers run by the United States military. Over the years it has grown to over 100 million users, each with a computer address and each with access to all the public material on the computers connected all around the world.

What's a service provider?

Service providers are large commercial organisations set up to route information on-line for a fee. They offer you access to all the information and forums – groups of users with an interest in common – that are controlled by their own computers, a gateway to the Internet and your own unique e-mail address which you can use to send and receive files and messages to and from anywhere in the world.

The service providers promote themselves with adverts in computer magazines or give away their software on the covers of magazines, so you will easily be able to find where to contact them and get an idea about what services they offer and how much they charge. If you know people already on-line, ask them about the service they use.

Super software

The big advantage of the service providers is that they give you dedicated Windows communications software that makes it very simple to access all parts of their system or the Internet.

With the software provided by your on-line service, you can click on the icon and your computer will automatically dial the number and join the system with your name and password. It then automatically presents you with a screenful of choices.

The cost

The increasing competition among service providers means that they are offering cheaper services. Most on-line services have now removed their setup cost or membership fee as a way of attracting new users. But each provider will still charge you a monthly subscription whether you use the service or not. The fee will include at least a few hours on-line time for free per month. Some, in fact, include unlimited usage. For others, there is an additional hourly charge when going on-line and still others charge on-line fees only for some of their services.

You have to pay for your phone call to the service provider's own phone links (called nodes). If you are in a city, there will nearly always be a node just a local phone call away. It doesn't matter where you are sending a file, you only pay for the call to the service provider's node.

Which service?

The number of major players in on-line services is continuing to grow, and the options and services they offer are continually being improved. Some names to consider are:

On-line services
- BBC Networking Club
- Cityscape
- CIX
- CompuServe

ISPs
- Delphi
- Demon Internet
- Direct Connection
- Frontier Commuications
- Microsoft Network MSN
- UK Online
- AOL

What you get

The aim of the service provider is to provide you, the customer, with as much in the way of interesting, stimulating and informative on-line services as possible. Many users find them so comprehensive that they hardly ever move on to the Internet.

Forums, messages and conferences

One of the most consistently active parts of any service provider's facilities is its forums. These are used by people with a common interest, such as photographers or musicians or people interested in family history. There are forums for hundreds of different topics. In a forum, you can have open or private e-mail conversations, access a large catalog of files on the topic or even contribute by uploading some of your information. An electronic conference is just like a real conference, with lots of people on-line together, each contributing opinions and ideas. A conference can involve a lot of people or can be as simple as a chat between you and just one other on-line forum member.

Investigate **what others know about the subject or add to the worldwide knowledge base with your own information.**

Talk **with others in the forum. Hear what they have to say and add your contribution at the touch of a key.**

Locate other *forums* **that might be of interest to you.**

ALE & LAGER

Welcome

The Ale & Lager Forum is built around the brewing business and current beer movement through adding and updating press releases and new material. Personal greetings to the (very successful Ale & Lager Guest Book Sign in BBS) messages left by the members are answered daily for personal attention offered to each interested member who signed the "book". The Ale & Lager Forum encourages members to build, discuss, and input their information relating to Ales & Lagers. This is the way to get the members to feel ownership of the Ale & Lager Forum to use

Games and entertainment. **You can find news about movies and stage shows. If you enjoy playing games, you can find on-line games and download samples.**

News. **Get all the news as it is happening with the electronic news service. You can say what types of news you are interested in. Your personalised news service will then be automatically e-mailed to you each day. Check the weather and sports news, too.**

Arts, nature and history. **The whole world at your fingertips. Investigate other countries with on-line tours. Keep up-to-date with the latest in international politics. Get in touch with some of your favourite musicians and explore new musical themes together.**

Self, health and wealth. **How to get the most out of your life, your house, your family and your finances. You can find lifestyle magazines, advice and information on anything from choosing wine to managing your time.**

Especially for the kids. **Fun and comics that explore the teenager's world. Kids can explore ideas and talk about common interests with other teenagers around the world. The Internet makes the biggest playground imaginable.**

On-line magazines. **The line that separates on-line services from magazines and even TV is getting thinner all the time. Look for a range of on-line magazines.**

The Internet

If all you could do with the Internet was exchange messages, it would be of only limited interest. But all these network routes from your computer to any other on the Internet are also available for you to use like a computer-oriented phone system. You can dial remote computer sites and look at the information and files that they have stored especially for public access and either just view them or download the files for your own use. The Internet has its own file-transfer protocol, the Internet Protocol (IP), which ensures that the data gets to you intact.

This is the point at which the Internet starts getting complicated. As the system grew, several different ways of accessing other computer sites were established. There are newsgroups that are very similar to FTP sites that have large stores of files, discussion groups and the Internet Relay Chat (IRC) system – the on-line equivalent of CB radio. So, instead of having just one type of on-line phone system, you have to negotiate several different types of access systems if you want to get at all the computer sites that are available on the Internet.

Service providers **make surfing the Internet simple and fun.**

All webbed together

The good news is that an idea called the World Wide Web, called WWW or the Web, developed by the European Laboratory of Particle Physics (CERN) in Switzerland, makes access to many of these systems infinitely easier.

Not only does the WWW remove much of the complex typing needed to get to a remote computer system, it does two other important things to make the Internet really work for you. The first is that it offers a Windows-like graphical interface that can deliver images, sound and even movie clips directly from a remote computer site to your desktop PC. This makes using the Internet very attractive and accessible to anyone who can operate a simple computer system. The second feature is that it can automatically make links to files located at many different sites by just clicking on a section (a 'hot' button) of the WWW page you have on screen.

Wandering the Web

Service providers give you all the software you need to browse through the millions of pages of information and entertainment that are available on the Internet. The software for browsing around the Web is called, naturally, a Web browser, and there are now two main browsers: Microsoft Explorer and Netscape Navigator. Many Internet sites add sound or animation features, which need additional software to play them. These additional software modules can be downloaded from a Web site and then plugged into the browser you are using.

Home sweet ome page

An increasing number of individuals and companies like the idea of their own home page, which can display information and pictures about themselves and has links to direct you to other sites of interest. With a little effort in learning HTML, the computer language that makes many Web pages work, you can create your own Web page, which your service provider may well put into its system either for free or for a small charge.

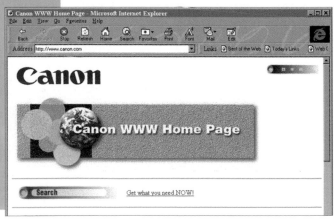

Clicking on a *hotspot* will whisk you off to another Web page.

The amazing Web site

A Web site is a treasure chest of information and entertainment. When you go to a site you'll see a starting menu page with words and images that are linked to hotspots. When you click on one of these hotspots, you are whisked off to another Web page that takes you deeper into the topic. This may be on the same Web site or it may be a link that automatically sends you to another Web site on another computer, maybe in another continent.

Everyone is getting on the Web-site bandwagon. Whatever your interest, there'll be a Web site that has something to say about it. Want to know more about the latest films? Most major movies have their own Web pages. Want to shop? There are Web sites that will sell you anything from a bottle of wine to an airline ticket. Just want to be entertained? There are a vast number of just plain fun Web sites that have great graphics and now add animation, sound and even video if you've got a fast enough modem – a modem of at least 28,800bps is needed – to get them to run smoothly.

Servers and clients

On the Internet, a server is the computer that serves you Web sites, files and messages, and you are the client. The problem with having so many thousands of Webs sites and servers is how do you find what you're looking for?

You certainly can't go looking at every site in turn and look to see if there are any files with likely-sounding names. It would take years on-line. Fortunately there is a team of gophers ready to come to your rescue...

Gopher it

Gophers (who get their name because they *go for* information for you) are search systems that have lots of lists of Internet sites and many of the files they contain. They use a list of key words that give you a good idea of what the files and sites are about.

If you know the name of the file you want, you can ask the gopher to find it for you. Or if you have a general topic of interest then you can type in a key word and the search system will give you a list of sites that may be of interest.

Once you've found a few useful Web sites, you'll see that they have lists of other, like-minded sites. For your convenience, the Web site's hotspots will link you directly to the new sites at the click of the mouse button.

Those Internet types

There are different types of Internet sites. Your service provider's software will have separate gateways to allow access to most of them.

- **Newsgroups** Accessed using the Usenet. Bulletin-board-type sites covering computers, specialist and human-relationship topics. Name clues: alt.*, rec.*, misc.*, sci.*, talk.*
- **IRC** Accessed on IRC service. More than 1,000 CB-radio-type channels.
- **File-transfer sites** Accessed using WWW. Archives of files on a huge number of topics. Name clues: ftp://*
- **Telnet** Accessed on Telnet and WWW. Lets you work on remote computers. Name clues: telnet://*
- **World Wide Web** Accessed on WWW. Interactive sites able to deliver multimedia data, produced by commercial and other organisations. Name clues: http://*
- **Gopher** Accessed on WWW. The systems that search out files for you. Different gophers cover different topics. Name clues: gopher://*

E-mail

The Internet creates a way for computer systems to link their messaging and file-exchanging functions. If you are connected to a service that offers the Internet, you have your own personal gateway to the Net, with your own e-mail address. With Internet e-mail you can send text messages to anyone in the world who also has an e-mail address. The message can be as long as you like and it will arrive at its destination within minutes of being sent.

Just text

E-mail is essentially a text system. It combines the friendliness of a phone call with the efficiency of a fax. If you are sending a document to someone who has a different word-processing system from you, it is important to convert it into what's called ASCII text first. All word processors can handle ASCII text, but you may lose formatting features, such as type style and size. If the recipient has the same word-processing system as you, click on attach, then click on the file you want to send and it will be sent with your e-mail.

Addressing your electronic envelope

When you join a service, you are asked for your own electronic name and address. Some service providers, such as CIX, let you use a shortened version of your name. Others give you a long number, although this practice will change with time. The address lets the Internet know how to get the e-mail to the right person and follows an established format:

The message goes on the *Internet*.

There is always the @ *separator* to separate the name from the address.

The type of service provider. Co. means it is a *commercial service*.

Internet: smithjones@demon.co.uk

The person's *e-mail* name.

The name of the *service provider*.

The *country*.

Finding people on the Internet

The easiest way of finding someone's e-mail address is to ask them. Call them up or fax them. If they have sent you a message, their address is included in it, and all you have to do is click on it with your mouse and add it to your e-mail address book.

Failing that, you have a problem, as there is no comprehensive e-mail equivalent of a telephone directory. There are several directory systems that can be used, but none offers a comprehensive listing of the millions of e-mail addresses.

Return to sender

E-mail can take a rather tortuous route to get to its destination, going through several different computer centres before it gets there. The exact route is added to the start of the message, so if there is a problem, you have some chance to track where the hold-up was. If the mail doesn't get through, the computers report back to each other and you will get a message that the e-mail failed to arrive.

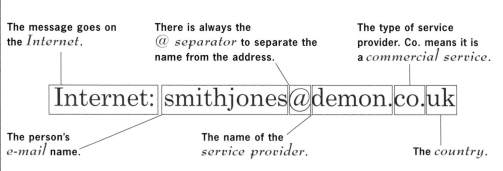

Etiquette

The vast majority of e-mail messages are polite, courteous, informative and fun. And, like any other club, the on-line community has its own rules of etiquette to keep it that way. When you join any on-line group there is always a FAQ file about the group and any etiquette that applies to it. FAQ stands for Frequently Asked Questions. This will give you guidelines to what is expected of you. If you are unsure, ask the Sysop, moderator, or anyone else who happens to be in the forum. You will also find other users helpful.

Little and often

Keep your messages short. You can make a point in a few sentences. This will be quicker to read and is more likely to get a response. You have plenty of opportunities to cover different topics in separate mailings rather than try to cover a lot of ground in one. Because other users won't necessarily have seen the start of your on-line conversation, it is sometimes nice to include a snippet from the mail you are replying to.

Junk mail

You can use the on-line systems to broadcast a file or message to many people. But don't do it unless you have a good reason. It clogs up the system with unwanted messages and files, and no one likes unnecessary mail.

There is a gentleman's agreement not to use e-mail for junk mail. While the system is open to anyone to use this way, what tends to happen is that those who receive the junk mail send it right back, clogging up the sender's in-box, so it is self-regulating up to a point.

Don't SHOUT!

If something is taken the wrong way, YOU CAN SHOUT BACK WHEN YOU ARE TYPING BY USING CAPITAL LETTERS. It's not much fun to try to read too many capitals, though.

Flaming last resort

Some messages provoke a heated reaction. If you see something that really gets on your nerves you can respond in heated verbal terms. Letting off steam in this way is acceptable, and is called flaming. If you want to use immoderate language, flame in a private e-mail. But don't forget that to libel someone in e-mail is just as much an offence as it is in any other written form.

☺ Smileys

When you talk to someone face-to-face or on the phone, there are all sorts of clues you get about the real meaning behind the words, whether what is being said is meant nicely, affectionately, humorously or angrily.

On-line, only the words come on the screen, so it is quite possible for your light, humorous remark to be taken as a deadly insult. One way of solving this is to add <s> or <g> at the end of the sentence, meaning smiling or grinning. There are also the smileys, which use keyboard characters to create the picture of your face as you are writing.

Here are a few of the more useful smileys. Turn the page on its side to see how they work.

:-)	Happy	:-(	Sad
:-D	Laughing	:-||	Angry
:->	Devilish grin	:-o	Shocked
:'-(	Crying	;-)	Winking

Here are a few less useful, but fun, smileys to describe people. See if you can figure out what they mean (the answers are below).

:-i	=:-)	:-[
8:-)	8-)	:-)>

:-) Smoker   8:-) Little girl   8-) Wearing glasses   :-)> Beard
:-i Vampire   =:-) Punk   :-[

Faxing

To store & to print

Your fax/modem will store all the received faxes on your hard disk. You can have your PC print them as soon as the fax has been received or leave them stored in the computer until you are ready to print them out later.

If you've looked through the ads for modems, you will have seen that they include a fax function. The fax machine is already one of the most important methods of communication in business. It is simple to use and can send pages of documents anywhere in the world in seconds.

A business has little difficulty in justifying the cost of a fax. But at home it is different. For the convenience of sending or receiving an occasional fax you wouldn't consider buying a fax machine, let alone finding the space for it and adding a second telephone line. But with a fax/modem all these problems disappear. You get the fax function for free with the modem. It doesn't take up any space and it will have voice/fax switching built into its software so you don't need an extra phone line.

Where do I put the paper?

Rather than scanning a real piece of paper, your fax/modem software takes the image created by your Windows program and turns it into a file of fax data ready to send. This is all done inside your PC. Apart from the convenience of not having to print the page first and then feed it into a fax machine, the fax/modem produces a better-quality fax, simply because the page hasn't gone through the printing and scanning process.

Using Print or Send

Nearly all Windows software packages let you fax your document directly using the Send or Print command in the File menu. This saves you having to load up Exchange or your fax software. Select Send, and Windows will start up Exchange so that you can choose where you want the fax to go. The alternative is to use the fax like a printer. Select the fax/modem as the printer and continue with your usual printing routine.

Fax incoming

Receiving a fax is even easier. The fax/modem is connected to the phone line. When the phone rings, the software will automatically detect a call and answer it. If it is a fax, your PC will receive and store it; if it is a normal phone call, it will pass it on to your telephone.

You can set up your fax/modem software in lots of ways. If you only rarely get faxes, you can tell the fax/modem to ignore all incoming calls. If you pick up the phone and find it is a fax, you just select Manual Receive from your keyboard and the fax system will take over. This is a lot nicer for your friends and relatives, who can find the squawk of your fax trying to talk to them very irritating.

Background faxing

Faxing, like printing, can be done as a background operation. Having told your PC to send a fax, you can go back to doing your normal work on the computer while, behind the scenes, your PC is busily creating the fax pages and sending them off.

On the move

By the end of the decade, over half the PCs being sold will be laptops, so going on-line away from the home will assume greater importance than it does now. On-line on the move can be looked at as either using a laptop from any phone socket in any building or going for the ultimate portable use, linking the laptop PC with a mobile phone so you can be hooked up to an on-line service from just about anywhere.

Mobile modems

Whichever way you want to work, you will need to add a modem to your laptop PC. The external portable modem is like a regular external modem, only smaller. It connects to the laptop PC using the standard serial connector and has a socket for a phone lead to connect to the telephone socket. Although their box is smaller, portable modems use the same basic electronics as the larger desktop PC versions, so they can work at high speeds and offer fax and modem transmission.

The credit-card modem

Modem miniaturisation is taken to an extreme with the new generation of internal modems. Instead of using a standard internal expansion slot, laptop PCs are adopting the PCMCIA adapter standard. A PCMCIA modem is a small credit-card-sized device that plugs into a slot on the side of the computer; the slot can take a whole range of different plug-in peripheral units. The slot-in-and-use convenience of the PCMCIA standard makes it ideal for portable communications.

The great on-line from the great outdoors

External and PCMCIA modems both need to be connected to an ordinary phone line. But because of the increasing number of portable-phone users, someone had to think up the idea of connecting the laptop to the mobile phone to go on-line from anywhere. Unfortunately, the existing analogue portable phone system works poorly with modems, so it hasn't been a great success. But the next generation of digital portable phones works very well with computers, and the digital system bypasses the traditional modem. Several digital mobile phones are now equipped with special adapters to connect the output of the laptop computer directly to the mobile phone, giving fast and reliable mobile on-line connections. Such phone systems are still quite expensive, but as digital mobile-phone systems become more popular, the prices will really start to come down.

The trend towards using *cellular phones* **with laptop computers and credit-card-sized modems means you can be on-line while you are on the move.**

Home and away

Many of the larger service providers, such as Microsoft Network, have access points throughout the world. You should be able to log on using a local or national call, rather than having to call back to your native country. You should always check where the nearest access sites are before you leave home. When you call and log on with your password, the system will react exactly as it does at home.

Shopping

Many banks and stores think that on-line shopping and on-line banking will be important to every household in the future. If you have a PC and a modem, you can already contact a variety of stores to browse through what's available, order what you want and have it delivered to your door.

You won't need a PC

On-line shopping is too big to offer just to households with PCs. With the arrival of hundreds of digital TV, satellite and cable TV stations, little black boxes connected to your TV that contain a modem and computer processor will hook up to the telephone socket. With a simple remote control, you'll be able to highlight any product being shown on screen and press the Order button, and the system will automatically make the call and electronically place the order for you.

On-line with your CD-ROM

More and more CD-ROMs are coming out that have on-line links to the outside world. On the face of it, these hybrid CD-ROMs seem like standard software, such as a reference book or a home-finance package. But you'll find they also include software that will use your modem to contact a special Web site to pull in more information for you. Both the '97 and '98 versions of Encarta and MS Money are hybrid CD-ROMs, and they use the on-line connection for quite different uses.

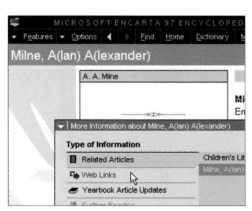

With Encarta, pressing Update will call up an on-line site with all the new entries that have been created over the past month. It then downloads them on to your hard disk, so your reference CD is always up to date. MS Money uses its links with banks to upload and download all your latest financial details, so bypassing all the hard work of entering details from your bank statements. You can also complete simple transactions like paying bills, using Money 97 with its on-line connection.

Secured nets

Many on-line stores give you a phone number to call to place your order using a credit card. Ideally you should be able to do the whole transaction electronically from your screen by typing in your address and credit-card number and whizzing that over the Internet to the Web-site shop. The reason this is only just being introduced now is that the Internet is an open, public service, which means that it is possible for some good hackers to tap into these transactions and get hold of all your credit-card information.

To combat this, electronic shopping and banking systems now encrypt the information into a secret code before it leaves your PC. Your information can only then be unscrambled by the electronic store or bank. To everyone else it is meaningless. The key that unlocks the encryption can have up to 18 billion billion combinations, so it's about as secure as you can get.

Quick draw

Take anyone new to a computer and what are they likely to want to try first? Their painting and drawing skills. There is a big attraction in using a PC and fooling around with stick men and funny faces if you're not too good at drawing, or producing amazing pictures if you are. So whereas some software is just useful, painting and drawing are both useful and fun.

For kids – and many older first-time PC users – it is also a way of exploring the workings of Windows and how to build up control of the mouse. Nothing increases your rodent control more than trying to draw a perfect straight line or circle completely freehand.

But painting and drawing isn't just for fooling around after your real work is done. You can produce illustrations, images and graphs that support the most serious documents or something a little more lighthearted for everyday use.

We are surrounded by computer-generated images in magazines, newspapers and TV. There are simple cartoon-like pictures and magical, almost impossible images – all made possible by painting and drawing programs that can run on your PC.

Drawing systems are also an important part of industry. A huge amount of what is manufactured or built – from the smallest toy to the largest building – starts life as a drawing on a PC. By using these tools designers can experiment with lots of alternatives and come up with better designs than could be done with paper.

Computer graphics are also used to liven up reports with graphs and simple pictures. With the latest generation of drawing and presentation software, anyone can make very professional-looking images, regardless of their abilities.

Painting and drawing are two different ways of making pictures. We'll show you what the differences are, and which to use.

This is the time to play around with all the different ways of drawing and painting. You can do as much as you like without wasting any paper, running out of paint or needing to sharpen a pencil. And your only limitation is your imagination. ●

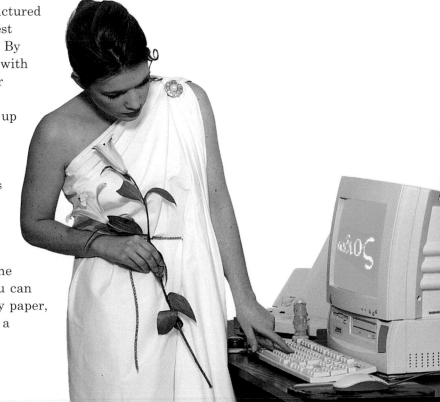

Painting and

Painting and drawing have developed as two entirely different ways of producing pictures on your PC. Painting is the artistic approach for producing pictures that look like real paintings and for working on photographs and other scanned images. Painted pictures give you a full range of brush and paint effects so you can sketch or paint in any way you like. You can take real images, scanned or downloaded into your PC, and change and alter them in ways that cannot be detected. And you can produce spectacular effects using the various mixing, merging and filtering tricks.

Drawing, on the other hand, is for making more technical looking images, graphs and plans. Everything you see is made up of a series of straight lines, curves, squares, circles, rectangles and ovals. While a drawing program can make excellent cartoon-type pictures, it won't let you re-create the 'Mona Lisa' on your computer screen. What it will do is let you make good-looking illustrations, graphs and drawings to be used in documents, either for home or office use, no matter what your drawing skills are.

Bit maps and vectors

If it looks like a photo or a painting, then it's a painted (bitmapped) image. Each coloured dot, or pixel, is given a number that tells the computer what colour it is and where it is on the screen. The sharpness, or resolution, of the image depends entirely on the number of dots, or pixels, used to make up the picture – the more pixels per square centimetre, the better the image will look.

A picture that fills the screen at normal Windows resolution will be made up of 600 rows of 800 dots in each row (nearly 500,000 pixels in all), and since every pixel is listed in the image's file, these files can get pretty big. Several megabytes or more is not unusual.

Pictures created by drawing programs are called vector files and store the picture information in a totally different way. They tend to look like cartoons or graphs. If you've placed a square on the screen then what is stored is information about your square's size, position and colour. The description of a big square or circle takes up no more file space than a few bitmapped pixels, and so vector files take up very little disk space.

Because everything you draw is stored in the file as a separate item – a square in this position, a curve there, a straight line here – even after you've finished drawing you can still pick out any of the elements and change their colour, position and size or remove them altogether without affecting anything else in the picture.

Paint **programs produce bitmapped images that can look just like real photos or paintings.**

Vector **programs give less artistic-looking results and are better suited to producing simple things like graphs.**

drawing

Zoom

If you zoom in on a bitmapped picture, the quality of the image declines as you begin to see the dots – just like looking at a newspaper through a magnifying glass. But when you make a vector drawing bigger or smaller, you are telling your PC to recalculate the position and size of the squares, lines and circles in the picture. So when you zoom in on a vector drawing, the picture is recalculated and displayed or printed at the best quality your PC can produce.

A vector drawing should look *smooth*, no matter how much you magnify it.

Display your work

If you want to work on your photos and images and get them exactly right, you will need the best colour resolution you can get out of your PC. Go to the Windows Display and make certain the colour settings are set to at least High Colour (16-bit), as this will approach photographic quality.

As you increase the number of colours shown on screen, you will notice your PC reacts more slowly. If you are doing a lot of drawing and painting work, you should think about using an accelerator video-display card. Increasing the amount of RAM in your PC or the memory in the video-display card will also help to speed things up.

Put it on paper

All printers will produce reasonable black and white copies of your images. Printers are getting better all the time, but they won't be able to produce prints that are as good as a well-printed magazine or a photograph. Having said that, the best inkjet printers working on the latest high-gloss 'photo' papers will produce near-photo quality. But if you want it printed out perfectly, go to a good DTP bureau which should be able to produce a high-quality print or photographic slide from your PC's picture file.

Input devices: Your PC's brushes and pencils

- A mouse or trackball *1* can be used for both bitmapped and vector drawing.
- A graphic tablet *2* is a book-sized tablet with a pressure-sensitive surface that can detect the point of a stylus being drawn across it. The tablet is the nearest a graphic artist can get to real painting on a computer.
- Scanners *3* are used to turn a photo or picture into a picture file that your PC can work with. For near-photographic quality, you need one that can capture the picture's subtlety of shading and colour, preferably a 24-bit scanner.
- If you have a video capture card, you can capture stills from your TV, VCR, or camcorder. These are then stored as bitmapped pictures just as though they had been scanned.

Paint tools

Atypical paint program is MS Paint. In Paint, you open a new picture and you'll get a blank sheet of electronic paper. Click on the pencil icon and start drawing on the screen by holding down the left mouse button and moving the mouse. Doodle as much as you like until you get the hang of it.

Once you've got the idea, click on the brush. This time you get a choice of brush sizes and shapes, and each has its uses. Click on an angled brush and see the calligraphic effect it gives to curves.

Have you ever wanted to be a graffiti artist in the comfort of your home - and no cleaning up afterward? Then click on the spray can. You've got a choice of three spray positions. The smallest is like holding the can close to the paper, with a small but very dark spray. Going to the larger sprays is like moving the spray can farther away, giving a lighter spray over a wider area.

And, as with a spray can, the longer you hold the can in one position, the more paint you spray on. Try moving the spray across the screen going very slowly first and then speeding up.

Outlined or filled in

When you draw a rectangle or an oval you can show them as an outline, you can have the outline filled in with colour, or you can have a coloured shape without an outline, depending on which box you select. The line colour is always the foreground colour. You choose a fill colour by changing the background colour.

Write on!

Adding text is easy. Click on the text button and then map out the space you want the text to fill – usually a long thin area. Now you can type the words. Click on the right mouse button and call up the Text toolbar to change fonts and sizes. When you are happy with your writing, clicking on any other tool

Lines, curves, squares and circles

Circles, ovals, squares and rectangles – in fact anything that needs perfect curves or straight lines – are easy to do in Paint, as it has special buttons dedicated to doing just these things.

To do *straight lines,* use the line button and select how thick you want it to be. Put the cross-hair where you want the line to start. With your finger on the mouse button, move the mouse, and a line will be created. With your finger still on the button, you can move the line and make it longer or shorter. For a perfect corner, release the button momentarily and press it again to start the next line at the end of the first. To get lines that are perfectly horizontal, vertical, or at a 45° angle, hold down the Shift key while you are drawing the line.

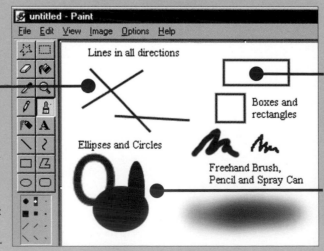

For *rectangles* and *squares*, click on the screen where you want one of the rectangle's corners to be. Click on the rectangle button and, as you drag the crosshair across the screen, you create a rectangle. Holding down the Shift key will produce squares rather than rectangles.

Ovals work in the same way. Click on the oval button and drag the crosshair across the screen for wide/fat ovals, or up and down for tall, thin ovals. Holding the Shift button down turns ovals into circles.

EasyART PROJECT

Use the oval button to create a filled circle. Try a skin colour by going to Edit Colour and typing in the values 20 for hue, 200 for saturation, and 210 for luminosity.

Use the oval for one eye (don't forget to change foreground and background colours) and add a black circle for the pupil.

Put a select box around the eye, then press Control-C to make a copy of it and Control-V to paste the copy onto the screen. Move the eye to the right position. If the eye becomes pink, it's because you are still in transparent mode.

Use the curve tool to make the bottom and top lines of the mouth. Choose a suitable colour and use the paint can to colour the mouth. If the whole face changes colour, it's because the lines that make the top and bottom of the mouth aren't quite touching. Use Undo to clear the fill, find the gap (using Zoom if necessary), and connect the ends with a small line. Now it's freehand time. Do your best for the nose with the pencil or brush and add the hair with the spray can. Now try the other tools to fill in the background.

button will place the text permanently into your picture. But remember, once you have exited the writing mode, the words become part of the image, just like the writing on a drawing. If you want to change anything afterwards, you have to rub out the words and replace them.

Cleaning up

If you've slightly overshot a corner or made other little mistakes, you can clean up your picture with the eraser. This will rub out anything just like the eraser at the end of a pencil. For large areas, click on the big eraser. For fine work, use one of the smaller options. For really careful work, zoom into the picture using Zoom in the view menu. The thumbnail (right) shows where you are in the picture. You can also use the pencil to correct single pixels.

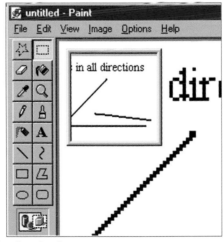

Oops!

You use the eraser to clean up a picture, but simple mistakes can be eliminated as they happen. Say you are drawing a line and it goes too far. If you are still holding the left mouse button down, pressing the right button will remove the line you have just drawn. Now start again.

If you have finished the line and let go of the mouse button, but then decide that the line isn't right, go to Undo in the Edit menu (or press Control-Z). Undo undoes the last drawing action. You can use it to remove the last three additions to your picture.

Manipulating

Once you've done some painting you still have a whole set of tools to alter what you've done. You can change the whole picture or select a part of it for changing by using the select buttons. You can cut and paste parts of pictures as you choose. Simply surround the part you want to use and Copy or Cut it out and then choose Paste. You will see a new copy in the top left-hand corner of your picture, and you can drag and drop this anywhere you like. By pressing Control-C repeatedly you can use Paste like a rubber stamp.

Paint also gives you a fancy drag/paste effect. Copy and Paste a single element in your picture in the usual way, but hold the Shift key down as you move it around. Paste will leave a trail wherever you move.

You can flip an image over or spin it around with Flip/Rotate. Flipping is like reflecting the image in a mirror and rotating spins it around.

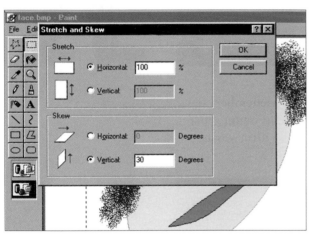

Squeeze me

Any part of the picture can be stretched or squeezed. Draw around it using the select tools. You will see a dotted line rectangle with small square handles on the corners and the centre of each side. Place the crosshair over the handle and use the mouse to squeeze or stretch the image. If you use the corner handles, you can shrink or enlarge the image without distorting its shape.

You can do the same thing using the stretch/skew menu, this time typing in, as numbers, the new size. From this menu (shown left) you can also skew the image, squeezing it sideways or upwards.

It's not obvious

The normal Cut and Paste takes a part of your picture, together with its background, and places it somewhere else in the image. But then it is quite obvious that there is one part of the picture laid on top of another. However, if you copy something that started life against a plain background, you can make that background completely transparent. Then, when you do the Pasting, you can't see where the part was added.

Foreground **colour to paint with.**

Background **colour for the paper and fills.**

Colours

Paint and draw programs give you control over both the foreground and the background colours, and you can change them as you go along. The foreground colour is your paint can colour – the colour that appears when you use the brush, pencil or spray can. The background colour is what lies underneath – the colour of the paper you are working on. The background colour also sets the colour used to fill squares and circles. When you use the eraser to rub something out, the background colour is revealed from underneath.

In most programs – we use MS Paint for this example – you choose your foreground colour by clicking on the paint can with the left mouse button. To select a new background colour, click on the paint can with the right mouse button.

images

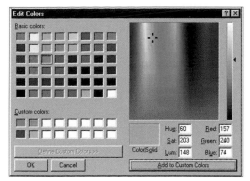

You can create your own colours in MS Paint using *Define Custom Colours* under Edit Colours in the Options menu.

In MS Paint you'll have a range of 28 paint pots to choose from, but you can also mix your own colours with Edit Colours in the Options menu. This gives you another 20 cans of colour to work with.

Go to Define Custom Colours and select your own custom colour by moving around the colour matrix block until you find the one you want. You can use it immediately or save it in a custom-colour paint can that you can use again.

Add black or white

To darken or lighten a colour, go to Define Custom Colours and move the Shade slider up or down. It's just like mixing in more black or white into your pot of paint.

Pick a colour

If you want a perfect match to a colour in a picture, then click on the dropper button. Now put the tip of the dropper over the colour you want. Click the mouse button to take a sample of the colour and your paint can will be magically filled with the right colour.

Kids painting

Children soon get the hang of painting and drawing programs, but if you want to stimulate an early interest in on-screen artwork, try a program designed specifically for kids. Kids' programs add in all kinds of extra fun and exciting features and make good use of multimedia, so sounds can be linked to images and simple animations can be produced with little effort.

Shortcut

To work with the background colour when you are painting, press down the right mouse button.

You can reverse the colours and produce a complete *negative* version of your picture.

Drawing

Although drawing programs share a lot of functions with MS Paint, there are some very important differences. Pictures created with drawing programs are full of shapes – each one entirely separate – that are put together by you to create the picture. Rather than painting on a piece of paper, drawing is more like making a felt picture, in which pictures are made by laying different small shapes on to a background card. In MS Draw, these shapes are called Objects. They are typically lines, curves, wedges, circles and squares.

One advantage of MS Draw is that, even when you think you've finished the picture, you can still go back to it and move single pieces around, change the order in which they are laid on top of each other, and add more pieces.

The draw screen looks very similar to the paint one. There are the drawing tools down the side and paint pots at the bottom – although these are now called line and fill colours.

Make a circle in the same way that you do in MS Paint and fill it. Make a couple more. Now if you go to the pointer tool and put the arrow over one of the circles you can select it, move it around the screen, and change anything about it you want. Stretch it, shrink it, squash it, change its colour – whatever you do affects only the object you've selected.

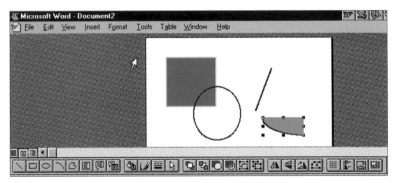

Drawing programs construct pictures using any number of different shapes, or *objects*.

From A to B

Instead of using the mouse's movement to make marks on your picture, in MS Draw you are setting the start and end points of the line. Click on the line button, then click anywhere on the screen – that is your line's starting point A. As you move the mouse around, the line is automatically drawn to the cursor. Click again and you've set your line's end point B.

With Draw you can alter those points at any time. Use the arrow button and click on the line. You can move it, change the start and end points, change its colour and thickness, even turn it into a dotted line.

Circles, wedges and squares

The same applies to any other object in MS Draw. When you create objects, you are telling the computer what shape and colour it is. Your PC uses these instructions to recreate your picture every time you call it up.

Create a star and make a *copy* and colour it. Click on the copy and put it behind the original.

Layer upon layer

Just like a felt picture, what you finally see depends on which objects or shapes sit on top of each other. Each time you draw an object it will automatically be placed on top of anything that is already drawn on the paper. But you can change the order in which objects are layered by using the Send to Front or Send to Back instructions in the Edit menu.

Grids

If you are producing graphs or other technical illustrations, you will find it important that you place blocks or other objects in straight lines. Doing this by hand is very difficult, so MS Draw gives you a grid to work with. The grid is really just like graph paper, except with paper you always see the squares. In MS Draw the squares appear only on your monitor. So you can easily make sure your columns and lines start and stop in the right place.

But maybe you are still not sure your control of the mouse is good enough, even with the grid lines to help. Then switch to Snap to Grid. As you draw, your PC will automatically place your lines on the grids, so even if you have only moderate control of your mouse everything will always be positioned accurately.

A choice of fillings

In MS Draw, you have a wide range of fillings that you can put into your shapes. There are solid colours, patterns, lines and graduated tints, which move slowly from one colour to another. Gradations can make an ordinary image look very professional. Gradations give a 3-D feel to your objects, turning circles into balls and squares into almost tangible cubes.

Join the group

Often you will need to handle a selection of objects as though they were a single item. You can do this by collecting them into a group. With the point button and the Shift key held down, use the mouse to click on all the objects you want to group. Now select Group in the Draw menu. Try moving the group around and you'll see that now everything moves together. Anything you can do with a single object – moving, resizing, copying, layering, changing colour and so on – you can also do with a group.

You may have created a group to move a whole part of the picture from one point to another. Now if you want to change something within the group, Ungroup it back to its separate parts.

Write-on

Unlike MS Paint, which turns text into part of the picture itself, MS Draw treats text just as a word processor does. You can type in your words and change their size, font and colour. You can align the words left, centre or right. Best of all, you can always come back and change the text at any time you like.

Line styles

When you are drawing lines in MS Draw, you can change both the thickness of the line and its style. You are not restricted to a continuous line: with MS Draw you can just as easily produce a dotted or dot-dash line by selecting these in the Line Style menu.

Freeform

MS Draw does give you a freehand drawing tool that works like the pencil in MS Paint. As you draw, the freeform tool creates your shapes out of numerous short lines.

Which draw program?

Because drawing is such a convenient way of creating illustrations and graphs to be included in a presentation, you will often find that good word processors, databases and spreadsheets include a drawing facility of some sort. The drawing examples here use MS Draw, which is included with many Microsoft programs. There are several stand-alone drawing packages and several business presentation tools that use draw techniques to produce graphs and images for business presentations. These can be printed or used for on-screen presentations. There are also several shareware draw programs, but check that they store their pictures in a format your other Windows programs can use.

Special effects

Some paint systems are designed to go beyond basic drawing to retouching and altering existing images and photographs. These all have the drawing functions of MS Paint but let you do other things with existing images to make them look more interesting or even make them look better than the original.

Filters

Those who own cameras with different attachments will know all about filters. They are the special lenses put on the camera lens to change the colour or give the image a different look. Photo-retouching software also comes with a wide range of filters – some of them simple, others very complex indeed.

Many of the filters produce special effects for creative work, for example, when you want to turn a picture into something entirely different.

Deformation of character

It's not only the colour and overall look of your picture you can change. You can also change its shape. We've already come across the idea of stretching and rotating the image, but these effects can go one step further. Put your picture through a fisheye lens or wrap it around a cylinder. The more sophisticated— and expensive – the photo package, the more options you have.

Posterisation **reduces the image to large dramatic areas of colour.**

Embossing **highlights the edges of the picture and makes it look as if it has been embossed in metal.**

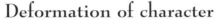

Mosaic **works out the average colour of all the pixels within a small square and replaces them all with a single small block of colour.**

Solarisation **produces a half negative effect.**

13 MULTIMEDIA

No limits!

Multimedia is the reason that most families buy a PC for their home. Your multimedia PC can merge information, images, movies, music and speech into a single program that can inform, educate and entertain – all at the same time.

Multimedia programs can be educational and take young children through the basics of reading or maths. For older children, there is a wide range of software on topics from dinosaurs to music. And for everyone there are the multimedia reference works that go far beyond the usual text of an encyclopaedia. Mixing sound clips, colour pictures and movies, multimedia turns learning into a more entertaining experience. Learning can be so much fun that users have coined a new name for these types of software: edutainment

For the business user, multimedia can radically overhaul the way information is presented. A sound clip of just a few words can be used to explain the complexities of a graph. Adding multimedia to a presentation – mixing animated graphs, sound and even video – makes a great difference in the impact the presentation makes on an audience.

And then there is pure entertainment. With a multimedia PC games can offer real sound and fast-moving video. You can even turn your PC into a TV. Multimedia not only brings you into the world of playing multimedia programs from CD-ROM discs, you can also make your own. With multimedia you can do virtually anything with your PC, from adding short sound bites to a word-processed document to making your own multimedia TV show.

Interactivity is a key element of many multimedia programs. It means being able to move all around the available information, with the PC helping you to navigate, rather than dictating where you have to go next. It is a bit like a reference book, in which you look up references and move around the book to delve deeper into a topic. But an interactive multimedia program will do all the searching for you and come up with a whole range of text information, images, video and sound clips to explain the topic more clearly. You can harness this power to a high-quality colour monitor and a sound card that can record and play to full CD quality. There is virtually no limit to what a multimedia computer can offer. ●

Multimedia

Take a good PC, add a CD-ROM player to run the latest multimedia software and a sound card and speakers to play sound and music and you have the essence of a multimedia PC. Most new home computers have all the important multimedia functions already built into them, so all you have to do is plug in the PC and you are ready to go.

Speakers

Some PCs have built-in speakers, which are convenient since you don't have to find any more desk space for them. You can also connect your computer's self-powered speakers to your sound card to further improve the sound, as your computer is capable of hi-fi-quality sound.

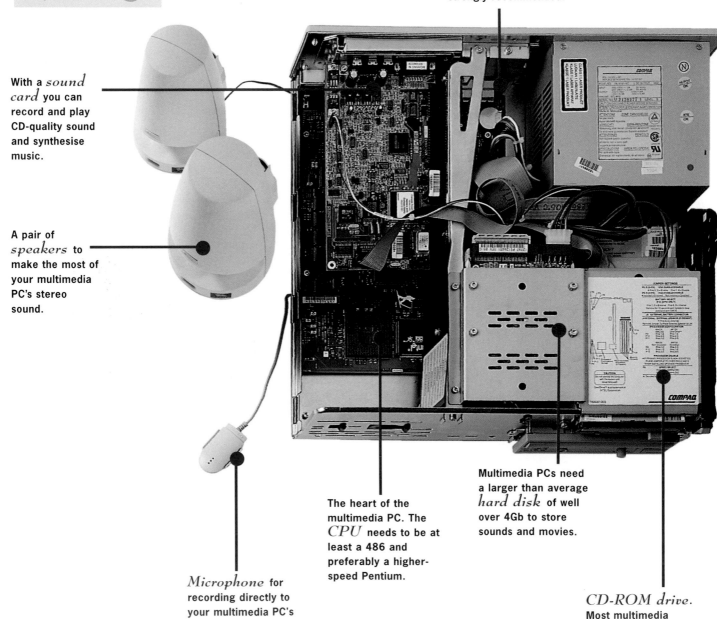

You need at least 16Mb of *RAM* to run multimedia software, and 24Mb to 32Mb is strongly recommended.

With a *sound card* you can record and play CD-quality sound and synthesise music.

A pair of *speakers* to make the most of your multimedia PC's stereo sound.

Multimedia PCs need a larger than average *hard disk* of well over 4Gb to store sounds and movies.

The heart of the multimedia PC. The *CPU* needs to be at least a 486 and preferably a higher-speed Pentium.

Microphone for recording directly to your multimedia PC's hard disk.

CD-ROM drive. Most multimedia programs are now made on CD-ROM.

Software

Inside your multimedia PC you will find all the essential elements that make it perform: the CD-ROM drive, to access the programs; the sound card; and the powerful central processing unit and SVGA video card. You will also find a larger hard disk so that you can comfortably store multimedia programs, audio and image files.

The reason for buying a multimedia PC is to run multimedia software. These amazing programs mix information with pictures, sound, animation and video clips in a way that makes the most complex topics accessible and interesting. There are thousands of multimedia titles available, ranging from educational and reference works to games. Although home multimedia has only been around for a couple of years, many of these titles are quite well put together.

Education
Kids can learn to use the PC to draw, write, make music or learn about their world. Multimedia encyclopaedias and dictionaries are designed to capture their attention and enthusiasm. These edutainment programs make education fun.

The more sophisticated edutainment software goes straight to the heart of subjects being taught in the National Curriculum. Such programs are particularly useful for special projects, background information and hobbies.

Adults, too
Multimedia is not all kids' stuff. Some of the most successful titles are bought by adults. Grown-ups' CD-ROMs range from computer golf to adventure games. Art, movies and music are particularly well represented. Other edutainment titles include architecture, history and astronomy.

And if you ever wanted a complete set of encyclopaedias but never had the wall space or the cash to buy them, a multimedia CD-ROM disc will give you the equivalent of a 30-volume set with the bonuses of sound and video.

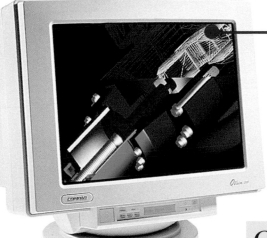

A good display card and *monitor* make the most of multimedia's full-colour images and speed up video playback.

Controller
Multimedia is as much about games as anything else, and multimedia computers often include a socket for a joystick controller. It is much better suited to game playing than the mouse or the keyboard.

Kit stop

MPC is short for *Multimedia PC*, **but not all companies bother to stick the logo on their boxes. So don't assume that your PC isn't up to scratch with MPC just because you can't see the logo on the box.**

As well as a CD-ROM drive and a sound card, your PC needs to have the right combination of processor power and memory before it will properly play multimedia programs. This is because the computer's workload increases dramatically when you want to hear and see high-quality sounds and pictures. For example, a photographic-quality colour image that uses nearly 17 million colours will demand three times more memory to store and display than a simple 256-colour image.

PC performance

Any PC that uses a 386 or lower processor won't work at all for multimedia, and a 486-based PC will play only the oldest programs. Only Pentium PCs will work with all of today's multimedia programs. These very fast processors are able to handle the large amounts of picture and sound information being played from a good multimedia program. The amount of internal memory that your computer has will also dramatically affect how smoothly it will play multimedia. Your computer must have at least 16Mb of internal RAM to handle multimedia programs. However, at least 24Mb to 32Mb is recommended if you are serious about using your PC for sound and moving images. There are sets of specifications called MPC1, MPC2 and MPC3 to make your life easier when choosing either a multimedia computer or the software that you will run on it. You will find that the MPC logo now appears on many

Minimum Standards

The MPC2 and MPC 3 multimedia PC standards set out the minimum requirements for playing a multimedia program. These are the basic requirements for both standards.

	MPC2	MPC3
Central processor	486SX	Pentium 75MHz
Memory	4Mb (8Mb recommended)	8Mb
Floppy drive	1.44Mb 3.5in	1.44Mb 3.5in
Hard drive	160Mb minimum	540Mb minimum
CD-ROM	2-speed	4-speed
Sound card	CD-audio, 16-bit On-board synth	CD-audio, 16-bit On-board synth
Graphics	640 x 480 resolution with 64,000 colours	640 x 480 resolution with 64,000 colours
Video	None	MPEG1
Keyboard	101-key keyboard	101-key keyboard
Mouse	Two-button mouse	Two-button mouse
Software	Windows 3.0 plus M/M extension or Windows 3.1	Windows 3.11
Inputs/outputs	Serial & parallel port, MIDI I/O port, joystick port	Serial & parallel port, MIDI I/O port, joystick port

computers and multimedia software. MPC1 is a very basic multimedia specification, established several years ago and is now completely out of date. The MPC2 standard reflects the quality of PCs that the current range of multimedia software need. It says your PC should have at least a 486 processor, a good graphics card and a basic CD-ROM drive. The more advanced multimedia software is working to MPC3 specifications, which can deliver smooth, good-quality video and sound. If you are buying a new PC, it should meet all the MPC3 requirements and be capable of running the current range of multimedia titles and games.

Look to the future

As time passes computers will continue to become more powerful and multimedia software will make more demands on your PC. Inevitably a PC that is right for today's multimedia programs may not be able to handle programs being produced in a few years' time. Yet all is not lost, because you can upgrade your computer to meet future needs. If you need more memory, you can simply plug some more in. If you need a high power, movie-type display card, you can replace your existing card with a new one. For more sound features, just replace the sound card. Invest wisely now and you will have a PC that can grow as the technology changes.

Better pictures

The normal Windows screen works well with 16 colours, but photos can contain millions of different colours, shades and hues. If you are using a 16-colour display, the PC will do its best to convert the full-colour picture to an image that is made up of only 16 colours. If you want to have more than 16 colours in the image, the number of calculations involved increases enormously. This can slow down the screen display. Accelerator display cards have their own sophisticated processors that take on a lot of the display calculations, so you can show more colours without slowing down the PC. Most multimedia software packages use 256 colours for their images, so running your system in a 256-colour mode should give the best ratio of picture quality to speed.

Bits of colour

Sometimes the colour performance of a PC is described as 4-, 8-, 16- or 24-bit. This tells you how many binary bits are used by the PC to describe the colours in each dot, or pixel, on your screen.

8-bit colour = Up to 256 colours	= Minimum for multimedia
16-bit colour = Up to 65,536 colours	= Video quality
24-bit colour = Up to 16.7 million colours	= Photographic quality

Music

MIDI

The MIDI (Musical Instrument Digital Interface) data system creates a simple set of instructions that tells the synthesiser about the note you want to play. MIDI instructions contain information about the note's pitch, length, dynamics and the type of sound that you have chosen. Because these are stored as simple instructions, rather than complete recorded sound samples, they take up very little disk space. MIDI synthesised music will need 30Kb of hard disk space per minute of music, compared to 600Kb per minute for even the lowest-quality recorded sound.

Your sound card's built-in synthesiser not only produces the sounds for most of your computer games, it can also be used to make your own music. If you don't have a musical instrument you can use your computer keyboard and a mouse to create your own tunes using the sequencer software that is often bundled with the sound card.

Instead of recording the actual sounds of a music track, the sound card's internal synthesiser plays the tune from a simple set of instructions using the MIDI system, which was developed for electronic-music keyboards.

These MIDI instructions tell the synthesiser which notes to play and for how long. They are stored as a MIDI file with the extension .mid. Games and multimedia software use MIDI and the sound card's synthesiser to create music and sound effects.

Sing-along-a-PC

You can buy floppy disks with a range of MIDI music files of popular songs. You just load the file from the floppy disk and the PC will play the music for you. Because these are files of instructions you are in total control. You can speed them up or slow them down or change the pitch. You can also change the instrument sounds, turning a keyboard solo into a guitar solo or altering the balance between the different synthesised instruments.

These MIDI disks are available in music shops so you can use them as an accompaniment to your own musical efforts – on another instrument or just singing along in karaoke mode.

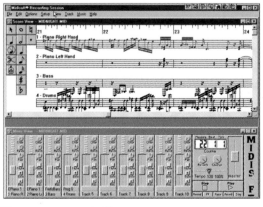

The *sequencer* is like a word processor for sound.

FM and Wave

The most common type of synthesiser chip on a sound card is an FM synthesiser, which recreates sounds by merging different tones. More advanced sound cards use WaveTable synthesisers that use a store of very short recorded clips of musical instruments. Because you are listening to real sound, the sound cards with WaveTable synthesisers sound much more realistic.

Making music

You create and store your own synthesised music using the sequencer, which is a word processor for music. Instead of typing in words and setting font size and styles, with the sequencer you enter notes and choose what type of instruments they should sound like. Many sound cards have an extra socket that can be used either for a games joystick control or as a MIDI connection to an electronic keyboard.

With a keyboard connected to the sound card you can play music directly into the sequencer, and the PC will store every note exactly as you play it. If you make a mistake, you can then use the sequencer to manually edit out or change any wrong notes.

Images

A multimedia PC can handle a wide range of images, both still and moving. Photographic-type images are usually bit maps, where the picture file contains information about the colour of every pixel (or bit) in the image. Drawn pictures are often created using vector drawing packages. These make a picture from circles, lines and squares that are stored as mathematical equations which tell the PC to display, say, a square of a certain size, shape and colour in a particular position. While the bit map images are good for photos and scanned images, they do take up a lot of disk space. The vector drawings are good for simpler images and take up less room on the hard disk.

Getting a new image

If you want to make your own presentations, there are lots of ways you can include images. You can create your own drawn images using either a painting or a drawing program. You can scan in your own photos and pictures with a scanner or you can go out and buy some. Most computer stores stock CD-ROMs full of photographic and drawn images.

Another way to get images is to use a video-capture system. Some multimedia PCs have video features, and some include an internal TV tuner so you can use the monitor as a TV. With video capture, as you see the images from the TV or your VCR, you can capture a single frame and use that as a picture.

Talkies

Still images are only half the story. Many multimedia CD-ROMs also contain animations and video clips. All multimedia PCs can play these using software programs that read and create the images. But the quality is often dependent on the speed of the computer's central processor and the amount of memory it has installed.

Real TV produces 25 images every second, but slower Pentium PCs may not be able to read, decode and display 25 full-screen pictures or frames that fast. So on your PC you will get a smaller image that plays at about 10 frames per second. Many VGA cards now have movie electronics to take over these image calculations so you get smoother playback. This is called hardware decoding. Specialised image-capture systems let you record video clips onto your hard disk so you can add home movies to your own multimedia shows.

Off to the movies

Many multimedia CD-ROMs include TV-quality video, using a system called MPEG1. Although there are software-only programs to decode MPEG1 images, they will suffer from jerkiness unless you have a very powerful PC. To get full-colour, full-screen video images with stereo digital sound there are VGA display cards that include MPEG decoding, or you can add a separate MPEG decoder card. There is a range of video-CDs of movies and TV programmes that use the MPEG1 system. These look just like audio CDs but contain movies instead of music.

Your CD

Your CD-ROM drive is very similar to an audio CD player, but with fewer buttons. You can control all the drive's functions from Windows. If you are running a computer program from the CD-ROM drive, your PC will operate the control of the CD-ROM all on its own. If you have a CD-ROM with individual files, treat it like any other computer drive and use My Computer or File Manager to locate the files. Playing audio CDs may just be a matter of inserting the disc, although there are now many CD jukebox software packages, such as the Windows CD Player, that give you more control over the choice of tracks to play.

Some CD-ROM players have a play/next-track button for playing audio CDs. For more sophisticated control you would run your CD-player software on your computer. The CD-ROM needs an interface to work with your computer. Although you can use a dedicated CD-ROM controller, most sound cards now also include the CD-ROM controller electronics. IDE CD-ROMs, which use a spare connector from your hard disk controller, are also becoming popular. The alternative is to use a CD-ROM with the more advanced, flexible (and more expensive) SCSI interface. SCSI (pronounced 'scuzzy') stands for Small Computer Systems Interface, and many sound cards and PCs have a built-in SCSI port ready for your CD-ROM drive.

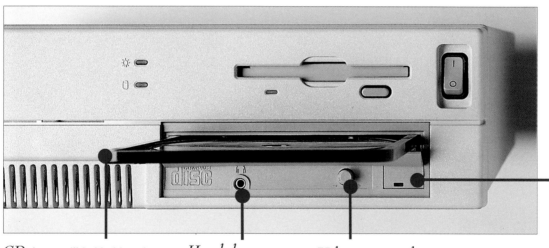

Front panel button to open or close the CD tray.

CD tray will hold either the standard 5in CDs or the small 3in discs sometimes used for portable CD-ROM applications or CD singles.

Headphone socket for playing audio CDs.

Volume control only alters the level of the sound going to the headphones.

Recordable CDs

Recordable CDs (CD-Rs) are a special type of CD that have a distinctive gold or green data layer. The CD recorder can be used to store files from your computer in the same way as a floppy disk. But unlike a floppy disk, on which you can continually delete files and write over them, once the information is burnt into the CD-R disc, it is locked in permanently and is impossible to erase.

Because of this, CD recording is called a WORM format: Write Once, Read Many.

CD-R is used in many professional applications. Software developers use CD-Rs to test their CD-ROM software before they go on to press thousands of discs, and radio stations use CD-R as a simple way of storing and playing their jingles. Blank CD-Rs are not expensive and audio

CD-Rs are now available for home use.

CDs that can be erased and reused are available, but these rewritable CDs (CD-RWs) need a dedicated drive, and not all CD players can read CD-RW discs.

Faster and bigger

The audio CD pulls data off the disc at a rate of 150Kb a second. So a large image file of several hundred kilobytes would take several seconds to be retrieved using a single-speed drive. To speed things up, CD-ROM drives work at higher speeds to make sure that there are no hold-ups in running multimedia programs. Now eight-speed (8x) drives are the slowest available and the fastest go up to 32x. Also look out for the next generation of CD-ROM – the DVD-ROM. These discs and drives look like standard CD-ROMs, but they contain five or more times the amount of data. DVD-ROM drives are able to play both DVD discs and standard CD-ROMs. DVD-ROMs carry more and better quality sound pictures and video.

In the driver's seat

Your computer is happy to work with a CD-ROM drive or a sound card, provided it knows how to control it and get data out of it. This is the job of the device driver, which is a small software program that tells the computer all about the new hardware and how it functions. Device drivers are usually transferred automatically to your PC's hard disk during the new hardware's installation and set-up procedure. After that, they are automatically loaded every time you switch on your PC.

The computer also needs separate software drivers to know what to do with specific types of multimedia such as CD Audio, MIDI or video files. Usually, these are also automatically placed into the device manager section of the system (or in Drivers in the Windows 3.1 control panel) when new multimedia software or hardware is loaded. These drivers will be automatically loaded when Windows is run.

Keeping it clean

The small laser beam inside your CD-ROM drive is focused on the playing surface of the CD using a tiny optical lens which can get dirty over a period of time. You can easily clean it by using one of the many CD cleaning disks that are available in computer or music stores. A cleaning kit designed for audio CD players will do just as good a job on your CD-ROM drive.

CDs you can and can't play

Your computer and CD-ROM cannot play every type of CD available as some discs need special additional electronics to work. Some need special drives and other discs are not designed to work on the PC at all. Here is what you need to play the various types of CDs.

Disc	Suitable CD-ROM Drive	Additional electronics needed
CD-Audio	Any drive	No
CD-ROM	Any drive	No
CD-i	Green Book (very rare)	Yes
Photo-CD	Multi-session, CD-XA (nearly all, check first)	No
Video-CD	White Book Compatible (all new CD-ROM drives)	Yes
Saturn CD	All new drives	Yes
DVD-ROM	Special DVD-ROM drives	Yes
3DO CD	All new drives	Yes

Multimedia

The CD was launched in the early 1980s, at the same time that the first PCs were coming into the shops. The main plan of its inventors, Philips and Sony, was to replace the LP with a longer-playing, better-sounding, scratch-proof, digital audio disc. But they also realised that it could be used to hold computer programs, since the CD is simply a carrier for digital information – a vast number store. On music CDs, these numbers carry digitised sound. But they could just as easily be carrying digitised images, digitised movies or the data that make up a computer software program.

CD-ROM

The proper name for a music CD is CD-A, which stands for Compact Disc-Audio. Computer CDs are called CD-ROMs, which stands for Compact Disc-Read Only Memory. The Read Only part means that the information on it is pressed permanently into the disc itself when it is manufactured. It is not possible to record on to it from your PC.

A CD-ROM is capable of holding at least 650Mb of data, which is the equivalent of 900 standard 3.5in floppy disks. And it is only a little more expensive to make. This is what has made CD a runaway success for delivering storage-hungry software such as multimedia programs.

Inside a CD-ROM

The CD-ROM is made of polycarbonate pressed with small pits in a spiral track and backed by a reflective aluminium layer. These pits represent the binary ones and zeros that the computer uses as data. If you stretched this track out it would be nearly 6km (3.7 miles) long. Unlike the spiral track on an LP which starts on the outer edge and works inwards, the CD's groove starts in the middle and works its way out to the edge.

Green CDs

Polycarbonate is a plastic that does not naturally break down very easily. There is a lot of waste polycarbonate during the manufacturing of a CD. Most CD plants try to recycle as much of their waste polycarbonate as possible, to save them from having to buy more raw material. Some countries are making strict laws about what happens to such recyclable products as CDs when they are no longer wanted by the consumer. In Germany there are moves to make CD manufacturers responsible for the correct disposal of unwanted CDs.

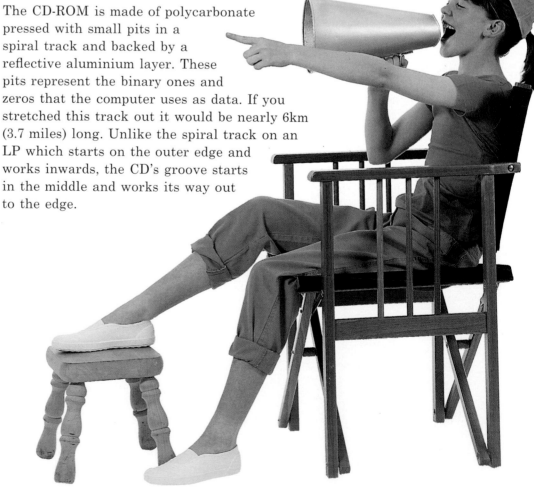

CDs

This aluminium layer is extremely thin and would fall apart if you tried to handle it, so it is coated on to tough, clear plastic.

When you put the CD into the CD-ROM drive, the small solid-state laser focuses a beam of laser light through the plastic on to the aluminium layer which then reflects the light back on to a light sensor. When the laser beam hits a pit in the surface, less light is reflected back. The sensor can read this as a 0 or a 1 and passes the data on to the computer.

Correcting errors

One of the reasons that a CD is not easily affected by surface marks is that the data recorded on to it also contain error-correction information. Instead of putting the data on to the disc as one long continuous stream of numbers, it is split up into tiny bursts, or blocks, of information. Each small block includes a way of letting your computer check that all the data has been read correctly. If there is a small scratch that hides some of the CD's data, the computer can recalculate what is missing.

What's ahead

CD and graphics technologies will continue to evolve. Most console games have already switched to CD and the introduction of Windows 95 made it much easier to run console-quality multimedia software on your PC. The quality of video playback is improving, too. The simple AVI-type video used in multimedia discs will slowly be replaced by the better quality MPEG1 video, and then there are DVD discs which are able to deliver better-than-TV-quality video on your PC screen. Games are going from flat (2-D) graphics to solid-looking 3-D graphics, and sound is moving from very basic radio quality up to CD-stereo quality with cinema surround-sound, too. Multimedia is no longer confined to CD. More and more Web sites are adding sound and moving images, so you can dial up full multimedia on the Internet.

High-density CD

The 650Mb capacity of CD may sound like a lot of storage, but this can soon be eaten up by multimedia software, especially if it contains a lot of audio and video clips. The next development for CD will be the high-density CD which will have between five and 15 times the capacity of today's CDs.

Whereas the high-density floppy took you out of kilo (thousand) bytes of data storage into mega (million) bytes of storage, high-density CD moves up into the world of giga (a billion) bytes of storage.

Sound and data

There has been a recent addition to the CD family that will be able to put data, program, image and movie files that your computer can read on to ordinary audio CDs. The CD-Extra discs will play their music tracks perfectly well on an ordinary CD player, but when you load one into your computer's CD-ROM drive you will be able to get all sorts of extras, such as photos or videos of the performers, background information and the lyrics or libretto displayed while the music is playing.

Handling CDs

Despite the early claims of indestructibility, CDs can still be damaged by dirt and grime. If the surface becomes badly marked, the laser will not be able to read the information buried inside the disc. So always handle the disc by its edges or by its centre hole and try not to touch the playing surface. Put the disc back in its case when you have finished and don't leave it in the CD-ROM drive. If the disc gets dirty, clean it with a soft cloth dampened with warm, slightly soapy water.

Edutainment

Here is an example of an edutainment multimedia CD-ROM. This is taken from Microsoft's Ancient Lands, and many other CD-ROMs work in a similar way. They use a mix of traditional index systems and point-and-click to find information. The beauty of these programs is that you can follow your own train of thought. You can go from one topic to another, with the computer doing all the searching for you. The images are all full colour and can be printed out, so they can be easily included in school projects. Unlike a book on history, Ancient Lands provides sound effects and sound clips.

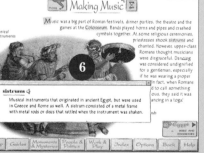

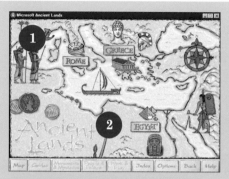

1 This doesn't look much like a computer program. Rather than square control buttons and information boxes, the screen uses the different *parts of the picture* to switch to other parts of the disc.

2 Click on Egypt or the Pyramid and you switch over to one of the different *topics* relating to the Egyptians. Getting hold of the Romans or the Greeks is just as easy.

3 Alternatively you can use the *text bar* at the bottom of the picture to move to the sections with more detail.

4 You can click on any of the *images* to find out more about how the Egyptians used to live.

5 If you want to swap nations mid-stream, just *click* here to go to the Romans or the Greeks and compare how they lived.

6 Clicking on a *new word* will display more information about it. Clicking on a *sound icon* will play an example of the instrument or speak the word so you know how it is pronounced.

7 You can choose your own *guides* who will talk you through their world. Different guides give talks about how they experienced life so you can get a feel for how it was for the highest and the lowest in the land.

EDUCATION

A class act

Computers used to be impressive luxury items for schools. Now they are just another essential feature of school life used by every child. Far from making children passive users of high technology, replacing a good understanding of basic skills like reading, writing and arithmetic, computers are helping kids to improve their skills in every area and enabling teachers to produce more individualised teaching materials.

Using the computer is seen by children as a reward in itself, especially as educational software is designed to feel more like computer games than lessons. Nevertheless, tucked into all the colour graphics, animations and sound effects is a huge amount of information to reinforce the teaching being done in class. And, as children move up in the school, the computer becomes just as important for finding information. Multimedia CDs on topics from dinosaurs to robots use sound, pictures, animation and video clips to make even the most complicated topics understandable and accessible.

The pattern looks as though it is going to be repeated in the home now that the cost of computers is dropping to a level that has brought them within reach of families, and the advances in technology have made them very easy to use. Using a PC as an educational tool is the most powerful reason for investing in a computer for the home. Parents, quite rightly, know that their children can use the computer at home to build up their expertise in many areas, from the basics of reading and counting in the earliest years to helping prepare for exams.

And it's not just the younger generation that can broaden their horizons with a home PC. Adults can use them for this, too. Whether you want to grapple with a foreign language for your holiday, go through a multimedia guide on wine, or learn more about classical music and art, there is a wide range of titles to choose from. So sit back and start learning about learning with the aid of your PC. ●

The educated

Home education and edutainment software are among the most demanding software in terms of what hardware you need to run it. Educational titles nearly all run under Windows and use it to integrate sounds, pictures and movie images, all in one package. This makes it essential that you have a good-quality multimedia PC.

The *screen and video driver card* for the monitor should be at least SVGA standard. Most titles will work best using the 600 x 800 setting and at least in 256 colours. Future software will use more colours, so a good video card is advisable.

The sound quality on the discs has often been poor compared to the picture quality. But things are changing, so opting for good *speakers* will make a noticeable difference, especially in those titles that deal with music-related topics.

The *CD-ROM drive* will be working hard on many educational titles to deliver all the audio, data, text, animations and movie clips contained on the discs. Look for a 12-speed drive or faster.

There is an amazing amount of information available from the Internet and the various on-line service providers. A fast *modem* will give you access to computer files all around the world.

Many educational programs need a *printer*. Learning word processing or drawing on a PC loses its appeal if you can't print out the results. Images and text can be printed out from all the reference works. A laser printer offers the best quality, but the results from an inkjet are almost as good. Inkjet printers are generally cheaper and have the advantage of colour printing.

Use a *CD rack* so that the discs are always handy and don't have to be searched for each time you want to run the program.

Most *sound cards* will work very well with educational titles, as nearly all are 16-bit, which is CD quality.

Speed is needed to make sure images come on screen quickly and to avoid any hold-ups inside your PC when sound and movies are being played. A *120MHz Pentium* processor is a good starting point, but a faster *Pentium* or a *Pentium II* is ideal.

Lack of *memory* can also slow down your edutainment titles a lot. You should consider 16Mb as the minimum RAM, with noticeable improvements when you go to 24Mb or more.

Although most of the software comes directly from the CD-ROM, each title will put some controller files on to your hard disk, with each title using around 2Mb of hard disk space. Titles that come on floppy disk will also take up a lot of space, so it is wise to have as large a *hard disk* as possible. Consider 2.4Gb (2,400Mb) as the minimum; 6Gb (6,000Mb) or 8Gb (8,000Mb) are not excessive.

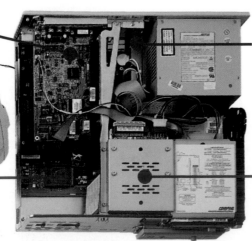

PC

Start at the beginning

It is a good idea to get your child used to switching the computer on and off, loading the programs, putting in floppy disks and CD-ROM discs and getting the printer going. These are basic skills that are fun, satisfying and add to a sense of responsibility and control over the PC. It also means they can get everything up and running without having to be supervised all the time.

K is for keyboard

Learning how to use a keyboard is best done while writing things in the word processor. Most of the ways a keyboard works are easily picked up, but one technique that does have to be learnt is using two keys together, such as pressing Alt and F at the same time to get the file menu and, more important, getting a capital letter by holding the Caps key down with one finger while pressing a letter.

Children, and many adults new to a keyboard, press the Caps Lock key to lock the keyboard into capital letter operation, press the letter and then press the Caps Lock key again to cancel Caps Lock. This is slower and it is easy to forget to switch off the Caps Lock. So try to build up the two-finger approach.

> **Shut Down Windows**   ☒
>
> Are you sure you want to:
>
> ⦿ Shut down the computer?
> ○ Restart the computer?
> ○ Restart the computer in MS-DOS mode?
>
> [Yes]   [No]   [Help]

Saving

As well as learning to switch on the computer, you should also go through the switch-off routine of saving the work, closing down the program, closing down Windows, and then switching off the computer and the mains supply. Going through a shut-down routine not only is good practice but also makes it less likely that any work will get accidentally lost because it wasn't saved before the computer was shut down.

Change a letter, not a word

When children find they have made a typing mistake they tend to use the Delete button to erase everything back to the mistake and then retype it. Get your child used to using the keyboard arrow keys to move to the mistake and delete the wrong letter. It's easier to do this with the arrow keys than with the mouse, as it can be hard to highlight a single letter with a mouse.

Considering how much time most kids will spend using the computer later on in life, typing skills are very low on the list of computer education priorities. While one-finger typing can reach reasonable speeds, real typing will always be faster and easier and can be mastered with learn-to-type software.

A large *track-ball* will help get fingers used to working with a PC.

Mouse time

Learning to use the mouse may take a little time. It is quite natural for little hands to hold the mouse a little way above the mouse mat and move it, not realising that the ball underneath has to be in contact with the mouse mat. Use drawing programs to get used to moving and clicking the mouse and using the mouse to access different functions in the menu bars. When using a word processor, refine using the mouse to highlight specific letters, words and lines, and use it to move things around.

Educational

Because educational software is aimed at the family rather than computer enthusiasts, it can be found in a wide range of shops. However, computer stores and computer games stores usually offer a wider range of titles. In the high street, check out newsagents and stationery retailers, radio/TV suppliers and bookshops. More specialised software is often available by mail order, so look through some of the computer magazines. Your school's computer or multimedia specialist will also be able to advise you on where to get specific titles if you are having trouble getting educational software.

Although the disc and packaging you get costs little to produce, the price you pay has to cover the development of the software, and this can run into large amounts for each title. Because they are now seen as a common consumer product, like games cartridges, educational CD-ROMs are gradually coming down in price. Some do cost more, but that may be because of the type of information they contain.

If you make a mistake when *loading software* from a CD-ROM, your PC is always ready to give you a helping hand.

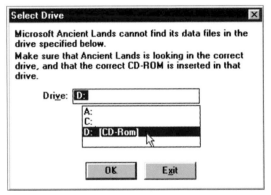

Loading your software

Some educational software is supplied on floppy disks. You put the first disk in the disk drive, type Install and the software takes over and loads itself on to your hard disk. Once loaded, all you have to do is click on the title's icon to run it. CD-ROM discs work differently. You put the disc in the CD-ROM drive and type Install. The software will then automatically load a relatively small set of programs that will control the CD-ROM software. When it has finished loading, the control program will be on your hard disk and you will have an icon to click on when you want to start the software.

When you want to run the software you must first put the CD-ROM disc into the drive and then click on the appropriate icon. The control software will then investigate the CD-ROM drive and start loading the pictures, sound and text from the disc. If you have forgotten to put the disc in the drive, or put the wrong one in, then you will get a message telling you what to do.

Teachers' Packs

Software companies are starting to produce packs for teachers so that they can use standard software in the classroom. Microsoft has what it calls Resource Packs for Education. These consist of a selection of classroom activities that accompany a particular program, such as the Encarta encyclopaedia. Each pack includes teacher's notes, pupil worksheets, a wall chart and templates on disk for teachers to develop their own activities. It also includes a video to show how technology can be used in the classroom. If you are interested in finding out about teachers' packs, contact your local education authority.

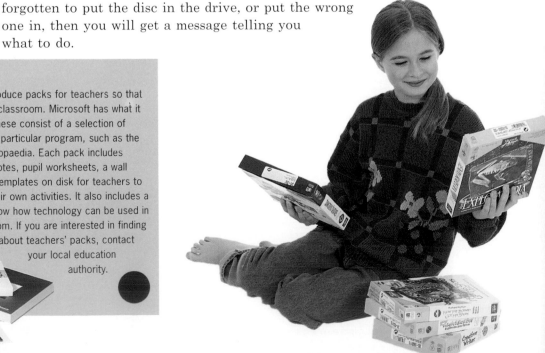

software

Noises

You might be wondering why children's writing or drawing packages still need a multimedia computer with sound. For a start, they use lots of noises to accompany on-screen activity such as selecting menu items. While you may find these noises irritating after a while, kids love them. Many of these programs include multimedia elements, so that noises, effects and music can be added to the on-screen text. Drawing programs often have the ability to create animations with accompanying sound and music.

Software on the cheap

When PCs were first developed, there were no software programs available on individual topics, such as learning a new language or how to manage your money. Fortunately, some people with computer-programming experience solved this problem simply by writing their own programs. Each of these amateur programs has some value and may exactly match something you want to do by yourself or with the children.

The reason they are cheap is that they are shareware programs, which you can try first and then send money to the authors if you like them. Freeware is software that people have produced for the fun of it rather than for profit, or just simply low-cost programs. Such programs vary in quality enormously. Although some are very simple, others can give commercial software a run for their money. Look in computer magazines for shareware companies, and for shareware CD-ROM discs in computer stores, or investigate the Internet forums on your particular area of interest.

Key stages

You may see some software referring to Key Stages and Attainment Targets. This is all terminology relating to the English National Curriculum. Your child's total school syllabus is split up into four separate phases, Key Stages 1 to 4. The Key Stage sets out what is being taught in any particular school year. The details of what is to be taught in each of the core subjects are set out in the National Curriculum. The school tracks what each child has covered and this is ticked off as an Attainment Level. So these show what has been taught at school and learnt by the child.

Different teachers cover areas of the syllabus in a different order and children naturally learn at different rates, so there will be considerable overlap of the Attainment targets reached by each child. At the end of primary school, your child could be studying anything from Attainment Level 2 work up to Attainment Level 5 work.

KEY STAGE	AGE RANGE	SCHOOL YEARS	ATTAINMENT LEVELS
1	5–7	1–3	1–3
2	7–11	4–6	2–5
3	11–14	7–9	3–7
4	14–16	10–11	-

Young kids

Very young children can use the computer to help develop the basic language, maths and science skills that are essential to their development in the early years at school. There is a lot of software that will grab children's attention and reinforce these skills while they think they are just playing on the PC.

For young children, up to the age of about eight, the most important thing is for you to work with them on the computer. Despite the sophistication of your PC, the instant computer teacher is still a long way off, and the PC should be used alongside books, magazines, television, radio, cassette tapes and video as one of the many wonderful ways to help your child grasp the basics.

Writing and drawing

Words and pictures are all around us, not just in books, but in cards, animations, leaflets, notes, magazines, comics and on badges. These can all be brought into play to help teach writing and drawing and stimulate the imagination. Many programs can produce quick and attractive results, such as a colourful birthday card for Grandma. But they also have enough depth and flexibility for working on longer and more elaborate projects. Software packages like Fine Artist and Creative Writer build up ability in both areas.

Creative Writer

Creative Writer helps children who already have some grasp of writing to expand their horizons. You don't need to read a manual to understand how to use it. Max, your funny-looking on-screen friend, will explain what the buttons do and offer general advice. There are loads of colours and special effects, which can all be easily accessed.

Creative Writer starts off with an *ideas generator* to begin a story.

There are lots of ready-to-run sections for making *badges*, *posters* and *cards*.

Write the words, add in pictures and go over the spelling. Then use the *spell checker* to see which words weren't corrected.

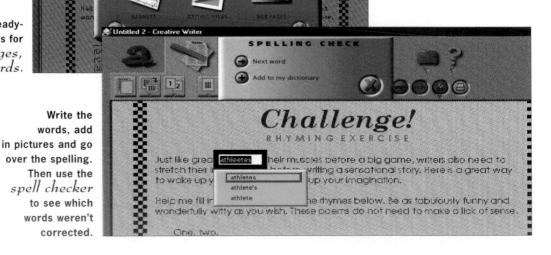

Spelling

Spelling is an area that computer software enhances by posing questions (disguised as various forms of games), keeping track of the scores and repeating areas that are problematic. Programs have key vocabulary lists and work through the words moving from simple ones to more complex and difficult spellings.

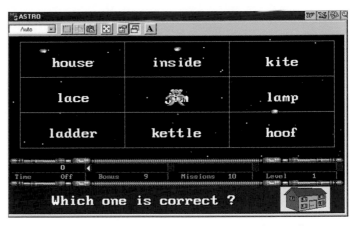

Structured Spelling mixes spelling exercises with arcade games.

Art

Art and drawing programs are good for experimenting with shapes and colours. There are hundreds of patterns and painting tools in software programs. There are 3-D tools for creating drawings that use perspective. Experimenting increases the appreciation of what different types of drawing and painting materials do.

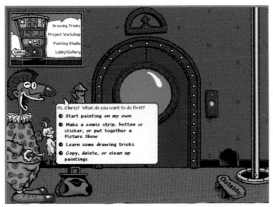

A good *drawing program* covers a lot of things beyond just making simple pictures on screen.

Reading

The multimedia computer is ideal for helping with reading. It can deliver the words on screen at the same time that the words are spoken through the PC's sound system. It's just like a read-along tape, but with total control and a lot more visual impact. These programs often add in other functions such as painting, so that there is more than one reason for wanting to use them.

Make *comic strips* without having to completely redraw each frame from scratch. Each image can be built up from different backgrounds and characters.

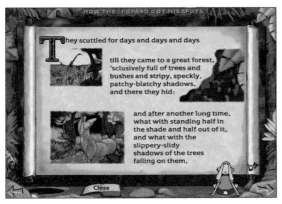

Click on any part of the picture to see and hear its name. Words are highlighted as the story is told.

Science

Topics like space and how your body works may seem a bit advanced for primary school children, but with a good story, lots of graphics and sounds, and a game or two, the topics come to life in a very accessible way. The number of software packages on specific topics aimed at younger children is still fairly limited, but the numbers are growing, as families no longer wait until their children are 9 or 10 before investing in a PC.

Exploring the *solar system* on Microsoft's Magic School Bus opens up the skies with animations, photos and video.

For your

The edutainment software that you are most likely to come across first is the reference CD-ROM. Encyclopaedias, dictionaries, and a whole range of specialised topics, from films to dinosaurs, have some very informative and entertaining software that covers the topic in reasonable depth and in a way that is easily understood by adults and older children.

A complete reference library

A single disc can contain all the basic reference books you'll need for everyday use: a dictionary, thesaurus, atlas, almanac, timeline and dictionary of quotations. A combined software system lets you cross-refer between the different reference works at the click of a button.

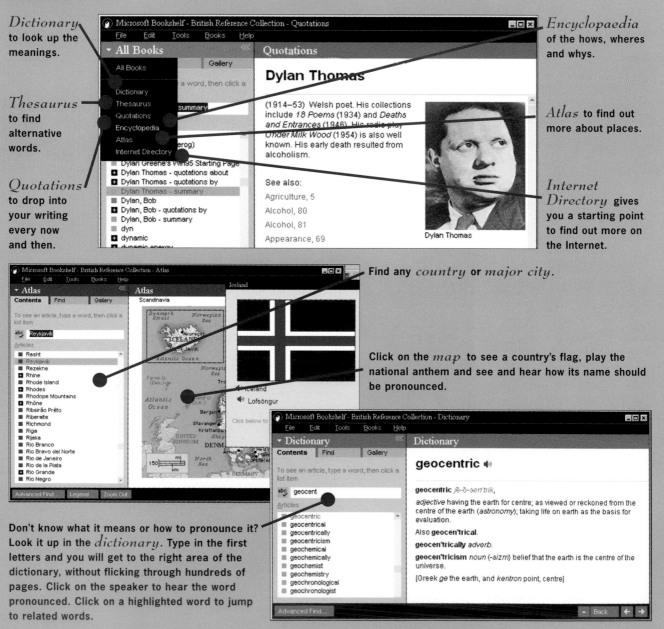

Dictionary to look up the meanings.

Thesaurus to find alternative words.

Quotations to drop into your writing every now and then.

Encyclopaedia of the hows, wheres and whys.

Atlas to find out more about places.

Internet Directory gives you a starting point to find out more on the Internet.

Find any *country* or *major city*.

Click on the *map* to see a country's flag, play the national anthem and see and hear how its name should be pronounced.

Don't know what it means or how to pronounce it? Look it up in the *dictionary*. Type in the first letters and you will get to the right area of the dictionary, without flicking through hundreds of pages. Click on the speaker to hear the word pronounced. Click on a highlighted word to jump to related words.

reference

Work your way around

Most reference CD-ROMS work in a similar way. Once you've learned to use one, you'll find the rest are easy.

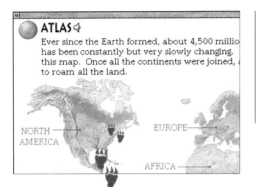

ATLAS
Ever since the Earth formed, about 4,500 millio
has been constantly but very slowly changing.
this map. Once all the continents were joined,
to roam all the land.

NORTH
AMERICA

EUROPE

AFRICA

Microsoft's Dinosaurs (below) is typical. It starts with an *opening menu* that shows you the general areas that you can delve into. Sometimes the menu looks like a Windows menu, but mostly they look like this.

If you want to approach the subject from another direction, look up the different *places* or *times*.

TIMELINE
The history of the Earth is divided into larg
All dinosaurs lived during the Mesozoic era, and
en 160 million years, the Mesozoic era was a sr
history. Eras are further divided into smaller blo
There were three periods during the Mesozoic era

PRECAMBRIAN ERA | | Cambrian | Ordovician
4,500-570 | | 570-500 | 500-430
| | | Million Years A

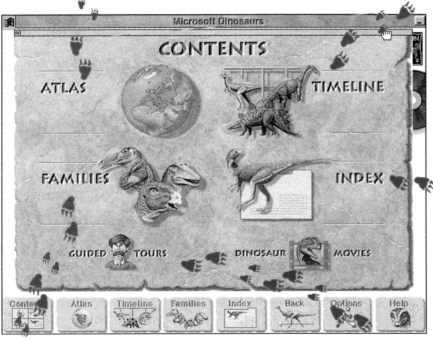

Microsoft Dinosaurs

CONTENTS

ATLAS
TIMELINE
FAMILIES
INDEX
GUIDED TOURS
DINOSAUR MOVIES

Conte | Atlas | Timeline | Families | Index | Back | Options | Help

If you know what you are looking for, go straight to it using the *index*.

INDEX

V

Velociraptor

The fossils clearly showed Velociraptor grasping the head

FOSSIL
The remains of an organism or creature of a past geologic age, usually in the form of bones (skeleton), shells, and occasionally in the form of an imprint, such as a footprint or plant embedded in rock.

Click on a *word* to find its full meaning.

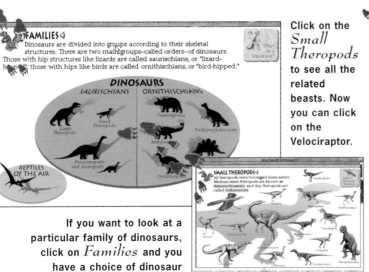

FAMILIES
Dinosaurs are divided into groups according to their skeletal structures. There are two main groups–called orders–of dinosaurs. Those with hip structures like lizards are called saurischians, or "lizard-hipped"; those with hips like birds are called ornithischians, or "bird-hipped."

DINOSAURS
SAURISCHIANS | ORNITHISCHIANS

REPTILES
OF THE AIR

Click on the *Small Theropods* to see all the related beasts. Now you can click on the Velociraptor.

SMALL THEROPODS
All theropods were two-legged meat-eaters. Medium-sized theropods are known as deinonychosaurs, and tiny theropods are called coelurosaurs.

If you want to look at a particular family of dinosaurs, click on *Families* and you have a choice of dinosaur families to investigate.

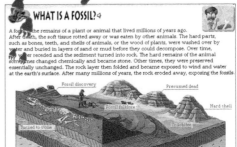

WHAT IS A FOSSIL?
A foss is the remains of a plant or animal that lived millions of years ago. After death, the soft tissue rotted away or was eaten by other animals. The hard parts, such as bones, teeth, and shells of animals, or the wood of plants, were washed over by water and buried in layers of sand or mud before they could decompose. Over time, the water receded and the sediment turned into rock. The hard remains of the animal sometimes changed chemically and became stone. Other times, they were preserved essentially unchanged. The rock layer then folded and became exposed to wind and water at the earth's surface. After many millions of years, the rock eroded away, exposing the fossils.

Fossil discovery | Presumed dead
Hard shell
Turned to stone
Trilobites

Want to know how fossils are found? Then take a *guided tour* that tells you everything you need to know.

Encyclopaedias

A big set of encyclopaedias costs a lot and needs a whole shelf to itself. But you can get more on a single multimedia CD-ROM encyclopaedia for a fraction of the cost. And there is the bonus that you can see how things work and listen to sounds and speeches, hear the words pronounced and look up what you want in a matter of seconds. Then you can go to other related information.

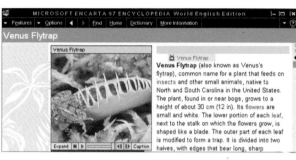

Watching the Venus flytrap closing is much more gripping than seeing a still picture.

Art for art's sake

Want to find out what makes great art? An art CD-ROM title becomes an interactive art catalogue that explains in detail the story behind the pictures and the secret references often hidden inside them.

Bacchus and Ariadne

Narrative Sources

The programme of the series was probably devised by a *humanist scholar in the service of Alfonso d'Este. The subject of *Bacchus and Ariadne* is derived from the classical authors *Ovid and Catullus.

*Bacchus, god of wine, emerges with his followers from a landscape to the right. Falling in love with Ariadne on sight, he leaps from his chariot, drawn by two cheetahs, towards her.

Ariadne had been abandoned on the Greek island of Naxos by Theseus, whose ship is shown in the distance. The picture shows her initial fear of Bacchus. He raised her to heaven, represented by the stars above her head.

Science fiction meets science fact

Some reference software manages to mix fact with fiction. You can read Isaac Asimov's robot books on screen with Microsoft's Isaac Asimov's The Ultimate Robot and also learn all about real robots, how they are made and how they are used. You can also call up many of the most famous fictional robots or listen to Asimov discussing them.

Reference for the young

Some reference works are aimed directly at younger users. Microsoft's Explorapedia makes use of pictures that can be clicked on to animate and bring up more details of a particular item, such as sharks (right). The facts are kept simple and the language is easy to understand.

Hunting Machines

The great white shark is the largest fish that hunts. Most great whites are about 21 feet (6.4 m) long but some are as long as 35 feet (10.6 m). The great white shark eats any kind of meat, alive or dead, and often swallows its prey in one gulp.

Shark skin is covered with *placoid*, or tooth-like, scales. It rips whatever it touches.

Your specialised topic

Some multimedia CD-ROMs are focused on very specific topics and go into the subject in great depth. Here the work of architect Frank Lloyd Wright is explored in Microsoft's The Ultimate Frank Lloyd Wright. Although the topic may be specialised, the disc accesses information using the same sort of graphics and words as more generalised software.

To Wright, the circle represented infinity. What better a form, then, from which to create "a temple of spirit," as curator Hilla Rebay requested for the Guggenheim Museum (New York, 1943-59). In the museum, which was designed for non-objective art, Wright canted the circle to create a continuous spiral. Thus not only

Glossary

A Jargon-Buster's Guide

A:
The letter used to denote the first floppy-disk drive on the PC. A PC can have two, three or sometimes four disk drives. There's one floppy-disk drive called A: and one hard-disk drive called C:. If you have a second floppy-disk drive, this is called B:, and a CD-ROM drive is D:. When talking about the different disk drives, you can say 'drive A' for the floppy drive, but you would usually write 'A:'. (*See also C:, Floppy disk, Hard disk.*)

Active window
The section of a screen that is currently being used. To make a window active in Microsoft Windows, click on it and it will appear in front of any other window you have open.

Adobe Type Manager (ATM)
Software that defines the shape and sizes of fonts – the typefaces – and allows you to change to different type sizes without losing image quality.

Align
To make text appear with a straight margin. When text is left-aligned, for example, all the characters line up on the left-hand side, but don't on the right-hand side. (*See Justify.*)

Alt key
A key on a PC's keyboard used in combination with other keys to activate special functions quickly. For example, many programs allow you to press Alt and S to save your file.

America On-line or AOL
The world's largest on-line service that provides access to the Internet and a range of other services, including newsgroups, chat forums and e-mail. Subscribers gain access via phone lines with their modems.

Anti-aliasing
A technique used to reduce the jagged edges that appear when circles or curves are displayed or printed out. Anti-aliasing masks the jagged edges with a shade of the relevant colour to give the impression of a smooth curve.

Application program, application software
An application program, or application software, is a program, such as a word processor or a spreadsheet, that makes the computer do useful work.

Archive
To transfer completed files that you want to keep on to a separate storage system, such as a floppy disk or a Zip disk. (*See Backup.*)

Arrow keys
The set of four keys on a keyboard that move the pointer up, down, left and right.

ASCII
Stands for American Standard Code for Information Interchange and is pronounced 'askey'. This is a standard set of numbers used to represent characters on a keyboard, used by almost all computers and software.

Attachment
A file that you transfer with an e-mail message. For example, you might send a spreadsheet file called ACCOUNTS.XLS to your accountant as an attachment to an e-mail message.

Audio file
A file containing a digital recording of a sound. In Windows, audio files usually have a .WAV extension.

AUTOEXEC.BAT
One of two special text files that control the startup process of a PC. (*See also CONFIG.SYS.*)

Backup
A second, safety copy of a file. You should always have regular backups of your important files in case of accidental loss. Keep the backup disks away from the computer.

Bad sector
A fault in a floppy disk or hard disk. If you have a bad sector, it means the disk surface has been damaged at this point and that the disk drive cannot read the data there. To fix it, use the disk tools in Windows or use a special program like Norton's Disk Doctor.

Base font
The font and point size automatically used by a word processor if you have not selected a particular style. (*See also Default.*)

Baud or baud rate
Describes the number of signal changes per second that occur in data transferred in a communications system such as the Internet. This is not the same as the quantity of data sent every second. (*See Bits per second.*)

Binary
Base two maths. In binary, the smallest unit is a bit (short for binary digit). This can have one of just two values: 0 or 1. PCs count using the binary system, since the values are easy to represent electronically.

BIOS
Basic Input/Output System. This is a series of instructions to manage the basic functions in your PC. The BIOS looks after how the keyboard works and makes sure the right character code is sent when you press a key. It also manages the disk drives and the monitor.

Bitmap
A bitmap image is made up of tiny dots or pixels. If you zoom in, the dots grow larger.

Bits per second (bps)
The number of single bits of data that can be sent every second over a network or a communications system such as the Internet. If you are checking the specification of a modem, make sure it is describing bits per second and not baud rate.

Boot, boot up
To start up a computer. When your PC boots up, a sequence of instructions permanently stored on the BIOS chip searches – first on the A: drive, then on the C: drive – for the main operating system, and instructs it to start loading.

Buffer
An area in memory that's used for temporarily storing information. For example, if you send a file to print before you have switched the printer on, the data is stored in a print buffer until the printer is ready.

Button
A button-like image displayed on screen. You move the pointer over a button on the screen and click on the mouse to make something happen.

Byte
A group of eight bits – that's eight binary digits – which is the usual form in which data is manipulated within a computer. For example, each letter of the alphabet has a special numerical code that describes it (*see ASCII*), and this code is stored within one byte. One byte can hold numbers between 0 and 255, so your computer can identify 256 different characters. (*See also Kilobyte, Megabyte.*)

C:
The letter that is commonly used to denote the hard disk on a PC. When talking, it's usual to refer to the hard disk drive as 'drive C' but you should write 'C:'. The other disk drives are A: (floppy disk), B: (second floppy disk, if you have one) and D: (CD-ROM). (*See also A:, Floppy disk, Hard disk.*)

Cache
A section of very high-speed memory that temporarily stores data before it is used by the PC's processor, increasing the speed at which data is read from a hard disk.

Cancel
A button usually displayed on a screen next to an OK button to allow you to stop the task you were about to do.

Capture
(1) If you want to store the image that is currently displayed on the screen in a file, you can 'capture' it. In Windows, you can save the current screen as a graphics image by pressing the Print Screen key on the keyboard. (2) If your PC is on a network that shares one printer and you want to print, you can 'capture' that printer using the Printer icon in the Control Panel group.

Case sensitive
Software that can detect the difference between lower-case (small) and upper-case (capital) letters. You're likely to find this in the Search and Replace function in a word processor.

CD-ROM
A type of compact disc that contains up to 650Mb of data. The name stands for Compact Disc-Read Only Memory. All multimedia programs and many software programs come on CD-ROMs. A normal music CD can also be played on your CD-ROM drive, using the Windows MediaPlayer and either speakers or headphones. You cannot save data on to a CD-ROM. (*See Read-only.*)

CD caddy
A flat plastic container that holds the compact disc for insertion into a CD-ROM drive. Another type of CD-ROM drive uses a motorised tray on which the compact disc is placed.

Check box
Small boxes that are displayed to give you a set of options. To select an option, move the pointer on to the check box and

click once; the box will now have a cross in it. If you don't want the option, click a second time and the cross will be deleted.

Chip

A small thin piece of silicon crystal on to which is etched a tiny circuit with hundreds of thousands of components. These components will do simple mathematical operations, such as adding and subtracting numbers (in a processor chip) or storing numbers (in a memory chip).

Click

To move the arrow pointer over an icon, button or menu option and press on a mouse button. One click selects, two clicks open. So to open a document or software program icon, double-click on it, making two rapid clicks on the left-hand mouse button. Windows uses a click on the right-hand button to display a menu of options that apply to an icon, such as its name and properties. *(See also Double-click, Drag and drop.)*

Clip art

A collection of ready-made images, borders and icons for use in your own presentations or desktop published documents, sometimes supplied with a software program.

Clipboard

An area of memory that is used for temporary storage of data, for example when you cut some text to paste it elsewhere. In Windows, the Clipboard can store any type of data, including text, audio and images.

Close

A menu option, usually under the File menu, that will close the document that's currently open, but will not quit the application. If you have not saved the document, the application will give you the chance to save any changes before closing it.

Colour

Any colour displayed on a monitor is made up of three tiny dots. The colours from these three dots combine to create millions of different colours, according to the capability of the graphics adapter that controls the monitor.

COM1

Name used in PCs to represent the first serial port. If you plug an external modem into the first serial port, you are connecting it to COM1. There are usually two serial ports (COM1 and COM2) in a PC, although it can support four. Some PCs have a mouse plugged into the first serial port and the modem plugged into the second port.

Command prompt

A symbol that tells you that the software is ready to receive the next command. In DOS, this is usually called the 'C:>' prompt, which denotes the hard drive. Since the development of Windows, you no longer need to use the command prompt to work with a PC.

Communications software

A software program that works with a modem to send and receive information over a phone line to and from other computers and on-line services.

Compatible

One version of hardware or software that will work with another type or version of hardware or software.

Compression

To reduce the size of a large file by encoding the data. Compression software programs can reduce the size of files but you have to use decompression software to read the files again.

CompuServe

An on-line service that can be accessed via phone lines with a modem. CompuServe offers its subscribers a range of services, including e-mail, information services and databases.

CONFIG.SYS

One of two special text files that are used to configure the operating environment of the PC when it starts up. If this file is present, then the special commands stored in it are automatically executed when your PC starts up.

Configure

To set the functions of software or hardware so that it works the way you want it to. For example, you can configure Windows so that it displays a different colour background on the desktop.

Context-sensitive help

Usually accessed by pressing the F1 key, this will display helpful information about the particular thing you are trying to do.

Control key (Ctrl)

A key on the keyboard that is used for special functions, usually when pressed in combination with another key. There are two control keys – in the bottom right and left corners of the main character pad. They both do the same thing. Ctrl-S will save the current document, Ctrl-N will create a new document, and Ctrl-P will print the document out.

Control Panel

A collection of icons that allow you to configure the basic functions of Windows and your PC. Within the Control Panel there are icons that give you access to the fonts that are installed on your computer, the colour of the background to Windows, the type of printer that's installed, how a network works and a range of other options.

Copy

To make a duplicate version of a file or section of text (using the Copy command). If you want to copy a section of text, highlight it, choose Edit/Copy, move your cursor to where you want to add the copied text and choose Edit/Paste. The copied selection will appear in the new location.

CPU or central processing unit

An electronic device that contains millions of tiny electronic components that carry out basic arithmetic and control functions. Each of the actions of a CPU is controlled by machine-code instructions used in software programs. The computing power of a CPU is usually defined by its speed in MHz (Megahertz), which roughly defines the number of instructions that it can process each second. A 166MHz CPU can process around 166 million instructions per second, for example.

Crash

This is what happens when your computer freezes up and won't respond. The only way to get out of this is to switch off or reset (using the reset button or by pressing Ctrl-Alt-Del at the same time). Unfortunately, you will lose anything you've input since you last saved your work, so make sure that you save your work regularly.

Cursor

A flashing shape on the screen that shows you where the next character you type will appear. When entering text, the cursor is usually a flashing vertical bar. Don't confuse the cursor with the pointer. *(See also Pointer.)*

Database

Software that lets you enter information into a file so that it can be organised and searched. For example, a database could contain names and addresses or details of your recipe collection. Each separate entry is called a record, and each individual part of a record is called a field.

Default

The options that are used if no others are specified. For example, if you run a word processor and start typing a letter, it will use the default typeface and the default paper size and margins. You can always change the default settings.

Defragmentation

A program that will reorganise your hard disk so that all the files are stored in continuous areas. When a file is saved to disk, the operating system does not necessarily save it all in the same place. If the disk is full, it can split files and save them in chunks in different places, making it slower to retrieve them. A defragmentation program will solve this problem.

Delete

To select text or other data and remove it from a file; to remove a file from your disk. If you delete a section of text, you can immediately undelete (using the Edit/Undelete) function. If you delete a file from your disk, you can sometimes undelete it, depending on your PC's setup. *(See Undelete.)*

Desktop

What you see on your screen when Windows first starts up. The icons, status bar, Start button and the Recycle Bin sit together on the Desktop.

Desktop publishing, (DTP)

The design, layout and printing of documents, books and magazines using special desktop publishing software.

Dial-up connection

The process of connecting to another computer via a telephone line. A dial-up connection is the most common method of accessing the Internet via an Internet service provider.

Dialogue/dialog box

A small box that appears on screen in Windows, usually to display a message from the computer's operating system or software. Sometimes it is a warning. At the bottom of many dialogue boxes are buttons. OK and Cancel are the two standard buttons, but there may be others depending on the message that's displayed.

Digital

Numbers and signals that can be processed by a computer. *(See Digitise.)*

Digitise

To convert an analogue signal, such as speech, sound or light, into a numeric form that can be processed by a computer. For example, if you digitise an image using a scanner, you convert the reflected light into an array of dots, each one a number that represents the brightness at that point.

Directory
An organised list of files on a disk. A good way to think about directories is to imagine a filing cabinet: the cabinet is the disk, each drawer a directory. If you open a directory, you'll see lots of folders that are sub-directories. Look in a folder and you will see documents or files.

Disk
A flat, circular piece of plastic coated with a substance that stores digital information in a magnetic form. A hard disk consists of several rigid plastic disks arranged in parallel; a floppy disk has one thin, flexible plastic disk.

Disk tools
A set of software programs that help you monitor the performance of your hard disk, maintain it, and ensure that it's storing data efficiently and is in good condition. (*See also Defragmentation.*)

DOS
The standard operating system for PCs before Windows was developed. DOS is difficult for beginners to use because it is controlled through a command-line interface, which means that you have to type in words to get the computer to do something.

Dots per inch (dpi)
The number of individual dots that a printer can print on an inch of paper. More dots per inch give a more detailed printout. Most laser printers can print at 600 dots per inch, the better ones print at a higher resolution of 1200 dots per inch.

Double-click
To click twice in rapid succession on a mouse button. For example, you run an application by double-clicking the left-hand button with the pointer over the application's icon. (*See also Click, Drag and drop.*)

Download
To copy a file from a remote computer to your own computer. If you use e-mail, you collect it from your Internet Service Provider by downloading it. Many Web sites allow you to download images and even software.

Drag and drop
A feature of Windows that lets you move a highlighted icon or piece of text from one place to another. For example, you can highlight a section of text in a

word-processing document and then click and hold down the left-hand mouse button to move that section of text to another place in the document.

Drive
A mechanical unit that holds a disk, which could be a floppy disk, CD-ROM or a hard disk, and responds to the instructions of a controller card. The drive has a motor that spins the disk and an access head that is positioned over the disk.

Drive letters
A PC can have two, three or sometimes four disk drives. There's one floppy-disk drive called A: and one hard-disk drive called C:. If you have a second floppy-disk drive, this is called B:, and a CD-ROM drive is D:. More advanced PC configurations can use additional drive letters, to identify areas on a network, for example.

Driver
A special piece of software that translates the instructions from Windows into a form that can be understood by a peripheral piece of equipment such as a printer.

DVD
A new CD format called Digital Versatile Disc. It can store seven times as much as an ordinary CD ROM (4.7Gb) and future versions will be able to store 17Gb. Its main attraction is to play movies and advanced multimedia titles.

E-mail
A way of sending and receiving messages on a network. If you are connected to the Internet, you can send messages to any other user who is also connected to the Internet.

Embedding
A feature of Windows that lets you drag a document, picture or sound into another document. For example, if you type a letter in WordPad and then want to add your signature, you start the Paint program, draw your signature and drag it into the WordPad document.

Error box or message
A small window that pops up to tell you an error has occurred – for example, if you have tried to do something that the program does not understand or if an error has occurred in the program.

Esc key
A key on a PC keyboard that is sometimes used to cancel an action. In Windows, pressing the Esc key is the same as selecting the Cancel button.

If you press Alt and Esc simultaneously within Windows you will cycle between any program windows that are currently running.

Exchange
A program that's supplied with Windows 95 to manage your communications. Exchange can control a fax modem and can send and receive e-mail messages.

.EXE file
The three-letter filename extension – short for executable – that indicates that a file is a program that can be run without using another application.

Expansion card
A set of electronic components on a plastic card that expands the functions of your PC. For example, if you want to connect your PC to a network, you will need to add a network expansion card. If you want to fit external speakers to your PC, you will need to add a sound card.

Export
To convert a file so that it can be read by a different program. For example, if you have written a letter in Microsoft Word and want to give it to a friend who uses WordPerfect for Windows, you need to export the Word document to a WordPerfect format file using the File/Save As option in Word.

Extension
The three-letter code at the end of a file name that generally indicates the type or format of the file. For example, a file name in MS-DOS might be Letter1 with the extension .doc. The three-letter extension, .doc, shows the file is a document. Similarly, .bmp means a bitmap file, .exe means an executable program file, and so on.

Field
An individual box in a database that can hold a particular type of information. For example, in a database of names and addresses, there would be separate fields for the name, address, phone number and other data.

File format
The way data is stored in a file. Each program stores information in its own format, which means it can be difficult to read a file that's been created by a different program from the one you are using. To get around this, you can either use the Import function or one of the standard file formats that lets you exchange data between programs.

File Manager
A program supplied with Windows 3.1 that lets you manage the files stored on a disk. With File Manager you can copy files, move files from one directory to another, create new directories and rename or delete files. To start File Manager, open the Accessories group and double-click on the icon. Windows 95 users have a more sophisticated utility called Explorer.

Find
A feature of Windows that will search any disk – on your PC or, if you are on a network, on any other PC – for a particular file.

Floppy disk
A portable storage device on which information is stored as a series of magnetic signals on a thin, flexible disk in a rigid plastic case. Each 3.5in disk can store 1.44Mb of data. Older 5.25in size disks are rarely used.

Font
A set of characters in the same typeface. Windows has TrueType fonts that can be printed and displayed in almost any size and printer fonts that can be printed in predefined sizes.

Format
To arrange text, define margins and columns, and include special fonts in a word processor or desktop publishing program.

Function keys
Twelve or more keys that run along the top of the keyboard. These have different uses according to different applications. However, most use the F1 key to display help information.

Gb or Gigabyte
A measure of the data capacity of a storage device, such as a hard drive, equal to 1,024 Megabytes (Mb). Most of the newest computers have hard disks with a capacity of 4Gb or more.

.GIF file
Stands for Graphics Interface Format. This is a commonly used format for storing images and bitmapped colour graphics, now one of the most popular formats for images stored on the Internet.

Graphical user interface (GUI)
A method of representing files, functions and folders with little images called icons. With a GUI, such as Windows, you can point and click on an icon using the mouse rather than typing in the name. This makes a PC easier to use.

Hacker
A person who is trying to break into a computer system for illegal purposes.

Hand-held scanner
A small scanner that contains a row of light-sensitive cells along its bottom surface. When you drag the scanner over an image, it reads the amount of light reflected from the image or photograph and converts this into a digital form that can be displayed on your PC.

Hard copy
A printed document or copy of a picture that's stored on the computer.

Hard disk
A rigid magnetic disk inside your computer that stores your software, operating system and files. In most PCs, the hard disk drive is called drive C: and can usually store anything from 500Mb to 2Gb of information.

Header
The line of text that appears at the top of each page in a document, such as the page number. In Microsoft Word, look under Header/Footer in the View menu.

Help key
The key to press to access a window that will display text to help you do what you are trying to do. Most Windows applications on a PC have standardised the F1 key as the Help key.

Highlight
To select a word or section of text in a document by moving the mouse pointer over the word and double-clicking on the mouse button. In Microsoft Word, a double-click will highlight the word you are over, a triple-click will highlight the line, and a quadruple-click will highlight the paragraph.

Hot key
A way of selecting a menu option or command by pressing two or more keys at the same time. For example, instead of selecting the File/Save menu option, most Windows programs use a hot key shortcut of Alt-S (the Alt key and the S key pressed at the same time) to do the same thing.

Icon
A small picture displayed on screen to identify a command or file. In Windows, each application you install has its own icon. Its associated data files often use the same icon.

Import
The function in a program that allows you to use a file produced by another program. For example, to read a WordPerfect document in Microsoft Word, you need to choose the Import menu option.

Inkjet printer
A light, quiet and relatively cheap printer that produces pages by squirting a stream of tiny drops of ink at the surface of the paper. This is the most popular printer for home use. The quality is better than a dot-matrix printer, but not as good as a laser printer.

Input
To put information into a computer. When you type text on your keyboard, you are inputting data into the computer. Other examples are using a scanner or using a mouse to draw on screen.

Install
To copy and set up an application program on your hard disk. The steps include copying the files from the floppy disks or CD-ROM (on which the application is sold) on to your hard disk, then configuring the options for your requirements.

Internet
An international network that links thousands of computers using telephone and cable links. Users connect via a modem to server computers often called Internet Service Providers, which are like local phone exchanges. You can send e-mail and transfer files over the Internet around the world for the price of a local phone call. To get on to the Internet, you'll need a modem and an account with an Internet Service Provider.

JPEG
Stands for Joint Photographic Experts Group. This is a standard you may come across if you use graphic images. JPEG is a complex way of storing images in a compressed format so they take up less disk space.

Justify
To align text so that both the left and right margins are even. This is usually an option on your word processor and is done automatically by inserting tiny spaces between words.

Keyboard
The collection of keys, each one attached to a spring and a tiny electrical switch. When you press a key, the switch closes and this sends a signal to the PC. In addition to the main characters, there is a row of 12 function keys along the top of the keyboard. These do different things according to the program you are using.

Keyboard layout
Different countries have different keyboard layouts. Britain and America use a standard Qwerty layout, which refers to the sequence of the first keys on the top left corner of the keyboard. Other countries have key layouts according to their need for accents and other local requirements. If you want to change the keyboard layout of your PC, you can plug in a different keyboard and configure Windows to support this, using the Control Panel icon in Windows 3.1 or the Start/Settings menu option in Windows 95 and 98.

Kilobyte (Kb)
A measure of the capacity of a storage device that is usually written as Kb. A Kb is equal to 1,024 bytes. If you want to check the size of a file, highlight the file name in Program Manager in Windows. The size of the file is displayed after the file name. Although 1Kb is actually equal to 1,024 bytes, many people use it to mean 1,000 bytes. The reason that 1Kb has 1,024 bytes is that it is equal to 2 to the power of 10 – remember that PCs work in binary, base 2. (*See also Binary and Megabyte*.)

Label
To identify a floppy disk by sticking a paper label on it. You can also identify it by giving it an electronic label, called its volume name. If you want to give a short description to a floppy disk (which will appear in the My Computer window), highlight the floppy disk icon, select its Properties window, and type in the new name.

Laptop
A small portable computer. A laptop usually has a 'clam shell' construction with a fold-down lid that houses the screen, a keyboard (often slightly smaller than full-size) and a floppy and hard disk drive. An internal rechargeable battery pack provides power for a few hours.

Laser printer
A printer that produces very high-quality text and graphics using a laser beam. The beam draws the characters as tiny dots – normally 600 or 1,200dpi – on to a special drum. The drum then attracts a fine powder (called toner) to these dots that is transferred to a sheet of paper. The final stage is to heat the toner, which melts on to the paper forming a permanent image. Laser printers are more expensive than other types of printers, but are faster and provide superior print quality. (*See also Inkjet printer*.)

Line spacing
The number of blank lines that are printed between each line of text. The text in this book is printed with single-line spacing. If you print with double-line spacing, each line of text is separated by a blank line.

Linked object
A piece of data that is referred to in another file or application. If you open a spreadsheet program and a word processor in two adjacent windows and drag the spreadsheet data into your document, Windows creates a link between the two files. The spreadsheet file is called an object and is linked into the document in your word processor. (*See also OLE*.)

Local area network
A communications network linking several computers within an office or building so that you can exchange files or messages with other users or send files to a printer.

Long file name
A feature of Windows 95 and 98 that lets you give files a long name (up to 254 characters). Before Windows 95 was released, file names were limited to a maximum of eight characters.

Mail merge
To incorporate address details automatically from a database in any document, such as a standard letter, labels or envelopes. Almost all word processor programs let you carry out a mail merge with a database program.

Maximise
To increases the size of a window so that it fills the entire screen. To Maximise any window, click on the Maximise button – the up arrow at the very top right-hand corner of the window.

Megabyte (Mb)
A measure of the data capacity of a storage device that is equal to 1,048,576 bytes (which is equal to 2 to the power of 20 or 2^{20}). Megabytes are used to measure the storage capacity of hard disk drives or main memory (RAM). (*See also Kilobyte*.)

Memory
Electronic components that store data and provide the RAM in your PC. Electronic memory chips only remember data for as long as electricity is supplied. This is not the same as disk storage, which is long-term data storage on magnetic media.

Menu bar

A line of options available that runs along the top of a window. When one of the words in the menu bar is selected, a further list of options is displayed beneath the word (this is called a drop-down menu). For example, almost all Windows programs have a menu bar that starts with the word File. If you select File, it displays the options that include Open, Save and Exit.

MIDI

Stands for Musical Instrument Digital Interface. This is a way of connecting electronic instruments to your computer. You tell the instruments what notes to play through the computer.

Minimise

To shrink an application or document window down to the size of an icon. To do this, select the down-arrow button in the top right-hand corner of the window (or the first of the three buttons in a Windows 95 window).

Modem

A device to convert electronic signals from your PC into sound signals that can be transmitted by phone. To receive information the modem works in reverse and converts the sound signals back into digital electronic signals. Modems are used to connect to the Internet and for sending and receiving faxes.

Monitor

A device that displays the text and graphics from your PC. It looks and works like a TV set. Images are displayed as tiny dots on the screen (the smaller and closer the dots, the sharper the image).

Mouse

A small, hand-held device that's moved on a flat surface to control the position of a pointer on screen. A mouse usually has two buttons. In Windows, the left-hand button selects text or starts an application. The right-hand button displays options for the item.

Mouse pointer

In Windows, a small arrow that's displayed on screen and moves as you move the mouse. The pointer is used to select and start applications. It can also change shape to an 'I-beam' pointer.

Multi-tasking

The ability of Windows to run several programs at once. The trick is that Windows switches very rapidly between tasks, giving you the impression that they are running in parallel.

My Computer

The icon usually in the top left of the screen on a PC running Windows. It contains an overview of your PC. If you double-click on it, you'll see the peripherals linked to your PC.

Network

A way of connecting several computers and printers so that they can share data. To set up a network, each PC needs a network interface card and a cable. If you are linked to a network, you'll be able to send files and messages to other users. (*See also E-mail.*)

Object Linking and Embedding (OLE)

A system that lets you cut and paste data from one application to another, retaining the formatting and controls. You can select part of a spreadsheet, switch to a word processor and paste it in. To insert other objects, select Edit/Paste Special and you'll see a list of the types of objects that you can include.

On-line

(1) A modem that is connected to another modem via a telephone line and is currently transferring information. (2) A printer that is ready and waiting to print.

Open

(1) To access a file and read its contents using an application. Most Windows applications will read a file via the File/Open menu option. (2) To look inside a folder to view the list of files or sub-folders stored in it. Open a folder with a double-click.

Operating system

The software that controls the actions of the different parts of your PC. In older PCs, the operating system is called MS-DOS. In modern PCs, Windows manages the screen, keyboard, disks and printers.

Packet

A collection of binary digital data that also contains the address of the particular packet and its sequence in a transmission. Digital information is transmitted via the Internet in 'packets'.

Page break

The point at which one page of text stops and the next starts. In Microsoft Word, you can insert the character that stops one page by pressing Ctrl-Enter.

Parallel port

A socket at the back of your PC that lets you connect it to a printer. A parallel port sends data to the printer over eight parallel wires.

Paste

To insert a section of text or other information. To move a section of text in a document, select the text, choose Edit/Cut, move to its new location and choose Edit/Paste.

Path

The series of directories or folders that locate a particular file. If a file is in a sub-folder named Letters within a parent folder named Simon, on drive D:, its full path is D:\Simon\Letters.

PC

Stands for Personal Computer. Usually refers to an IBM-compatible computer that uses an Intel processor and runs MS-DOS or Windows.

PC-compatible

Software or hardware that will work on a standard PC that uses an Intel processor and has standard ports and expansion slots.

Pentium

A processor chip developed by Intel and used in most of today's PCs. It is software-compatible with older processors such as the 80486. Latest versions available include the Pentium MMX and Pentium 2.

Peripheral

Any add-on item that connects to your computer.

Phono connector or RCA connector

A plug and socket standard used to connect audio and video devices. If you have inserted a sound card inside your PC, you'll see two phono connectors on the back plate. They let you connect your sound card directly to your sound system.

PhotoCD

A standard for storing 35mm photos in digital format on a CD-ROM. The PhotoCD is usually created at the same time as the photographic film is developed by digitising each frame. One PhotoCD can hold 100 photographs.

Pixel

The smallest single unit or point on a monitor or on a printer the colour or brightness of which can be controlled.

Platform

The type of hardware or the combination of hardware and system software that make up a particular range of computers. For example, the PC-compatible platform usually means a computer that has an Intel-compatible 80 x 86 or Pentium processor running DOS,

Windows 95 or another popular operating system.

Pointer

A graphical symbol – usually a small arrow – used to show the position of a cursor on a monitor. If you are using Windows, the pointer changes shape according to what you are doing. For example, it is usually an arrow, but changes to an I-beam pointer when you are typing or editing.

POP

Stands for Point of Presence. A telephone access number for a service provider that you can use to connect to the Internet via your modem. Most of the major service providers have dozens of POPs scattered across the country so that you can connect to the Internet with a local-rate telephone call.

Pop-up window

A window that is displayed on the screen at any time on top of anything that is already there. When the window is removed, the original screen display is restored. These are most often used to display warning messages or to confirm a choice.

Port

Communications channel that allows a computer to exchange data with a peripheral. On the back of your computer, you'll see a range of connectors. They are all ports between your computer and peripherals. (*See also Serial port.*)

Portable

(1) A compact, portable computer that can be used with a battery pack or plugged into a mains power supply. (*See also Laptop.*) (2) Any hardware, software or data files that can be used on a range of different computers. For example, Adobe's Acrobat graphics file format can be viewed on almost any type of computer.

PostScript

A language used to describe how a printed page will look, including the size, position and style of text and graphics. PostScript was developed by Adobe Systems and offers flexible font sizing and positioning. It is most often used by DTP systems, high-quality laser printers and photo-typesetters.

Preview

To display text or graphics on a screen as it will appear when it is printed out.

Print queue

A list of files waiting to be printed. If you are using Windows, the printing is usually controlled by the Print Manager, which temporarily stores documents on disk until the printer has finished the previous document.

Printer
A device that produces text or images from a computer on paper using ink or toner.

Printer driver
A special file that tells Windows how to control a printer. Windows comes with hundreds of printer drivers which cover most printers. If you buy a new printer, make sure that it comes with the latest Windows printer driver.

Processor
Also called the central processing unit (CPU). *(See CPU.)*

Program
(1) A self-contained set of software codes that is used to accomplish a particular task, such as word processing. (2) In musical instrument digital interface (MIDI), data that defines a sound in a synthesiser.

Prompt
A display to remind you that an input is expected. DOS uses the C:\> prompt. In the case of DOS, the command prompt also displays the name of the current disk and sub-directory.

Properties
In Windows, the attributes of a file or object. To view or edit all the properties of a file, select the file with a single click to highlight the name, and click once on the right-hand mouse button. This displays a small menu of options. Select the Properties menu option and you will see the various properties for the object.

PrtSc
Stands for Print Screen on an IBM PC keyboard. It is the key that sends the contents of the current screen to the printer or copies a Windows screen to the Clipboard.

Purge
To empty the contents of the Recycle Bin in Windows. To do this, click once on the bin to highlight it, then click on the right-hand mouse button and choose the Empty option.

Query window
(1) Window that appears when an error has occurred, asking you what action you would like to take. (2) Window that is displayed with fields you can fill in to search a database.

QWERTY keyboard
English-language keyboard layout for a typewriter or computer, in which the top line of letters starts QWERTY.

Radio button
A circle displayed beside an option that has a dark centre when selected. Radio buttons are a method of selecting one of a number of options. Only one radio button in a group can be selected at any one time. If you select another in the group, the first is deselected.

RAM
Stands for Random Access Memory. The memory chips in your PC are RAM chips, since any memory location can be accessed by specifying its address.

Read-only
A file or memory device whose stored data cannot be changed. A CD-ROM disc is read-only; you cannot save data on to it as you can with a floppy disk.

Recycle Bin
An icon displayed on the Windows Desktop that looks like a wastepaper bin. If you want to delete a file or folder, drag it on to the Recycle Bin or press the Delete key. The contents of the Bin are not deleted from the disk until you purge it.

Red, green, blue (RGB)
High-definition monitor system that uses three separate input signals controlling red, green and blue colour picture beams.

Rename
To change the name of a file or folder. In Windows, click once on the file or folder that you want to rename and keep the pointer over the icon. After a few seconds, the description will be surrounded by a box and you can edit the name.

Rich text format (RTF)
A way of storing a document that includes all the commands that describe the page, type, font and formatting. RTF allows formatted pages to be exchanged between different word processors.

ROM cartridge
Software or fonts stored in a ROM chip that is mounted in a cartridge that can easily be plugged into a computer or printer. Often used to store extra font data.

Run command
A command in Windows that lets you type in the name of a program that you want to run or a DOS command you want to execute. To enter a command, select the File/Run menu from the Program Manager of Windows 3.1, or the Start/Run menu option from Windows.

Save
To store a document on a disk. Windows applications have a Ctrl-S shortcut for this function or you can choose the File/Save menu option.

Save As
A way to save a named document to disk under a different name or in a different format. If you have written a message in Microsoft Word and want to save it in plain text format so that it can be sent as e-mail, you would select the File/Save As menu option.

Scanner
A device that uses photo-electric cells to convert a drawing, photograph or document into data that can be manipulated by a PC. A flat-bed scanner has a flat sheet of glass on which the image is placed. The scan head moves below the glass. *(See Hand-held scanner.)*

Screen
(1) A display device capable of showing an image. (2) Grid of dots or lines placed between a camera and artwork that has the effect of dividing the picture up into small dots, creating an image which can be used for printing

Screen saver
Software which, after a short period of inactivity, replaces the existing image on screen and displays moving objects to protect against screen burn.

Scroll
To move displayed text vertically up or down a screen, one line or pixel at a time.

Search engine
The databases on the World Wide Web, which you can use to locate the information you are seeking. There are two types of search engine. Directories, such as the popular Yahoo!, in which the information has been sorted into helpful categories such as Education or News and Media; or Indexes, such as Alta Vista, which contain more information but require more perseverance to use effectively.

Search and replace
A function in a word processor or database that lets you search for a word or phrase and replace it with something else. In some word processors you can search and replace formatting or text.

Select
(1) To position a pointer over an object, such as a button or menu option, and click on the mouse button. (2) To find and retrieve specific information from a database.

Selection tool
In a paint or drawing program, the selection tool is an icon in a toolbar that allows you to select an area of an image that can then be cut, copied or processed in some other way.

Serial port
A connector and circuit used to convert data in a PC so that it can be transmitted in a single stream through an external cable.

Shareware
Software that is available free for you to sample. But if you want to keep it, you are expected to pay a fee to the writer. Often confused with public-domain software that is completely free.

Shortcut
An icon placed on the Desktop in Windows that links to a file, folder or program stored on the disk. The shortcut has the same icon as the original file except for a tiny arrow in the bottom left-hand corner. The shortcut is not a duplicate of the original – it is a pointer to the original.

Shut down
To switch off your PC. First exit Windows. This ensures that all the files are closed and that Windows sorts itself out internally before being switched off. To exit Windows, select the Start/ShutDown menu option. With some new PCs, this will also automatically switch off the PC. With older PCs you need to wait until the screen tells you it's safe to switch off the PC.

Sixteen-bit
A processor that handles data in 16-bit words, providing much faster operation than older eight-bit systems.

Software
Any program or group of programs that tells the hardware how it should perform, including operating systems, word processors and applications programs.

Soundblaster
A type of sound card for PC compatibles developed by Creative Labs that allows sounds to be recorded to disk and played back. It also has an FM synthesiser and a musical instrument digital interface (MIDI) port.

Sound card
An add-on device that plugs into an expansion slot inside your PC. The sound card generates analogue sound from digital data, using either a digital to analogue converter or an FM synthesis chip. It also provides functions to record

digital sound (using an analogue to digital converter) and control MIDI instruments. There are three major standards for PC sound cards: AdLib, SoundBlaster and Windows-compatible.

Sound file
A file stored on disk that contains sound data. This can either be a digitised analogue sound signal or notes for a musical instrument digital interface (MIDI) instrument.

Source file
In Windows, the file that contains the data referenced by an OLE object. For example, if you have an OLE object with a link to a spreadsheet, the spreadsheet file is the source file. (*See also OLE.*)

Spell check
A function of word processors and desktop publishing programs that checks the spelling of words by comparing them with words in a dictionary file.

Sub-directory
A directory of disk contents contained within another directory.

Super VGA (SVGA)
An enhancement to the VGA graphics display system, which allows higher resolutions than the basic 640 x 480 pixels with 16 colours. With a 15in or 17in monitor you would usually choose 800 x 600, or even 1,024 x 768 pixels, in 256 or more colours.

System software
The software that makes everything work correctly. The system software controls the hardware and manages programs. It looks after and controls all aspects of the computer. Windows is a form of system software, since it operates everything itself and does not rely on other software. This is different from Windows 3.1, which relied on MS-DOS to manage the hardware. In the latter case MS-DOS is the system software.

Tab key
A key on a keyboard – usually positioned on the far left, beside the Q key, with two arrows pointing in opposite horizontal directions – used to align the text at a preset tab stop.

Task bar
A bar that usually runs along the bottom of the screen in Windows and displays the Start button and a list of other programs or windows that are currently active. You can move the entire task bar to any of the four sides of the screen by

clicking on the bar and dragging it to another edge.

Template
A file containing a standard section of text, such as a memo or invoice, into which specific details, such as company address or prices, can be added.

Thesaurus
A file that contains a collection of synonyms that are displayed as alternatives. It is also a useful vocabulary guide when composing letters or any other type of document.

Tile
To arrange a group of windows so that they are displayed side-by-side without overlapping.

Toolbar
A window containing a variety of icons that allows you to access different tools. For example, paint programs usually have a toolbar that includes different icons for colour, brush, circle, text and eraser tools.

ToolTips
A feature of Windows that displays a line of descriptive text under an icon when you move the pointer over that particular icon.

Tree of folders
A view of all the folders that are stored on your hard disk, arranged so that the folders and sub-folders can be seen.

Undelete
A function of Windows and DOS that lets you restore deleted information or a deleted file. In DOS you can type Undelete and DOS will attempt to recover your file. If you have mistakenly deleted a file, do not save any other files on to the disk, but run the Undelete command immediately. In Windows 95, you can retrieve the file from the Recycle Bin.

Undo
A function of some applications that lets you undo the task that you've just carried out. For example, it can undo a paste or a delete operation.

Upgrade
To improve the performance or specification of your computer by adding more RAM, a larger hard disk or another kind of improvement. Software can also be upgraded from an old version to a more recent one.

URL
Stands for Uniform Resource Locator. The Internet system to standardise the way in which World Wide Web addresses are written. For example, the URL

of the Microsoft home page is http://www.microsoft.com.

VGA
Stands for Video Graphics Array. A standard of video adapter developed by IBM that can support a display with a resolution up to 640 x 480 pixels in 256 colours. Superseded by SVGA, which is an enhancement to the standard VGA graphics display system that allows resolutions of up to 800 x 600 pixels in 16 million colours.

Video memory (VRAM)
A section of memory fitted on a video adapter that is used to store temporarily image data sent from the PC's main memory, or to store an image as it is built up and before it is displayed on the screen.

Video disc
A read-only optical disc that can store up to two hours of video data. Usually used to store a complete film (as a rival to the video cassette) or in an interactive system with text, video and still images.

Virus
A software program created by a rogue programmer that can infiltrate your computer and cause serious damage. Some viruses are pranks, others are maliciously designed to destroy data and programs. They can get on to your hard disk from a floppy disk or by being downloaded from the Internet. Effective anti-virus software is widely available.

Wallpaper
In Windows, an image or pattern used as a background in a window. You can change the wallpaper from within the Control Panel/Desktop icon settings.

WAVE or WAV file
A standard Windows sound file that stores an analogue signal in digital form.

Window
(1) Reserved section of your computer's screen that is used to display special information which can be selected and viewed at any time and which overwrites information already on the screen. (2) Part of a document currently displayed on a screen. (3) Area of memory or access to a storage device.

World Wide Web
Abbreviated as WWW. Within the Internet, thousands of pages of formatted text and graphics that allow a user to have a window to the Internet rather than a less user-friendly command-line. (*See Internet.*)

WYSIWYG
What you see is what you get. A word-processing or desktop publishing program where what you see on the screen is exactly the same as the image or text that will be printed, including graphics and special fonts.

Zip drive
A type of disk drive that can use the 100Mb Zip disks developed by Iomega Corporation, which are becoming more popular for storing the larger files needed for graphics, video and sound.

Zoom
To enlarge an area of text or graphics to make it easier to see or work on.

Index